BUTTS

A Backstory

Heather Radke

AVID READER PRESS

New York • London • Toronto • Sydney • New Delhi

AVID READER PRESS
An Imprint of Simon & Schuster, Inc.
1230 Avenue of the Americas
New York, NY 10020

First Avid Reader Press trade paperback edition June 2023

For information about special discounts for bulk
purchases, please contact Simon & Schuster Special Sales at
1-866-506-1949 or business@simonandschuster.com.

The Simon & Schuster Speakers Bureau can bring authors to
your live event. For more information or to book an event,
contact the Simon & Schuster Speakers Bureau at
1-866-248-3049 or visit our website at www.simonspeakers.com.

Interior design by Lewelin Polanco

Manufactured in the U.S.A.

5 7 9 10 8 6 4

Library of Congress Cataloging-in-Publication
Data has been applied for.

ISBN 978-1-9821-3548-5
ISBN 978-1-9821-3549-2 (pbk)
ISBN 978-1-9821-3552-2 (ebook)

MORE PRAISE FOR *BUTTS: A BACKSTORY*

"Fascinating and frank . . . [with] top-notch reportage, assured and respectful voice, and invitation to butt-centric contemplation. . . . [Radke] guides readers on an impressively well-researched tour of butts throughout history, beginning with a functional analysis (hominids and horses take center stage) and ultimately alighting in the present (twerking, social media, and celebrity butts)."

—*BookPage* (starred review)

"Radke thoughtfully, and without judgment, addresses the complexities and contradictions that this body part evokes and delves into some surprising topics that may spark further curiosity in readers. Her captivating writing and witty approach to a taboo topic will appeal to a variety of nonfiction readers, particularly those interested in cultural history and gender studies. . . . A fun, fascinating, and surprisingly empowering exploration of the history and cultural significance of the butt."

—*Library Journal* (starred review)

"Whip-smart . . . Marked by Radke's vivacious writing, candid self-reflections, and sophisticated cultural analyses, this is an essential study of 'ideas and prejudices' about the female body."

—*Publishers Weekly* (starred review)

"A deeply researched and thoroughly fascinating look (ogle?) at a body part that has long captured the cultural imagination. Radke talks to evolutionary biologists, models, and fitness gurus, and dives into the history of the racist objectification of women like Sarah Baartman and Josephine Baker in an effort to understand our complex relationship with the butt."

—*LitHub*

"How did butts become both sexualized and mythologized? Why do certain body types fall in and out of fashion? Who even makes those decisions? In this cheeky (sorry) nonfiction debut, *Radiolab* reporter Heather Radke examines society's obsession with derrieres and how larger ideas about race, control, liberation, and power affect our most private feelings about ourselves and others."

—*PureWow*

"Here comes a story on the evolution and sensationalization of, you guessed it, butts! Radke takes a deep dive into the most emphasized human body part, taking a look at its physical evolution in relation to survival, as well as the part it has played in popular culture throughout the years. And you know Sir Mix-A-Lot's name will come up a time or two."

—*The Everygirl*

"Cheeky and entertaining."

—*BookRiot*

"An ingenious cultural study."

"As women we have always been asked—been *told*—to lie about our bodies. Our culture subjects them to laws, myths, race bigotries, class pieties, and sexual anxieties. With *Butts: A Backstory*, journalist and critic Heather Radke takes up these lies and takes them apart. The result is a bold and exuberant leap for womankind."
—Margo Jefferson, Pulitzer Prize–winning critic
and author of *Negroland* and *Constructing a Nervous System*

"Rigorous, generous, and utterly compelling. The range of its research is thrillingly expansive. . . . With humor, intelligence, outrage, and compassion, Radke excavates the social and historical forces that haunt our most ordinary moments. This fiercely intelligent, frequently witty 'backstory' is a journey through centuries of history that will transform how you think about the butt, and—quite possibly—how you consider the value of exploring those parts of ourselves we don't take seriously enough."
—Leslie Jamison, bestselling author of
Make It Scream, Make It Burn and *The Empathy Exams*

"From the first, I have been delighted and deeply informed by Heather Radke's writing. She has a mind like no other. This book contributes not only a great deal to the complicated discussion around women's bodies; it illuminates what unites us all: being human."
—Hilton Als, Pulitzer Prize–winning critic and author of *White Girls*

"Juicy and scholarly, *Butts* is a heck of a ride. At turns troubling, wild, painful, surprising, and flat-out fun, Radke's reporting unearths a set of largely overlooked historical figures with outsized effects on cultural evolutions. . . . Her book is teeming with rebels—drag queens and fat activists and twerkers—who flip supremacy the bird and offer another path through. Don't let the cute cover fool you; inside is a serious feat of reporting and scholarship."
—Lulu Miller, bestselling author of *Why Fish Don't Exist*

"A deeply thought, rigorously researched, and riveting history of human butts—Radke knows exactly when to approach her subject with levity and when with gravity. A pitch-perfect debut."
—Melissa Febos, bestselling author of *Girlhood* and *Body Work*

"Heather Radke takes a subject so familiar as to be practically invisible and trains a sharp reportorial eye on it, touring the reader through the centuries of cultural history that shape our feelings about what's filling out our jeans. She has amassed a trove of surprising and fascinating case studies, from bustles and the 'Hottentot Venus' to flappers, fit models, and Sir Mix-A-Lot. *Butts* is everything you want a piece of reportage to be: smart, creative, searching, deeply researched, political, and *fun*."
—Jordan Kisner, author of *Thin Places*

For my mother

Contents

INTRODUCTION   1

ORIGINS   17
Muscle   19
Fat   31
Feathers   36

SARAH   47
Life   49
Legacy   68

SHAPE   79
Bigness   81
Smallness   94

NORMA   111
Creation   113
Proliferation   125
Resistance   134

FIT 143

Steel 145

Joy 162

BOOTYLICIOUS 171

Kate 173

Mix 177

Jennifer 190

Kim 202

MOTION 217

Twerk 219

Miley 227

The Year of the Butt 234

Reclamation 239

CONCLUSION 247

Acknowledgments 253

Notes 257

Index 301

Introduction

The first butt I remember isn't my own. It's my mother's. At seven years old, I would sit on the fluffy toilet seat cover in my parents' bathroom and watch her get ready for the day, standing in front of the mirror in her bra and underwear, smearing lotion onto her body. She rolled Velcro curlers into her short brown hair: a few girthy pink ones on top, several smaller green ones on the sides. She cracked the window to let out the steam of the shower, and the Michigan morning air—cold and thin—woke me up. *Close your eyes*, she told me, and as I did, she'd liberally douse her hair with hairspray. I held my breath, fearing the sticky choke. Then, she took her glasses off and leaned in close to the mirror and curled her lashes, her butt sticking out as she leaned over the counter.

As a young girl, my mom's was the only naked adult body I had ever seen. I imagined all women's bodies looked like hers: shapely and short, with full breasts and an ample butt that filled out any pair of pants. I liked the idea that one day my body would look the same—a fate that seemed as inevitable as growing taller or getting my period. She was beautiful and free as she went about her morning ablutions.

The clear-sightedness of childhood allowed me to see my mother's butt for what it actually was—a body part like any other, something to love because I loved the human it was part of. It was not a problem or a blessing. It was only a fact.

What I did not know then is that butts are not so simple. They are not like elbows or knees, functional body parts that carry few associations beyond their physiological function. Instead, butts, silly as they may often seem, are tremendously complex symbols, fraught with significance and nuance, laden with humor and sex, shame and history. Women's butts have been used as a means to create and reinforce racial hierarchies, as a barometer for the virtues of hard work, and as a measure of sexual desire and availability. Despite (or perhaps because of) the fact that there is little a person can do to dramatically change the way their butt looks without surgical intervention, the shape and size of a woman's butt has long been a perceived indicator of her very nature—her morality, her femininity, and even her humanity.

But butts can be hard to see clearly. The fact that they are on our backside means they are somewhat alien to us, even as they are perfectly visible to others. To see your butt, you need the cocoon of mirrors of a dressing room, the cumbersome triangulation of a hand mirror in a bedroom, or an awkwardly held smartphone. And when you catch sight of your butt—or at least when I catch sight of my butt—there is always a bit of surprise: *That is what is trailing me?* There is a note of humiliation in this—we don't ever really know what someone else is seeing when they look at our butts, which makes us vulnerable. There is also a giving-over: in some ways, the butt belongs to the viewer more than the viewed. It can be observed secretly, ogled in private, creepily scrutinized. In order to know how a pair of pants fits, I must ask a salesperson how my butt looks because I cannot see for myself. A woman passes a man on the street and then his head turns to look at her butt. Although everyone else on the street may spot the greedy glance, the woman may not, and doesn't realize she is being assessed, criticized, objectified, desired.

Even the words for our backside resist clarity. The terms we use are always euphemisms, never sure things. I grew up referring to the two masses of flesh attached to the back of my hips as a butt. It is the word a kid uses, the word your obnoxious brother hurls at you. Butthead! Buttface! A hilarious idea—having a butt for a face—but it's not an insult that has much impact beyond the age of ten. The word *butt* is funny, but the humor is mild, familiar, and innocuous. A man slips and falls smack-dab on his butt; chuckles ensue. If the word *butt* were a noise, it would be the honk of a clown horn, or maybe a fart.

As I got older I experimented with other words. *Ass* felt a bit more grown-up, a bit more obscene—a word in the category we used to call "swears." But it's a light swear, the least of the offenders. You can say *ass* on TV, although you can't say *asshole*. There are many other terms for the body part in question: In the UK they call it a bum; in Yiddish they call it a tuchus. Sometimes people get a little highbrow and a little French and call it a derrière. These days, grocery store tabloids and TV talk shows usually call it a booty or a badonkadonk, words lifted from hip-hop songs and country music, used to connote sexiness, silliness, and race. There is also a whole category of words that refer to the physical positioning of the part on the body: *behind, backside, posterior, rear end, bottom*.

But what is the *proper* word? The fundamental word? What is our neutral term that signifies "the fatty, fleshy part of your body that you sit on"? Although there are boobs and tits and jugs, ultimately we know the correct, "official" word is *breasts*. We might call a man's sexual organ a dick or schlong, but we know there is a "right" word, and that word is *penis*. *Buttocks* seems to be the obvious choice, but it's a word rarely used in real life. You wouldn't say, "My buttocks are sore," after a tough workout, nor would you say, "My buttocks don't look good in these pants." I once asked a surgeon friend how his fellow doctors refer to it, thinking that I might find the most practical word in the medical lexicon. He told me the colorectal surgeons—the ones who likely spend the most time talking about it—use words like *rear* and *bottom*. One surgeon he knows employs the very scientific *gluteal cleft* when he means *crack*; another invariably calls the body part in question a tush. Even in the doctor's office, there are layers of euphemism. The muscle has a scientific name—*gluteus maximus*—but that term refers only to the sinewy bundle of fibers that stretches from the pelvic bone to the thigh. The fatty layer on top is called the gluteofemoral fat mass. No one calls it that.

Because of this triangulated, euphemistic relationship we often have with our butts (the word I've settled on as the most straightforward), our ideas about them often tell us more about the viewer than the viewed, the meaning determined by who is looking and when they are looking and why. As historian Sander Gilman puts it, "The buttocks have ever-changing symbolic value. They are associated with the organs of reproduction, the aperture of excretion, as well as with the mechanism of locomotion through the discussions of gait. They never represent themselves."

This idea—that the butt never represents itself—makes it a peculiar and peculiarly compelling object of study. Because the butt is capricious in what it symbolizes, sifting through and investigating the profusion of meanings and signification can tell us a tremendous amount about many other things: what people perceive to be normal, what they perceive to be desirable, what they perceive to be repellant, and what they perceive to be transgressive. Butts are a bellwether. The feelings we have about butts are almost always indicative of other feelings—feelings about race, gender, and sex, feelings that differ profoundly from one person to the next.

————————

Everyone has a different origin story for how they feel about their adult body. Like photographs pasted into a scrapbook, the way I feel about mine emerges from fractured memories of times when I felt my body being seen by others. But my earliest memories of my body come from just before puberty, when my limbs and muscles seemed useful and resilient, rather than like parts to be assessed. I rode my bike all over the neighborhood, sped down hills, and felt the humid summer wind fly through my nostrils. On one July afternoon, I tumbled face-first over the handlebars and scraped up my cheeks and forehead on the cement, breaking open the flap of skin that connected my lip to my gums. Blood poured all over the sidewalk and then the kitchen, where I sat on the counter with my feet dangling as my mother held ice to my mouth. The next morning, I was eating Cheerios in a purple polyester ballerina outfit, ready to ride again. My father took pictures of me at the kitchen table, smiling and cheerful. I wasn't particularly fearless, but I understood my body as a thing that would grow, would heal, would take me places. By the time the roll of film was developed, I only had a few scabs left.

When I was eight, I went with a friend to her parents' gym to swim in the pool, and I found myself for the first time in a locker room full of women in various states of undress. There were so many kinds of bodies, and since I had not yet learned to put bodies in categories, to rank and order them as good and bad, all I could do was observe. *Breasts can look like that?* I thought, catching glimpses of parts that didn't look like my mother's. *Hips can be straight? Butts can be bony?* The women in the locker room seemed misshapen. Dressed, they'd looked familiar, but underneath their clothes, they had been hiding all kinds of oddities, shaped in so many different ways.

At ten, I was riding my bike with a friend, around the same blocks we'd been circling for years, when two boys shouted at us from behind a bush. "*Nice butts!*" we heard them say. The comment had the bite of cruelty, but there was something else in it, a new and dangerous feeling, one I now know to be the particular anxiety of having your body seen and commented upon by a male stranger.

The fact that they said something unprompted about our butts felt uncomfortable and bizarre. Butts were not a body part I thought could be *nice*. I was aware that there were body parts that were considered beautiful and sexy and were coveted by others, but it had not occurred to me that the butt was one of them. It felt like they'd caught us with our pants down—as though they'd seen our *actual* butts due to some hilarious and humiliating mistake. We rode back to my house and told my parents what had happened. Somehow, they managed to track down the two boys—young teenagers with skateboards and heavy metal T-shirts—and confronted them about their catcalling. The boys nervously swore that they had shouted, "*Nice bikes.*" I remember feeling embarrassed all over again. Of course butts were not a thing that could be *nice*. Certainly not a thing someone would shout about down the street.

By middle school, I was the oddity in the locker room. I wasn't *fat*, exactly—the adjective that carried the most profound stigma in the dusty halls of Kinawa Middle School—but my body definitely didn't feel like it looked right. It was slowly turning into a youthful approximation of my mother's: my butt had grown, my hips had widened. Standing in front of the burnt-orange lockers, I no longer found myself in awe of the diversity of the female body; it was plain to me that there was a correct way to look, and the way I looked, and the way my mom looked, certainly wasn't it.

Around the same time, the PE department separated the girls and boys to teach us how to swim in the school's hyperchlorinated, crumbling pool. In an unusual gesture designed, I suppose, to level any class distinctions, the school provided us with black swimming suits made of cotton with very little stretch. We plucked them out of gray plastic bins, organized by size, each suit well worn by industrial laundry machines and by generations of anxious girls shivering within them at the edge of the pool. The sizes of the suits were indicated by the stitching: suits with yellow stitching were the smallest, the size for girls who still had the bodies of children. Orange was the most coveted color—the suit of a girl who had matured but had no roundness. Red stitching meant large, and white meant larger still—the colors for girls who had breasts and butts and thighs and bellies. Girls who had *substance*. The black fabric that covered us from armpit to midthigh expanded and grew loose when wet. My suit had red stitching, and I dreaded the looming specter of the white thread. I worried what it would mean about my body, my attractiveness, my place in the order of things.

In high school, I was confronted with even more concrete evidence that my body was somehow wrong. Although I could barely run a mile, I would occasionally fraternize with the tenth-grade cross-country team, attending their pregame spaghetti dinners, where we would heap gluey pasta with jarred red sauce on our plates and gossip about school. At one of these dinners, a friend pulled me aside to tell me a secret—the kind of secret no one should tell. She revealed that a girl on the team had been overheard at practice complaining about how fat she was getting. How her hips were *so* big. Another girl laughed at this and said, *At least your butt isn't as big as Heather's.*

I was shaken. I imagined the willowy and desirable blondes

of the cross-country team, laughing heartily and venomously about one thing they all knew to be true: Heather Radke did, indeed, have a big butt. And they were oh so glad they did not.

The story of my relationship with my body isn't a dramatic one. In fact, I'm interested in it primarily because it strikes me as fairly typical. There was no relentless bullying, no significant eating disorder, nothing that pushes my feelings about my body beyond the shame that seems to infect the brain of every seventh-grade girl, a hellish rite of passage so many of us had to get through to become semi-functioning adults. It's as though the ranking of bodies—and all the attendant humiliation and self-doubt—is normal, natural even. As though there actually *are* bodies that are better, and those that are worse.

The first time someone told me my butt was sexy was in 2003. I was twenty and it was summertime and I was pulling shots of espresso behind a coffee bar in a Midwestern college town. I was wearing a polyester, navy blue pleated skirt and a thrifted yellow T-shirt that I had cut the neck out of, in an attempt to make it look more punk. My hair was pulled back; grounds of coffee stuck to my sweaty neck. Since high school, my butt had grown ever larger. Every pair of pants seemed to fit me strangely, gaping at the waist even as they stretched tightly across my butt—I went from wearing a size eight to wearing a size ten, then twelve and fourteen. If a group needed to squeeze four into the back of a car, I would blurt out that my ass was actually too large to make it work and that someone should just sit on my lap. One day, my coworker at the coffeehouse—a quiet singer-songwriter boy who was tall and flirty—asked me, "Do you know what *callipygian* means?" I did. I'd learned it for the SATs and could still recall the flash card that made me blush. The word is Greek. It means "having beautiful buttocks." I supposed that art historians must have used it in describing statuary. "You, darling, are callipygian," the singer-songwriter told me. His delivery was definitely awkward and the line felt rehearsed, like he was testing out vocabulary that was just beyond his reach. Even so, I was frankly moved. He wasn't making fun of me. It felt like a sincere compliment.

He was only the first in a series of people I encountered in my twenties and thirties who seemed to regard my generous butt not as a drawback, but as a virtue. It became the frequent subject of catcalls; the word on a lover's lips as they whispered in my ear; the part of my body that elicited second glances from strangers and comments from men at work. In other words, I was becoming aware that my butt was—or had become, when I wasn't looking—a sexual object, a thing that other people (*some* other people; certainly not *all* other people) found desirable.

And those people were almost always men. Although I am queer, and although I dated both men and women during those years, the truth was that this change in how other people thought about my butt seemed to be emanating from straight, mainstream culture. Plenty of women commented on my butt, but they were mostly straight and seemed to be parroting beauty magazines in an updated, inverted version of the girl on the cross-country team who said she was so glad her butt was not like mine.

Although I told myself that what other people—especially men—thought about my body shouldn't matter, the truth was it really did. All of a sudden, a part of me that had felt shameful and ugly was the part that some people liked most. Although I didn't want to be admired only for my body, I certainly wanted my body to be admired. Like all people, I wanted to be wanted. And it felt good to be wanted by the sort of people who had once made me feel ashamed.

I wonder now how my peers in high school came to their

initial conclusion that my body wasn't one of the *good* ones, and how, a decade later, many of those same men and women came to feel the opposite. How could it be that what a butt means had seemed to change so radically, and so quickly? How could a body part mean so many different things to so many different people? Those are the questions that prompted the research at the heart of this book.

Before becoming a writer, I worked for a number of years as a curator at the Jane Addams Hull-House Museum in Chicago, a historic-house museum that also functioned as a contemporary art space and community gathering place for the city's activists. When I put together an exhibition at Hull-House, my job was to present stories and cultural experiences that helped to explain larger shifts and themes in history. This book is meant to work in a similar way: I will introduce you to figures from the past and present and tell specific stories that speak to important shifts in what butts have represented in the United States and Western Europe over the past two centuries.

Butts: A Backstory is an attempt to trace some of the threads of thought and meaning surrounding this enigmatic body part, and explore how they evolved and continue to resonate in the present. The approach is largely historical and chronological but begins with the scientific basics: What, exactly, *is* a butt anatomically and physiologically? Though butts have been around forever, my framework's historical starting point is the story of Sarah Baartman, once called the "Venus Hottentot," whose cruel and lurid display in life and death is foundational to perceptions of the butt for the past two centuries. From there, I explore a number of topics extending through the twentieth and twenty-first centuries, peering into the histories of fashion, race, science, fitness, and popular culture, encountering a procession of people who have shaped ideas about butts—an illustrator who defined the sleek look of the flapper, a model whose butt is used as the template for nearly every pair of pants on the market, a eugenicist artist who created sculptures of the most "normal" man and woman, the man who invented Buns of Steel, drag queens who design butt pads, and fat fitness instructors who used aerobics as a form of resistance and a way to find joy. Finally, I explore changing attitudes toward the butt in the last thirty years—a time when large butts gradually became integrated into the mainstream, white beauty ideal and the appropriation of Black bodies and culture hit a new peak.

A project like this could never be all things to all people. It can't begin to answer the question, *What is the history and meaning of every butt?* In this book, I focus on the history and symbolism of women's butts for the simple reason that I am a woman and I began this project because I was interested in how feminine identity is constructed, reconstructed, and reinforced over time.

My research also deals exclusively with the *butt*—the two protruding masses of muscle and fat situated between the lower back and thighs. There are a number of excellent books exploring the anus and rectum and their myriad associations and functions, but those are not my objects of study. Although there are relationships between the symbolic meanings of the anus and the butt, women's butts frequently carry their own, separate symbolism and aren't necessarily linked to the various functions of the anus, sexual or otherwise.

I am primarily interested in butts as construed and represented by mainstream, hegemonic, Western culture—the culture of those who hold political and economic power, those who dominate popular media and who are most responsible for creating, perpetuating, and enforcing broad standards and trends.

That is, I am often exploring how straight people, white people, and men have (mis)understood and enforced standards, preferences, and ideology on the butts of women of all races, and the meanings they have constructed about women's bodies in the process. Of course, these are general categories and may suggest binaries where they do not exist—the experience of living inside a body always constitutes multiple, intersecting identities—but it has often been people who identify as male, straight, and/or white who have been able to determine the meanings of butts because they were in positions of power.

I've decided to focus on these mainstream concepts of women's butts because I wish to understand where the often unspoken ideas and prejudices about butts come from, and to speak that history clearly. Because of the power they've long held in science, politics, media, and culture, white people, men, and straight people have always maintained an inordinate amount of influence and control over what meanings are applied to bodies. They have invented and enforced ideas of what is normal and what is deviant, what is "mainstream" and what is marginal. By looking closely at how people in power have constructed those meanings, my hope is that I will make visible something that often feels invisible: the deep historical roots of why women seem to have so many—and so many contradictory—feelings about their butts. I wanted to understand why butts have come to mean so much, when they could very well mean nothing at all.

One thing I found consistently throughout my research is that conversations about butts are almost always also conversations about race, specifically about Blackness and whiteness. From the earliest days of colonial exploration in Africa, European explorers and scientists employed pseudoscientific theories about big-butted Black women to construct and reinforce racial hierarchies and stereotypes (particularly the doggedly persistent stereotype of the hypersexual Black woman), a set of ideas that were amplified and reinforced in the wake of Sarah Baartman's death in the nineteenth century. Both Black femininity and white femininity are ideas that are informed by stereotypes of the body and the butt created by scientists in the eighteenth and nineteenth centuries, stereotypes that affect not only Black women and white women but women of all races. It is for this reason that this book is so often an exploration of Blackness and whiteness specifically.

Of course, any knowledge I have of what butts mean and have meant within communities of color, in other nations, and in cultures of the past is derived from reporting and research, not firsthand experience. My experience with my body is specific, and the shame I have felt about my butt comes from the particular context I grew up in. It is not at all universal. Many of those I've spoken with in my research for this book love their butts or grew up with very different ideas about what constitutes an ideal body than I did. In these pages, I've endeavored to include voices of those who can speak to experiences other than my own, and I've conducted interviews with women and non-binary people from disparate backgrounds as crucial foundational research. Ultimately, though, this book is an idiosyncratic one. It stems from the questions that most interest me about the butt: questions about gender, race, control, fitness, fashion, and science. It is not an encyclopedia of butts and does not attempt or claim to be comprehensive—it is not the final word on the subject, and there are many fascinating areas of research associated with butts that are not included in these pages. My hope is that by not only exploring historical context but also articulating my personal experiences and feelings, I can contend with my own body straightforwardly and help others to see that that which we do not name, that which goes unsaid, holds tremendous power. In that sense, this book is a political project as much as anything else: it is a way of teasing out and examining levers of power that aren't always visible.

"I personally do not find my butt sexy. I am self-conscious about its largeness," a white woman in her midthirties told me. "It's horrifying to imagine that there's someone in my life that knows what it looks like really well. But many strange men have made it clear they find my butt sexy. Since I was young, I have always known that men of all walks of life like my butt. Not all of them; skinny white guys don't like my butt very much."

"I'd probably think my butt was fabulous if I was white," says a small-butted Black woman in her fifties. "But like many things about me, it's one of the things that makes me sort of racially inauthentic. Whenever I say this, people get tense; they think I'm hating on myself. I just mean that I was plagued as a child by other people's assessment that I was not Black enough."

Another white woman in her thirties describes her ideal body for herself as "as androgynous as possible but still female—small breasts, no hips. Classic androgynous dyke. Jenny Shimizu." But she's attracted to big-butted women. "My first girlfriend had a big butt and I couldn't get over it. It looks good, it feels good, and it's nice to hold on to. It's the opposite of the body I have." Lately she's been wondering if her idealized body for herself is a problem. "I've started to wonder how much of this ideal is internalized misogyny. Why does it feel like a feminine body cannot house brilliance and sarcasm? Why am I hewing so closely to these sexist narratives?"

A Chinese American woman in her twenties describes her butt as "a good protrusion" on her "planklike shape." But she also tells me, "I'm continuously surprised when my butt is sexualized. I guess I have a fear that my sex appeal is rooted in having this girl-like figure. I wonder if my sexiness is some offshoot of pedophilia, [if] any interest in me is the sexualization of a schoolgirl." It's not something she's ever brought up with a partner, but it is always in the back of her mind.

Over and over again in my research, I've been surprised by how many different meanings one body part can contain. And yet, several of the women I talked to told similar stories about how they came to understand their bodies. For some, their mothers and grandmothers and aunts told them to cover themselves up. For others, those same relations taught them how to enjoy their curves. Catcalls and middle-school taunts told them where they stood in the order of things. Nearly every woman, regardless of the size and shape of her butt, told a story about a dressing room and the sinking feeling that there would never be a pair of pants that fit her correctly.

In so many ways, butts ask us to turn away, to giggle with hot-faced shame and roll our eyes. When I started writing this book, I wondered what would happen if I instead turned my full attention toward the butt, if I investigated its history and asked butt experts and enthusiasts of all stripes—scientists, drag queens, dance instructors, historians, and archivists—serious questions about what butts are and what butts mean. In doing so, I found stories of tragedy, anger, oppression, lust, and joy. And I found that in our bodies, we carry histories.

Origins

MUSCLE

. .

If you happened to find yourself near the arid shores of Kenya's Lake Turkana 1.9 million years ago, you might have encountered the first known hominid with a butt. This creature was closer to a modern human than an ape: His nose was distinct from his face, a cartilaginous appendage rather than two holes in his head. His face was flat, with eyes that looked forward. He had a bony brow ridge with a forehead that sloped steeply back. He walked, and ran, on two legs. And he had a protruding gluteal muscle at the top of each hip, the underlying flesh of a round, strong backside.

The area he lived in would have looked much like the African savanna as we know it now, with few trees and open grassland, a relatively recent change from the lush, dense, jungle-like forest his distant relatives had inhabited for millions of years. The ancestors of *Homo erectus* had bodies adapted to life in the trees: agile, flexible legs and feet designed for climbing, as well as apelike snouts, hairy bodies, and enormous jaws that allowed them to grind down massive amounts of vegetation. Their butts were flat and small—hardly butts at all. By the time this specific *Homo erectus* came on the scene, however, the bodies of hominids had adapted to their new, flat terrain. To succeed on the savanna, large gluteal muscles were a must.

Several millennia later, in the summer of 1974, Bernard

Ngeneo slowly paced the same eastern shore of Lake Turkana, peering intently at the dark, sandy soil. He was there as a member of what he and his colleagues affectionately referred to as the "Hominid Gang," a group of Kenyans working on the expeditions of Richard Leakey, a famous and often controversial paleontologist and conservationist. The members of the Hominid Gang were known for their expert ability to find human fossils buried deep in rock or hidden in plain sight among bones and shells—just two years earlier, Ngeneo had discovered a skull buried beneath a pile of animal fossils that was believed to be evidence of an entirely new species in the *Homo* family.

Ngeneo trained his keen eye on a rock cemented with pebbles and shells, remnants from the bottom of an ancient lake that had been covered by sediment for millions of years. There, among the solid remains of aquatic life, Ngeneo glimpsed something promising poking up out of the rock. A closer look revealed that the expert hominid finder had struck again. Ngeneo had found fossil KNM-ER 3228, a right hip bone and the last remaining part of a male hominid who had walked the shores of Lake Turkana 1.9 million years before, the oldest hip bone anyone had ever found (or has found since). And although there is no documentation suggesting that anyone thought much about this specific bone on the dig—it was one of many hominid parts found that summer—Ngeneo's discovery would give science a critical tool for understanding the purpose, and evolutionary backstory, of the human butt.

It was Dr. Daniel Lieberman, Edwin M. Lerner II Professor of Biological Sciences and chair of the Department of Human Evolutionary Biology at Harvard, who directed me to fossil KNM-ER 3228. Although scientists in the nineteenth century created a robust pseudoscience of the butt as part of a larger project of creating and justifying racial hierarchies, the butt wasn't a particularly rich topic of study for much of the twentieth century. For the past twenty years, however, Lieberman has been the go-to guy for the biology of the butt, and he's likely the scientist who has taken the most keen interest in fossil KNM-ER 3228.

When Lieberman encountered the fossil in the 1990s, he found a key to answering a question that few evolutionary biologists had ever taken seriously, and one that became Lieberman's singular point of focus for many years. It wasn't, however, a question about butts—or at least it didn't start as one. Instead, it was a question about running.

While in graduate school at Harvard, Lieberman had been taught that humans were terrible runners and that running was a relatively unimportant adaptation in the history of human evolution. Biologists understood human running as little more than fast walking, a byproduct of bipedalism that humans weren't particularly well suited for. Instead, they believed that the champion runners of the animal kingdom were sleek quadrupeds like antelopes and cheetahs, whose four legs allowed them to gallop and spring forth with all four feet off the ground, and gave them stealth and maneuverability. Because it's impossible to gallop with two legs, four-legged animals will always have an advantage over even the fastest humans. (For example, Usain Bolt can sprint at ten meters per second for several seconds, but an antelope or a horse can sprint at fifteen meters per second for several minutes.) Humans are good at a lot of things, evolutionary biologists thought, but running isn't one of them. During the course of his studies, however, Lieberman began to believe that the conventional wisdom might be wrong.

He came to this conclusion while conducting an experiment where he observed miniature pigs trotting on treadmills. One day, as Lieberman was conducting his pig exercise research, a colleague named Dennis Bramble stopped by to observe. Bramble pointed out that the pigs' heads flopped around when they ran, probably because they didn't have a special ligament (called the nuchal ligament) in the back of their skull to help steady their heads while in motion. All the great runners of the animal kingdom have this ligament— horses, dogs, cheetahs, jackrabbits. Animals that aren't great runners, including apes and chimpanzees, do not. But as Lieberman and Bramble talked, they remembered that one animal who was supposedly a terrible runner *did* have the ligament: humans.

Bramble and Lieberman were intrigued. They'd both read a paper—at that point dismissed by many biologists—that posited that running was actually a crucial part of human evolution, rather than a mere side effect of bipedalism. As they thought more about the nuchal ligament, they started to wonder if there might be something to it.

In order to figure it out, Bramble and Lieberman went to the Harvard Museum and started digging through fossils so they could figure out when the nuchal ligament became part of the story of human evolution and why. They quickly discovered that it appeared in the fossil record at a very important moment in human evolution—about two million years ago, when *Homo erectus* first came on the scene. *Homo erectus* was the first human ancestor to walk around on two legs, and also—critically—the first ancestor to have a large brain.

As they examined the fossil record, Lieberman and Bramble discovered that nearly all of the physical traits that make it possible for humans to run appeared around the same time our ancestors became bipedal. This fact suggested to them that hominids may have become bipedal, in part, in order to run. *Homo erectus* was the first hominid species to have short toes that could bend and flex when it launched itself forward; the first species to have arched inner feet and long Achilles tendons, which act like springs and shock absorbers; the first species to have hips that can twist and knees that can bear the load of the hard footfalls of a running creature. It was also the first species to have a butt.

This discovery led Lieberman to the extensive study of the butt in human running. He closely examined the anatomical differences between the butts of humans and those of their closest primate relatives and attached electrodes to the butts of human research subjects as they ran on treadmills in an effort to determine what, exactly, the gluteus maximus does when a person breaks into a jog. By 2013 he had become famous for his research and made an appearance on *The Colbert Report* to describe the butt's evolutionary purpose. "If you look at the butt of a chimpanzee, it's tiny. They have really, really pathetic butts," he explained. Humans, on the other hand, have enormous butts; our gluteus maximus is the biggest muscle in our body and we are still the only animals on Earth that have such a large gluteal muscle. Like the whites of our eyes and the arches in our feet, the gluteus maximus is a uniquely human feature. He encouraged Colbert to walk around with his palms firmly affixed to his butt cheeks so that he might feel how flaccid the muscles are when walking. Then Lieberman asked Colbert to run. "Do you feel it clenching up?"

When I spoke to Lieberman, he suggested that I perform the same test, though in my case I had to dig in deep to feel the muscles move because my butt isn't just, or even mostly, muscle. As I ran around in a circle in my apartment, my toes sprung me forward, my hips twisted, my butt clenched. Despite the fact that I can barely make it twice around the block at a slow jog, Lieberman assured me that my body was designed for the task, and that proof of this could be found in the Arizona desert.

Every October since 1983, in the thin air of Prescott, Arizona, a soulful blinds salesman named Ron Barrett has organized a race straightforwardly called Man Against Horse. According to Barrett, the race began as a bar bet between a local city councilman and a horse-loving police officer. The drunken city councilman asserted that a well-trained human could beat a horse in a foot race. The policeman disagreed and, feeling certain of his odds, suggested they put money on it. The two men set up a course, and for the next four decades, a version of that race has been an annual tradition. The concept is simple: a group of humans and horses traverses the desert in a daylong endurance race that pits beast against beast, human against human, and, most crucially, one against the other.

These days, humans and horses go head-to-head on Mingus Mountain, a 7,800-foot pine-covered peak thirty miles outside of Prescott. Although Barrett sets up 12- and 25-mile races, the real race—the one that attracts some of the world's best distance runners and endurance riders—is the 50-mile ultrarun.

Skeptical but curious, I traveled to the course to see what Lieberman described as a primordial battle unfold. Horses would hurl their 1,500-pound bodies (more with their rider) up a small rocky path, balanced atop four hooves, each smaller than a human hand. After completing the length of a full marathon along the same route, the runners would climb 1,700 feet up the back of the steep mountain, ascending "knee to cheek," as Ron Barrett describes it. Even then, they would only be halfway done—they would then need to run almost twenty more miles before they crossed the finish line. And then, after a day of primal competition, all the humans would gorge on barbecue.

When I arrived, I discovered that the event begins on a flat, arid expanse where runners and riders both set up camp the day before. One side of a small creek was the land of horses. Each animal arrived in an enormous trailer along with all that was needed to care for them: hay and hoof-picks and saddles and special shoes that looked like Crocs designed to protect the horses' small hooves from the rugged terrain. The riders set up makeshift paddocks, small fenced-in areas for the horses to rest and eat in. As they did, the animals huffed and whinnied, snorted and nickered, cutting a bold silhouette against the bright blue desert sky.

On the other side of the creek was the land of runners. They pulled up in energy-efficient Subarus, ate vegan gel that came in pouches, wore clothes that could be bunched up into a sack the size of a fist. "Tiny heinies" was what one of the endurance riders called the runners, and the runners almost all fit the description: small, lithe, and thin, with lean, muscular butts—butts built to beat the enormous and powerful beasts munching grass across the creek.

Despite the seemingly long odds, in every version of the Man Against Horse Race, at least one runner had beaten at least one horse. Lieberman himself had done it—the year he ran, he remembered, he bested "almost all the horses"—and he was "just a middle-aged professor!" But there had never been a human runner who had beaten all the horses. The year I attended, however, buzz floated through the camp about one runner in particular: Nick Coury, a software engineer from Phoenix, who happened to be one of the world's best ultramarathoners and was thought to just maybe possess the goods to win the ultimate human victory.

I met Nick on the morning of the race as he sat in the trunk of his hatchback, rubbing his eyes and yawning. After inhaling an entire sausage pizza on the late-night drive up from Phoenix, he had slept in his car. I asked him if he thought he might be able to beat the horses. He smiled and said humbly, "I don't like to get ahead of myself," before pulling on his shorts, lacing up his shoes, and darting over to the porta-potties. Even in the ultrarunning world, where fifty-mile runs are commonplace, this one was hard: Nick would have to climb 2,800 feet up a labyrinthine trail, confronting loose rocks and tough footing and significant temperature changes—not to mention the enormous, heaving equines running alongside him.

The run started at six a.m. The air was dry—I'd spend the entire day smearing my face with Vaseline in a Sisyphean effort to mitigate the effects of the high desert air—and the early morning sky was clear and pink. I had imagined a whinnying pack of horses pawing at the ground, bunched up with a group of focused runners at a ceremonial starting block, but both horses and runners preferred a less cinematic, calmer beginning. The runners stretched and jogged in place. Horses pranced around in a large, loose circle. The starting line wasn't much more than a small flag and a mark in the dirt. Ron didn't even shoot a starter pistol, because it might have scared the horses. He just yelled, rather inefficiently, "Man Against Horse Race starts right now! Here we go!" And then they were off.

The horses galloped out of the gate, but once they reached the foot of the mountain, they began to move slowly and carefully to avoid a fall. Nick and the other humans started at a slow jog and quickly found themselves literally eating their competition's dust. But although the horses had speed, humans had a different advantage: they had endurance. And this, according to Lieberman, is vital to the story of human evolution.

The human ability to run long distances, as Lieberman explains it, evolved when *Homo erectus* went from living in forests to roaming the grasslands, a lifestyle that demanded different capacities and capabilities. When animals live among trees, as gorillas still do today, there is plenty to eat: bugs, berries, and vegetation are all abundant. These foods are fibrous and hard to chew, but a gorilla's low metabolism makes it possible for them to live off of it. They can spend all day eating without having to worry about running out of nourishment.

Homo erectus, on the other hand, needed to figure out a way to sustain themselves without the inexhaustible gifts of the woodlands. Instead of eating bucketloads of berries and leaves, they turned to what was available: the flesh of animals, which, unlike the low-quality foods of the forest, offered significant quantities of calories and protein per bite. Nutrient-rich wildebeests and kudu dotted the savanna, but how could the relatively slow-moving *Homo erectus* keep up with, and hunt down, these speedy, four-legged beasts?

For more than a century, evolutionary biologists, including Darwin, surmised that *Homo erectus*'s ability to hunt fast-moving savanna creatures was due to one of the major advantages of bipedalism: *Homo erectus*'s hands had been freed up to make, and use, tools for hunting like spears, bows, and arrows. But recent archaeology has shown this to be unlikely. It is harder than you might think to penetrate a tough, leathery animal hide, and harder still to inflict the damage necessary to fell a racing, six-hundred-pound wildebeest. You'd need to use a stone-tipped spear or arrow to get the job done, but the best tools *Homo erectus* had available were wooden clubs and sharpened sticks. They would have had to be in very close proximity to an animal in order to kill it. So what did early humans do without sophisticated weapons? They used their butts.

According to Lieberman, the reason why Nick Coury would have any chance at all in the Man Against Horse Race is because early humans evolved a specific advantage over many quadrupeds: although a four-legged animal can run very fast, it can't run at high speeds for long stretches of time. Horses and other quadrupeds are incapable of panting when they gallop—they can only pant while trotting or walking. This means they can't keep themselves cool while running at high speeds. In intense heat, after ten to fifteen kilometers of galloping, they have to slow down to modulate their temperature. This is true as well of the animals that ancient humans hunted on the savanna, an environment much hotter and flatter than Mingus Mountain. An antelope running at full speed in high heat can't keep up the pace for long. Humans, on the other hand, can run at a slower pace for hours at a time, and a running human moves just a little bit faster than most trotting quadrupeds. This is possible thanks, in part, to the unique collection of dense muscle at the top of our legs.

The human butt muscles are part of a complicated stabilizing apparatus: the gluteus maximus equivalent in chimps is primarily a muscle that allows them to move their legs away from the body, but in humans it is an extensor—a muscle that allows an animal to straighten and extend a limb outward. It is a critical part of the system that keeps us from tumbling forward as we launch ourselves off our back feet when we run, and it helps to slow us down just a bit as our foot hits the ground so that we maintain control over our stride. The butt is an essential adaptation for the human ability to run steadily, for long distances, and without injury.

As evolution slowly crawled along, *Homo erectus*'s brain got bigger. It takes a lot of calories to maintain brain tissue; a breastfeeding mother would have required about 2,500 calories every day. This was a hard goal to meet on the savanna, and so hunting and running were necessary to continue feeding the evolving organs that would eventually allow hominids to use tools, create agriculture, read books, and make outlandish bets at bars. Lieberman believes that the butt, among other adaptations, allowed *Homo erectus* to chase after prey for miles until they tired and had to stop. Then *Homo erectus* would bash their prey over the head with a rock and eat the spoils, making it possible for them to eat a large, calorie-rich meal.

Dennis Bramble, Lieberman's old colleague from his days running pigs on treadmills, believes something slightly different, and slightly less grand: that the ability to run allowed *Homo erectus* to compete for the scraps of the savanna, not catch their own prey. After a lion or other large predator had made a kill, it would leave carrion behind, and the scavengers would need to run long distances to beat out the other scavengers and arrive before the dead flesh had spoiled.

Another group of scientists, led by Jamie Bartlett at the University of Colorado Boulder, has done a study that shows that although the butt is critical for endurance running, it actually has many other functions. Bartlett says the gluteus maximus is "akin to a multifunction Swiss Army knife" in that it helps humans to climb, throw, lift, and squat. Bartlett believes that the butt evolved to help *Homo erectus* traverse long distances, but also to help them escape predators—to scamper up the few trees available on the savanna, to squat behind bushes, to move quickly and nimbly away from a predator. She tells me this is fairly obvious if you take a look at a track team. "It's not the distance runners who have big butts, it's the sprinters, jumpers, and the throwers."

Although these scientists differ on the precise reason for the butt muscles' existence, they agree that it is a uniquely human feature that crucially contributed to our evolution. We are humans, you could say, thanks to our butts.

One point nine million years ago, the man whose hip bone would become fossil KNM-ER 3228 ran after a wildebeest. His large butt flexed, and the long tendons that attached his heel to the back of his knee catapulted him forward like a spring. His head, balanced on his spine, bobbed loosely as he ran, the S-curve in his back absorbing the shock of each footfall. His sparse body hair and ample sweat glands kept him cool, and he panted heavily through his mouth as he slowly, steadily, ran after his prey.

On a beautiful October day two million years later, Nick Coury runs up a mountain. His butt muscles flex, his sweat glands release perspiration, his tendons and joints propel him forward like a spring. He passes one horse and then another, climbing Mingus Mountain slowly, one footfall at a time. He uses his gluteal muscles to climb, and then he uses them to run. He doesn't think about the end, or the powerful animals around him. He thinks only about the few feet in front of him. And then, suddenly, Nick realizes that he is winning.

The mountain turns flat, and Nick can see the finish line in the distance. He feels euphoric, flush with the pleasurable endorphins that many call a runner's high (likely another evolutionary adaptation that helps make humans excellent runners). He starts to run as fast as he can, holding nothing back. Tears stream down his face as he crosses the finish line. It has been six hours and fourteen minutes since he started the race, the fastest any runner has ever completed the course. Like the man with hip bone KNM-ER 3228, Nick has outrun all of his four-legged competitors, the first human in Man Against Horse history to do so. Nick hasn't done it for food—he has his vegan goo and a barbecue celebration dinner waiting for him—but simply because he loves to run.

FAT

· ·

Muscles serve a certain physiological purpose—they expand and contract, moving bone and sinew up and down, back and forth, allowing us to sit upright, lean side to side, even digest our food—and, as a result, are the easiest part of the butt to study and to understand. But butts, especially women's butts, do not consist only of muscle. They also have a layer of fat that sits on top of the gluteus maximus—and for many (including me) that layer of fat is thick, and it is complicated.

In nearly every way, fat is far more difficult to study than muscle. A soft tissue, it decomposes after organisms die and leaves no long-term record behind, so evolutionary biologists can't know for certain how early humans or our hominid ancestors carried it on their bodies. It is very tempting to imagine ancient humans as thin and lithe, to see the earliest *Homo sapiens* as the blueprints for our current rendering of the ideal body, but the truth is that no one knows the size of the breasts or butt of the earliest human females, just as they don't know the girth of a male *Homo erectus*'s penis or whether he had a beard.

We do know, however, that humans living today are the fattest primates, storing significantly more "white fat"—fat that isn't easily converted to energy—than other primates, which carry more of the quickly and easily metabolized "brown fat." According to Duke postdoctoral associate Devjanee

Swain-Lenz, this difference is embedded in our DNA. A gene that converts white fat to brown fat is literally turned off in humans, making us biologically more susceptible to fat accumulation.

According to Morgan Hoke, who has studied nutrition in both contemporary and historical human populations in her role as assistant professor of anthropology at the University of Pennsylvania, this development began when nutrition was sparse and early hominids had to rely on fat reserves to survive. It wasn't so much that they were starving; there were just frequent and significant variations in what kind of and how much food was available. To survive, early hominids went through metabolic and genetic changes that allowed them to pack on fat that they could then use as a kind of caloric deep storage in case of emergency. This was necessary for the same reason it was crucial for *Homo erectus* to devise a way to hunt: larger brains need more calories. And although our gluteal muscles helped us to hunt and scavenge for high-calorie meat, we needed reserves of fat on our bodies to make sure that our brains could function even when it was very cold and when food was hard to come by. It is ironic, then, that in the twenty-first-century United States, it is almost impossible to conceive of fat in the way we think of muscle—as a part of the body with a job to do. Instead, fat in any form—whether in food or on bodies—carries layers of negative association: gluttony and decadence, rather than necessity and abundance.

Although all people need fat in order to stay healthy, women need it more than men. Most women have twenty to thirty pounds of fat on their bodies, which is a significant percentage of body mass and a lot of weight to haul around, which would seem to be an evolutionary disadvantage. Studies say the lowest level of body fat for a woman to have and still be considered healthy (that is, not starving) is 8–12 percent. For men, that number is 4–6 percent. One scientist I met with told me that even the thinnest women have a higher percentage of fat on their bodies than any other creature on Earth, with two exceptions: seagoing mammals, and bears just before they go into hibernation. After hearing this fact, I spent the next two weeks repeating it to other women I know. It somehow felt powerful—we have the kind of fat that keeps enormous seagoing creatures warm in Arctic waters, the kind that could get you through winter in a cave in the woods. It also felt delightfully outside of my control. This undeniable scientific reality became an antidote to the perpetual voice in my head that said, *Aren't you just a little bit too fat?* I felt like I had a solid rebuttal for once: *Fat is part of what it is to be female. My fat is what makes me like a nursing whale, like a mama bear.*

Of course, I am not a large seafaring mammal, nor do I hibernate. Nor do any of the other women I know. A whale cow's blubber may serve many functions, but one is very clear: she needs to stay warm in glacial waters. A bear going into hibernation needs significant reserves to get through the winter. But why does a female human need to store so much fat on her body?

"As a feminist it frustrates me, because I can't come up with any other answer," Hoke tells me, "but it has to do with reproduction. It turns out that pregnancy and breastfeeding are really expensive in terms of energetic cost." She further explains that, as with any animals that utilize sexual reproduction, there are going to be some biological differences between the sexes to accommodate the physical and energetic needs of creating new humans—and there is no question who takes on the primary biological burden. "A sperm basically costs nothing," Hoke explains. "An egg doesn't cost much either, but for humans there is a grueling nine months of childbearing and then breastfeeding, which can go on for a long time." The need for extra reserves is huge, because nutrition is going toward fueling two (or more) bodies and brains. Pregnancy requires the mother to take in approximately three hundred extra calories per day, and some studies indicate that breastfeeding can require even more caloric fuel. If there isn't enough food in the environment, a breastfeeding mother can rely on the fat she stores on her body to feed her babies.

Women may need a significant amount of fat to meet the demands of reproduction, but that fat could be anywhere. We could have fat globules hanging from our elbows; our shoulders and necks could be large and bulbous. But instead, fat gathers in the hips, butt, thighs, and breasts, creating a pattern of curves that now read to us as distinctly feminine—but why? The most straightforward possibility is physiological. We have to carry it where we do because to store it elsewhere might impede our range of motion and disrupt the center of gravity—to have a very fatty shoulder would make us top-heavy; to have very fatty knees would make it hard to walk.

There is also a body of research—conducted by Professor Hoke and other evolutionary anthropologists—that suggests storing fat in the butt and thighs is safer for us because it's far from vital organs, which don't react well to being surrounded by fatty tissue. Additionally, there is some evidence that women with bigger butts and thighs and smaller waists have fattier breast milk, a positive adaptation for helping babies to grow, particularly in places where there may not be ready access to significant fat in the diet. Hoke suggests that this may indicate that when human females are breastfeeding, they draw on the white adipose fat stored in the thighs and butt to nurture their babies.

The truth is, the butt is an anatomically simple part of the body: it is a joint attached to a few large muscles and covered with a layer of fat. But although we have a good understanding of why we have butt muscles, and even, to some extent, why they are covered in fat, it isn't entirely clear why butts are, for many people, so attractive and what, if anything, this has to do with evolution. In order to answer those questions, to the extent they are even answerable, we need to talk about peacocks.

FEATHERS

· ·

Imagine, if you will, a peacock—that grand and bright pheasant, originally from the Indian subcontinent, that now roams the grounds of children's zoos and eccentric billionaires' gardens the world over. The peacock is colorful—he has a bright blue head and opulent, iridescent tail plumage with a distinctive eyespot pattern best seen when he fans his tail high and wide—a tail that can extend up to five feet long. The tail alone makes up about 60 percent of his overall body length and weighs around eleven ounces, quite a bit on a bird that typically weighs around ten pounds.

"The sight of a feather in a peacock's tail, whenever I gaze at it, makes me sick!" Charles Darwin famously wrote in a letter to Harvard botanist Asa Gray in 1860. It wasn't the beauty that sickened him, but rather the fact that he was unable to explain the existence of such an enormous, conspicuous, yet seemingly useless part of an animal. Evolution, as we often think of it, prioritizes efficiency, and a peacock's tail is decidedly not an efficient addition. In fact, it is the opposite—a burdensome appendage, attracting predators with its shimmering color and making it difficult to escape.

Darwin's theory of natural selection tells us that the members of a species best adapted to their surroundings, and therefore more likely to survive and flourish, will also be more likely to reproduce. If a trait is heritable and helpful, it is passed down to a higher percentage of members of the next generation. In this way, random genetic mutations add up, resulting in organisms better evolved to succeed in their environment—survival of the fittest, as they say. But if it is true that those animals with favorable characteristics are more likely to survive, how do we explain an apparently unnecessary, or even counterproductive, ornamentation? "This is a real puzzle," says Chris Haufe, professor and philosopher of science at Case Western Reserve University. "You have all these animals with really costly traits—really bright plumage, bright scaling, bright faces, animals who are always making noise. They're doing stuff that seems idiotic from a survival perspective. And so you need a way of explaining why it is so widespread."

Darwin attempted to explain these traits in *The Descent of Man, and Selection in Relation to Sex*, his bold follow-up to *On the Origin of Species*. In it, he proposed that while natural selection chooses animals that are best suited to an environment, sexual selection plays a significant role as well. These heritable features, which Darwin called secondary sexual characteristics, make them more attractive to their mates (Darwinian evolution assumes heterosexual mating) and therefore make them more fit. In humans, female hips and butts are considered a secondary sexual characteristic, as are breasts, and may have been selected to look the way they do because of mates' preferences. That is, male humans, over centuries, *might* have chosen to mate with females who had particular kinds of butts that they found attractive, and thus indirectly altered the body part's evolution forever. But whether it actually functioned that way and what, exactly, this attraction might mean or how it might work remains unresolved, opening the interpretive floodgates for a separate—and often controversial—field of evolutionary studies.

Since the 1990s, the discipline of evolutionary psychology emerged as a popular method for understanding the relationship between sexual attraction and evolution. You can find evolutionary psychology studies in academic journals, but you'll also find them referenced in the pages of *Maxim* or *Cosmopolitan* or in long Reddit threads attempting to explain why contemporary behaviors or psychological traits—promiscuity, fear of spiders, or male desire for specific female traits, like big butts—may have been advantageous to early humans. These are also the armchair theories I most often hear when I tell people at parties that I'm writing a book about butts. "Don't big butts signal fertility?" someone will say as they search for another beer in the back of the fridge. "I've heard that women with big butts are smarter," someone else might add as they plunge their hand into a bowl of chips.

Although these acquaintances are surely just dredging up some half-remembered thing they read long ago in an internet wormhole, I find these comments telling because of what they seem to imply. There are two underlying assumptions being made: first, that big butts are biologically advantageous, and second, that sexual attraction to butts, particularly big butts, is innate and out of our control. Just as we crave sweetness because sugar sustains us, the partygoers seem to suggest that we desire big butts because they are good for us and help us survive. It is somehow natural, and in our biological best interests, to be turned on by prominent butts.

Because evolutionary psychologists often take on pop topics related to sex and attractiveness, magazines use their studies as the basis of click-baity articles like "High Heels Do Have Power over Men, Study Finds" and "How Make-up Makes Men Admire but Other Women Jealous." These articles offer watered-down evolutionary justifications for common behaviors—women are jealous of other women who wear makeup in the workplace because they perceive the makeup wearers to be sexually dominant; high heels compel a woman to arch her back, an ancient signal of her readiness to mate—instead of cultural ones. Evolutionary psychology isn't designed to grapple with the seemingly more obvious explanations of human behavior that are rooted in culture, identity, or individual psychological experience. For example, maybe the men in the study were entranced by women wearing high heels because they've spent a lifetime absorbing images that equate high heels with sexiness; perhaps women's jealousy of other women emerges because there are so few opportunities for women in many work environments and women are conditioned to interpret other women as rivals. These explanations are not considered as potential answers to the questions being posed in the studies.

This, then, is part of the reason why evolutionary psychology can be such a tempting mode of thought: it offers evolutionary explanations for behavior that may very well be dictated by cultural or historical forces, which can be a way of offering an excuse. If we took seriously that a lifetime of imbibing unrealistic beauty standards may be behind our thinking that high heels are sexy, we might feel a responsibility to interrogate ourselves and our assumptions, and even change our views. But if the desire for women in high heels is evolutionary, then there is nothing to be done.

Butts are a particularly rich subcategory for the evolutionary psychologists of popular media. The articles "The Science of Why You're an Ass Man," "How the Gluteus Became Maximus," and "Science Has Finally Figured Out Why Men Like Big Butts" were published in *Men's Health*, the *Atlantic*, and *Cosmopolitan* in 2014 and 2015, all based on the same evolutionary psychology study. The experiment was conducted at the University

of Texas by researchers who were looking to determine the evolutionary origins of sexual desire for women's butts. The researchers showed drawings to 102 men between ages seventeen
and thirty-four that depicted women curving their spines at different angles, sticking their butts out to various degrees. According to the response data, the men preferred women who held a
45-degree angle. Then, in a second study, researchers showed the
same photos but included drawings of women with larger butts.
The men still preferred the women sticking out their butts. The
researchers deduced from this data that a desire for larger butts
was actually a desire for women who have a slightly swayed back,
which they claimed was an evolutionary adaptation for early
hominid females because it allowed them to better support, provide for, and carry out multiple pregnancies. The mechanism for
that adaptation is a bit of a long walk: according to the researchers, pregnant females who had backs swayed at 45 degrees had
better torque when they reached down to forage for food, which
meant that they could gather more nourishment and better feed
their babies. It was to the male's advantage to choose a mate who
could provide the most food for their family, and a protruding
butt was the visual signal that a female could do just that.

For decades, many biologists have taken considerable exception to evolutionary psychology for a host of reasons. Paleontologist Stephen Jay Gould described the thinking that
undergirds these types of studies as the creation of "Just So Stories," a reference to Rudyard Kipling's book of children's fables
that offer fanciful explanations for traits like a leopard's spots
or a camel's hump. According to Professor Haufe, evolutionary
psychologists often use survey data and then create theories that
explain the results, whereas evolutionary biologists like Daniel
Lieberman rely on experimental research and the fossil record.
In the University of Texas study, for example, the researchers
came up with the theory that big-butted women were better

able to forage for food, but they provided no experimental data to back it up. This is a fundamental problem that many biologists have with evolutionary psychology: it doesn't adhere to the standards of other sciences that study biological evolution.

Another problem with evolutionary psychology is that it frequently rests on a fundamental assumption that may not be true: that mate choice is always based on detecting and selecting for positive inheritable genetic qualities. For example, a well-known evolutionary psychological theory about the peacock's tail is that only a very tough and resourceful peacock could drag around one of those immense tails, and hence the tail is a way to show the peahen how strong the peacock is. But, according to Haufe, there is no real evidence that mate choice is driven by the ability to detect genes with adaptive features. That is, peahens may not be making choices that have anything to do with virility or strength.

This may sound counterintuitive. It certainly did to me when I first heard it. Because I'd been so steeped in the idea that all animal traits must be adaptive, that every part of us—including our feelings of sexual attraction—must be built to accomplish something for some particular evolutionary purpose, it was hard for me to imagine any other reason why peacocks might have blue heads or human women might have fleshy butts. This mode of thinking is what Gould and evolutionary biologist Richard Lewontin refer to as "adaptationism," a mindset they criticized for decades because it cut off the possibility that certain traits may not serve any purpose, and that the purpose they might serve today may have nothing to do with why and how the trait originated. That is to say: the peacock's tail may not be an adaptation for anything, or it might be an adaptation for something peacocks needed thousands of years ago, but we should not assume that the tails of today's peacocks serve any particular function at all.

On a visit to the Peabody Museum of Natural History at Yale University, I open a drawer and find more than twenty green parrots, nearly identical, stuffed with cotton and resting belly up, wings tucked tight against their sides. The drawer smells surprisingly pungent, a combination of mothballs and preservatives, with a touch of something more earthy and animal. When I ask about the odor, Dr. Richard Prum—the William Robertson Coe Professor of Ornithology at Yale and, on this day, my guide to the museum—shrugs and says, "The drawer of penguins smells like oily fish." It is a surprise to me that the smell of a bird's food and rotting flesh can persist after decades of sitting in a drawer, but Dr. Prum is unimpressed. These are animals made of flesh. Rot is part of the deal.

Along with the odor come flashes of color: vibrant blue bird backs, opalescent heads, bright orange Mohawk-like feather crowns, a black bird of paradise body that Prum says is probably the blackest black found in nature. An enthusiastic bird lover, he explains how the pigment in the shiny feathers lines up like marbles in a bowl to create the uncanny sheen, how the feathers in the black bird of paradise's body are precisely angled so that no light can reflect outward, creating a hyper-matte black that offsets the gleaming teal feathers the bird displays in its elaborate mating dance.

The museum's bird collection is in a large, white room in the Environmental Science Center, full of floor-to-ceiling white cabinets. The lighting is fluorescent, the floor covered with industrial gray tile. The bounty of this room is a testament to what Prum calls the "stamp-collecting" element of biology. Biologists measure the variety of the world of birds in all its particulars, looking to understand the physics of feather pigments or what kinds of larynx allow for different types of song. Dr. Prum—a MacArthur "genius," a Guggenheim fellow, a professor with his own laboratory—has made a career out of asking these kinds of questions about birds, and in the process has made myriad exciting discoveries, including the fact that there is a direct evolutionary relationship between contemporary birds and dinosaurs.

But I'm not here to learn about feather pigmentation—at least, not explicitly. I'm here because Prum is the champion for a theory about the evolution of ornamentation that pushes against the adaptationist mindset. Building on Lewontin and Gould's ideas (as well as those of earlier scientists, including Ronald Fisher and Darwin himself), and pushing back against theories of evolutionary psychology, Prum believes that animals may come to adopt certain aesthetic characteristics not because those traits are adaptive but simply because they are beautiful. This may be because of a sensory bias in the brain—a neurological feature that just prefers shiny things over nonshiny things—or a preference for novelty. But these attributes don't necessarily signal that there is something *better* about the peacock with the extravagant tail. The peahen doesn't like his tail more than others because it suggests he's a strong and fit potential mate, but just because she likes how it's shiny, and blue, and large. Prum bases this theory on a lifetime of studying birds like those in the drawers at his lab, many of which have plumage, skeletons, or songs that make it difficult for them to fly or easy to be spotted by predators. When Prum realized just how poorly adapted many birds were from the perspective of natural selection, he began to wonder why else they might have such inconvenient and beautiful plumage. It was from his ensuing experiments and theorizing that he discovered a new way of thinking about beauty in birds, and, to some extent, in humans.

When I arrived at Dr. Prum's lab at Yale, one of the first things he said was that he was a little bit nervous to talk to me. Although he regularly gives lectures and talks with the media about bird beauty, human beauty is another matter entirely. It's one thing, he says, to put up a slide of a bird of paradise and say, "Look at this beautiful bird," but it'd be another thing entirely if he were to put up a picture of a woman and point to her as the pinnacle of human beauty, or to discuss why her features exemplify those humans innately prefer.

This speaks to one of Prum's problems with the dominant theories in evolutionary psychology: by arguing that peahens or humans are drawn to the physical attributes of potential mates for entirely biological reasons—health or strength or re-productive fitness—we erase the rich variety of ways that humans might be beautiful to one another and shut down the questions that we can ask about beauty. Suggesting that certain attractions are, evolutionarily speaking, "wrong" while others are "correct" takes away from the epic diversity of taste and preference, and simply doesn't comport with the realities of human—or bird—attraction.

Peacock tails might all look the same to us, but they likely look very different to peahens. But the science of how indi-vidual peacock variations and individual peahen preferences have together shaped the development of the peacock tail over thousands of years would be far too complicated to trace. Sim-ilarly, while the physiology of the butt is scientifically explica-ble, if the myriad forms it can take—and the myriad reactions it engenders—are the result of sexual selection, the causal history is too complicated to tell. Variation might be due to different adaptive needs or different aesthetic preferences, but anything that smacks of universals—there is one kind of butt that is most attractive, one kind of butt that is most fit—is almost cer-tainly not the case. This is because the contexts that determine our capacity to thrive—whether environmental, cultural, or personal—are always changing and differ for each one of us. As Haufe told me, "Any butt that is not killing you is probably good enough."

In fact, Haufe takes Prum's idea one step further. He says that there is no reason to think that big butts, or fancy feathers, are driven by mate preference at all. Big, small, flat, or bubble butts might just exist. And people may like them, or not, for reasons that have nothing at all to do with evolution or biology. Once again echoing Gould and Lewontin's critique of adaptationist thinking, Haufe says, "We all have preferences for stuff. I like Marvel movies, for example. I don't need to appeal to evolution to explain why I like them." Butts may not be so different. We understand the butt as a site of attraction, a site of revulsion, a body part inextricably tied up in associations of race and gender, but those associations don't come from the layers of bone, muscle, and fat that create the biological reality of the butt. They come from all the layers of meaning, and of history, that we've put on top of it.

Sarah

LIFE

• •

The National Museum of Natural History building sits on the southeastern edge of the Jardin des Plantes, which takes up seventy acres on the east side of Paris between the Grand Mosque and the Seine, on rue Cuvier, a street named to honor the man who collected the bones and rocks and seeds that are stuffed inside.

Georges Cuvier was, among other things, the most important comparative anatomist in the world in the early nineteenth century, a man who was a crucial part of the rigorous biological discoveries of the nineteenth and twentieth centuries, a man whose work helped lay the foundation for biologists like Daniel Lieberman and Richard Prum. He established the field of paleontology, and his discoveries helped to pave the way for Darwin's theory of evolution.

Cuvier's lifetime goal was nothing less than to collect a specimen of every single plant, animal, and mineral in the world and attempt to answer how they came to be. As I walked through the gardens and the buildings, it felt like he might have succeeded. The gardens were divided up into rectangular plots, with every tree and plant noted by an engraved placard displaying its species and region of origin. A cement pool full of *Glaux maritima*—sea milkwort—was situated next to a swampy patch of water cabbage. To me, they both looked like nothing more than weeds, but on the grounds of the museum they were tended, noticed, and named.

Inside, the museum was packed tight, cluttered with the bones of animals, from a miniature bat skull to the monstrous baleen of a blue whale. Most contemporary museums are places of careful curation, of choice: one chair, one skeleton, one coin stand in for many. The National Museum of Natural History was not that place. It was a place of almost gratuitous fullness, a place that seemed nostalgic for the time of its creation. Every corner of the vast brick hall was full, the skeletons of every animal I could imagine strung together atop wooden plinths, displayed behind polished glass, or suspended from the ceiling. Instead of informational placards designed to help visitors make sense of the jumble, the museum presented even more jumble: a monkey head floating in a jar, his neck splayed open to reveal the anatomy of his throat; the jaws of twenty different kinds of rats encased by individual orblike vitrines; the pancreas of a panther displayed in front of a large piece of blue velvet.

Human bones were littered among those of animals: a *Homo sapiens* skull was arranged next to a chimpanzee's to show both the similarities and the differences. We are all animals, the museum seemed to say; everything alive is part of the same family. But for more than a century, the museum said something else too: some of us are more animal than others. It is among these animal bones that it becomes clear that Cuvier's mission was never just to collect. It was also to establish a hierarchy, to tap into an imagined natural order and determine which species were "higher" and which were "lower," a system that became particularly important when it came to translating his studies to human beings. At the time, many scientists, Cuvier included, were obsessed with the idea that there were people alive on Earth that were in fact another species, a third category between human and animal. Most scientists thought this creature would be found in Africa, undoubtedly an attempt to justify their own assumed racial superiority with science.

"*Fetus humain*," read the cursive text on one yellowing label in front of five small human skeletons, unfurled and standing upright in the back corner of the museum. Nearby, a one-eyed cyclops kitten and a two-headed dog floated in jars of preservative next to a wax model of conjoined human twins. The label simply read, "*Monstres.*"

As I looked in this dusty corner, I didn't see order, I saw cruelty. What purpose could this display possibly serve beyond provoking shock and revulsion, particularly with no context, no attempt at education? But I felt uncomfortable not only because of what was there, but also because of what I knew had once been there. I'd come to Paris to learn about the life and legacy of a woman whose body, and butt, became central to Cuvier's project of ordering humanity. A woman whose remains Cuvier thrust into this collection in 1816, displayed as a prime example of what many at the time referred to as a "Hottentot," a term used in the eighteenth and nineteenth centuries to describe the people of the Khoe tribe of what is now South Africa.

Her name was Sarah Baartman, or at least that is the name that most scholars use when they write about her. Her real name, the one she was given by her parents, is unknown, as are many of the details of her life. The only documentary evidence of her life comes from the individuals and institutions that exploited Baartman and held her in their control: ship's logs, court transcripts, sensational newspapers, scientific textbooks, firsthand accounts by the only people who could write them down—the educated and the wealthy. Rarely does she emerge in the historical record to speak for herself, so in order to piece together her story, scholars have had to closely examine both what is in the archival record and what has been omitted, elided, and suppressed, doing work often called "reading against the grain." It is only through this process that they've been able to find a more complex story of her life.

Baartman, who was Khoe, was born in rural South Africa in the 1770s, a time when the territory was a Dutch colony. The Khoe were an Indigenous pastoral people from southwestern Africa—men herded sheep and cattle, and women gathered berries and insects—whose traditional way of life was disrupted by colonization and intertribal conflict. For decades before Baartman's birth, colonial explorers had sent reports back to Europe of their African travels, describing Khoe women as having long, pendulous labia, a lazy demeanor, and a habit of constantly smoking pipes. They also described what would become the most famous of the Khoe features in the European imagination: large butts. These descriptions would inspire Carl Linnaeus, the father of modern taxonomy, to classify the tribe as "homo sapiens monstrous," a category of half human that included mythical wolf-boys and elephant-headed men.

By the age of ten, Baartman had been captured by the Dutch and was living with her parents on a colonist's farm, working as a servant. Within another decade, both of her parents had died. In the mid-1790s, Baartman was sold to Peter Caesars, a free Black man who was himself a servant to a German butcher in Cape Town, a bustling, cosmopolitan port city full of soldiers, tradesmen, and travelers from all over the world. Under Dutch law, free Black people were not citizens or on equal footing with whites. They had to carry a pass when they walked the streets, they were required to dress simply, and they weren't allowed to make purchases on credit. When the British arrived in South Africa in

1795, the laws regarding credit changed, and free Black men like Caesars went into debt buying slaves and servants of their own.

In the first years that Baartman was owned by Caesars, she gave birth to three children, all of whom died. She may have, in some sense, been married, but if that was the case, that man likely died as well. She was, essentially, alone. It was during this time that Caesars decided he would conscript his young servant into a new kind of duty. He asked her to begin "performing" for sailors in Cape Town's military hospital to earn money and help pay off his debt. Historians don't know exactly what the show entailed, but it is likely that Caesars had Baartman display her large butt to the crowd. Soon, she became something of a local celebrity.

One of the people who saw the show was Alexander Dunlop, a Scottish military doctor with an entrepreneurial bent. Dunlop was low on funds and preparing to return to England, where he hoped to improve his fortunes, and proposed a plan to Caesars that he dreamed would make them both rich. The empire was growing, and explorers were returning with the bounty of their travels so that scientists, government officials, gentlemen, and the lower classes of London could see the fruits of the wars and voyages subsidized by their tax dollars. Botanical specimens, pelts, and even human curiosities were available for members of all classes to view at various museums, scientific societies, and freak shows.

Dunlop was eager to capitalize on this fascination with all things "exotic" and bring Baartman to England, where he intended to feature her in a Piccadilly freak show, wearing the clothes of her tribe as she played her guitar. It was a plan built in part on the fame Baartman had accrued in Cape Town, but also on Dunlop's experience in Georgian England, which had become fascinated with butts in general. Full (although not necessarily large) women's butts had, for centuries, been one

component of a voluptuous silhouette that became synonymous with femininity and beauty, in part because of the way
that silhouette was employed in both Paleolithic and Greek
statuary. The statues that displayed this shape, called Venuses,
named after the Roman goddess of love, fertility, beauty, and
prosperity, were a celebration of a holistic image of femininity
rather than a beauty ideal focused on one physical part (the
Venus Callipyge, or "Venus with the beautiful butt," being one
notable exception). European Renaissance painting had also
commonly represented women's butts, perhaps most famously
in the work of Peter Paul Rubens, whose depictions of full-
figured women were created at a time when thinness was increasingly equated with rationality. Thin men were considered
more intelligent, and the ideal woman—an irrational creature,
Rubens thought—was plump and round and "white as snow,"
part of a project of elevating whiteness (and suggesting that
women weren't very bright) that was already happening in the
sixteenth century.

Although associations between shapely butts and femininity, beauty, and irrationality were surely present in the Georgian London that Dunlop knew so well, in the early nineteenth
century there was a new mania for butts spreading through the
British capital. Londoners were obsessed with butts: there were
fart clubs where people gathered and drank different juices to
see what sounds and odors they would produce. Newspaper
cartoons were full of ample-bottomed white women—in one,
a big-butted woman is merrily taking a bath as a group of men
peer at her through a crack in the door. Dunlop's plan was to
provide Londoners with a living stereotype of a large-bottomed
"Hottentot" woman—a symbol of the growing empire and a
fantasy of African hypersexuality. His hope was that the endeavor would make him rich.

Some scholars think that Baartman was promised money

and opportunity before she left South Africa, although there is no documented contract between herself and Dunlop, or anyone else. Though evidence suggests that she refused to go without Caesars, it's hard to know whether she felt she had an actual choice in the matter, even if she agreed to the arrangement. Her freedom to make decisions for herself about where she could go and when had long been legally restricted, and her economic straits narrowed her opportunities further. In her lifetime, South Africa passed back and forth between Dutch and British hands, a period in which the laws governing slavery, race, and servitude existed in a state of uneasy flux. Although the British Empire abolished the slave trade in 1807, slavery itself was very much alive in the British Empire until 1833, and de facto slavery and forced labor lingered for decades longer.

What we do know is that in the spring of 1810, Baartman boarded the HMS *Diadem*, a decommissioned British troop ship that had fought in Spain. She was accompanied by Dunlop, Caesars, and a Black boy named Matthias whose status was marked as "servant" in the records so that Dunlop wouldn't be accused of transporting slaves. After a months-long Atlantic passage, during which Baartman would have likely been horribly seasick and trapped belowdecks as the only woman on board, the ship landed in Chatham, England, in July 1810.

When she disembarked, Baartman was wearing the same clothes she had been wearing when she left Cape Town—a servant's smock and rawhide shoes, hardly enough to protect against the harsh winds and salty spray of the long voyage. She took a stagecoach with Dunlop and Caesars from Chatham to London, clattering up the Old Kent Road with a trunk full of African goods and a smelly giraffe skin—another artifact from the cape for sale—strapped to the top.

By the end of the summer, a cartoonish image of Baartman was plastered on storefronts, street corners, and newspaper stalls across London, depicting her standing in profile, emphasizing an enormous bottom, large and high and round. In the drawing, her likeness is all but nude, wearing only vaguely tribal ornaments, her breasts obscured by the placement of her arm. A pipe sticks out of her mouth, and smoke curls from its tip. In large, bold letters, the poster advertised the show: "The Hottentot Venus just arrived from the interior of Africa; The Greatest Phenomenon ever exhibited in this country; whose stay in the Metropolis will be but short."

The first performance took place at 225 Piccadilly, in a part of town where Londoners came to experience the strangeness and newness of an expanding world through "freak shows"— exhibitions featuring albino children and so-called Siamese twins and giants. Piccadilly was a place where the scientific and the salacious merged, and everyone from the poor Irish immigrants who cleaned the city's hearths to the great men of finance gathered, creating a new kind of intermingled public space that brought many together to participate in the degradation of people like Baartman.

The daily show began the same way each time: Baartman emerged from behind a velvet curtain on a three-foot-high stage at the front of a well-lit room. She wore no corset or underwear—only a skintight, skin-colored body stocking, her nipples clearly visible through the fabric. The spectacle was later described in the London *Times*: "She is dressed in a color as nearly resembling her skin as possible. The dress is contrived to exhibit the entire frame of her body, and the spectators are even invited to examine the peculiarities of her form."

The producers wanted Baartman to look as "African" as possible, so they adorned her with ostrich-eggshell beads, jangling bracelets, and ostrich-feather cuffs, artifacts that had been brought from Africa but weren't all Khoe. She also wore her own small tortoiseshell necklace, a traditional token presented upon first menstruation to Khoe girls and one of the only authentic artifacts that would travel with her throughout her life. Around her waist, Baartman wore an elaborate girdle designed to highlight the parts of her body that her handlers knew Londoners would most want to see. They made sure her large bottom was visible and her genitals were enticingly hidden by a leather flap that echoed descriptions of Khoe genitalia sent back by explorers. They very often had her smoke a pipe.

When the show began, she entered a roomful of women with bows in their hair and men in high-necked collars, craning their heads for a look. Caesars would lead Baartman around the stage, commanding her in Dutch to turn, sit, and walk. She then sang Khoe songs, played the guitar, and danced, in what was perhaps an attempt to elevate the show beyond lurid spectacle to anthropological showcase. Finally, spectators willing to pay a bit more were invited to approach the stage and feel her bottom, pinching it to make sure it was real or poking it with an umbrella, turning Baartman into whatever they wanted her to be: a body to be reviled, a specimen to be studied, an object to be desired, a symbol to be controlled. As they squealed with delight and horror, she very often scowled.

Just as Dunlop had hoped, the show quickly became a must-see. Reports of the performance circulated quickly in newspapers, and Baartman soon began receiving invitations for private engagements. The audience was filled with both men and women, Black and white, from all socioeconomic classes. After a day onstage at Piccadilly, she would be carted off to the homes of wealthy Londoners, where she would display her body in ornate sitting rooms, singing before dukes and lords. On her nights off, Baartman worked as a servant to Dunlop and Caesars, cooking and cleaning alongside two African boys. Her days were long and likely lonely. It was imperative to the success of the show that Baartman be understood as a specimen rather than a person, so her social life was severely limited.

Soon, newspapers began to report that Baartman was becoming visibly distressed and angry during performances. Once, she tried to hit a male spectator with her guitar. Another time, she yelped and sighed audibly. "She frequently heaved deep sighs; seemed anxious and uneasy; grew sullen," the London *Times* reported. Baartman was doing what she could to protest, but her resistance only heightened her popularity, her performances evolving from a titillating and exploitative display of African sexuality to a live enactment of the master-slave relationship and the "natural order" of the races. The audience was only too happy to believe Caesars when he claimed that Baartman was a "wild beast" and that he needed to contain her for her own good.

When abolitionist groups learned of the situation, they took up Baartman's cause. Zachary Macaulay, one of the most famous British abolitionists of the day, called her "a foreigner, and a female, too, in worse than Egyptian bondage." Slavery had been outlawed three years earlier, but here was a slave in their midst, he argued, and she needed to be saved. For Macaulay and the abolitionist organizations he worked with, Baartman was a symbol and potential test case for the issues they'd been debating for decades. Still, to fully champion Baartman's cause was complicated. Most abolitionists at the time were motivated by traditional strictures of Christian morality, which meant they also had strong opinions about sex, nudity, and vice. Baartman may have been a captive, but they also saw her as a flagrantly sexual temptation.

By October, a very public debate raged in the London newspapers. Was Baartman free? Was she enslaved? A description in the London *Times* suggested something closer to the latter: "The Hottentot was produced like a wild beast, and ordered to move backwards and forwards, and come out and go into her cage, more like a bear on a chain than a human being."

By this time, Caesars had moved out of the shared home and was no longer involved in the show, so it was from Dunlop that Macaulay demanded documentation and witnesses from Cape Town who would corroborate their story that Baartman was in London legally and under her own free will. Dunlop pushed back, claiming that everything was aboveboard and that she could leave any time she wished. (No one asked about the other two African "servants" living with them.) As the men volleyed back and forth, Baartman's popularity continued to grow, as did Dunlop's profits.

On November 24, 1810, the case went to trial, but Baartman wasn't present. Her defenders—an abolitionist organization called the African Institution—were worried she would come to court dressed indecently, and the judge didn't know if they could find anyone in London who spoke the language they called "low Dutch" (Afrikaans) to translate for her. As the court came to order, she was busy performing to a packed theater in Piccadilly, forced to miss the proceedings that would determine her fate. Before long, however, it was decided that a verdict could not be properly reached without the complainant's voice. With minimal effort, they found two Afrikaans speakers—London was a diverse place, and the empire brought many South Africans aside from Baartman into its borders—and Baartman was summoned.

Dunlop must have realized that her testimony was going to be a problem, because, on November 27, he took her to a notary to sign a contract that was backdated to March 20. The contract explicitly addressed Baartman's primary concerns and promised that Dunlop would split the profits with her, eventually pay for her return voyage home, provide her with medical attention, and give her warmer clothes when she performed. She was shivering onstage with so little on.

Until she testified, no one had uttered Baartman's name

aloud, referring to her only as "a female of the Hottentot Tribe," the "Hottentot Venus," or just "the female." Baartman gave evidence in the apartments where she lived, dressed regally in European clothes. She told the examiners about her past—where she grew up, how her father died, and how she met Dunlop and Caesars—and testified that she was satisfied with her situation in England. She liked the country, she explained. She was paid by her masters and had no wish to return home. The notes from the trial say that the notary from the state asked Baartman "whether she preferred either to return to the Cape of Good Hope or stay in England and that she replied—Stay here."

It's difficult to know why, exactly, she testified as she did that day—perhaps she thought she had already gotten what she wanted, that the men who had brought her to England were good for the money they'd promised. Or maybe she felt that she simply couldn't speak freely, fearing retribution. There was also concern about what would happen to her if she were to be released from her captors. Though one abolitionist claimed, "There are persons ready to take her," it was a vague promise, likely offering little comfort to a woman who did not speak English, had no financial security, and was marooned in a strange, cold land.

The court determined that Baartman "was under no restraint, and she was happy in England." Thanks to all the free publicity the trial provided, her show continued to sell out through the winter, and after the details of her supposed financial agreement with Dunlop became public, the cartoon drawings of her included a new feature: piles of gold and bags of money.

Over the next three years, Baartman toured Britain, performing in London, Brighton, Bath, Manchester, and Ireland. While in Manchester, she was baptized, declaring her name as Sarah in the baptismal record. She traveled with Dunlop until he died in 1812, and then began traveling with a man named Henry Taylor. Little is known about Taylor or his relationship with Baartman beyond the fact that he took her to Paris in 1814, where she lived and worked around the edges of the Palais Royal, an area known for political unrest, vice, and pamphleteering. Baartman was already famous when she got to France, and false rumors about her spread quickly: some said she was secretly married, while others claimed she was a sex worker.

Baartman lived on one end of the Palais and worked at the other, doing a version of the same show she had been performing since her time in Cape Town. She danced and sang nearly nude, smoking a pipe and displaying her butt. The show proved once again to be enormously popular; France had its own stake in colonial Africa, and the nation, like Britain, maintained a feverish curiosity about what they perceived to be the highly sexual Indigenous people of that continent. To maximize profits, Taylor increased the number of hours Baartman performed every day from six to ten. At night, she continued her private performances for the wealthy and the powerful. Soon, she grew ill from exhaustion, and by 1815, she could no longer perform.

In January of that year, the *Journal Général de France* declared, "The Venus Hottentot has changed owners." The language used in this newspaper declaration revealed a stark difference between Paris and London. In London, slavery was illegal, an evil to be rooted out. In Paris, slavery was basically still allowed (although technically illegal since the French Revolution) and there was far less of a debate about the morality of buying, selling, and owning human beings. There was no longer any question about whether or not Baartman was a free person. She now belonged to a man called S. Reaux.

Reaux was an animal trainer with ties to Paris's scientific

community, who sold animal carcasses for dissection and study to comparative anatomists interested in hereditary links between species. Baartman's performances had always been vaguely scientific—Dunlop and Caesars had all but explicitly marketed her as a specimen of Africanness, a living link between humans and apes—and Reaux knew that Parisian scientists would be interested in examining her. He arranged for her to pose for a group that included Cuvier, his assistant, and three artists at the National Museum of Natural History in exchange for a hefty sum.

On the day that Georges Cuvier was meant to examine her, Baartman arrived at the Jardin in costume but was quickly asked by the assembled group to undress completely—something she had always refused to do. Cuvier and his colleagues argued that they weren't interested in what they saw as showman's artifice, a costume put together by Europeans and a skin-colored stocking that gave the illusion of nudity; they wanted to see her "objectively."

They asked to see Baartman's "organs of generation," which meant her butt and her genitalia—parts that, for two centuries, scientists and philosophers used to attempt to prove that the Indigenous people of South Africa were, in fact, a different species from Europeans. Cuvier and his colleagues were eager to make the determination for themselves. At first Baartman resisted, but eventually she agreed to pose mostly nude. Perhaps it was the large payment promised to her and Reaux, or perhaps it was because she had little choice. Whatever the reason, she posed in the halls of the National Museum of Natural History with only a handkerchief to cover herself. The men drew pictures of her in profile, her butt once again enormous and central in the renderings, but Cuvier didn't get the thing he most wanted: "She kept her apron concealed," he wrote later. "Either between her thighs or still more deeply." After days of examination, Baartman grew sicker and, eventually, either from physical pain or emotional exhaustion, began to more heavily drink the brandy that Reaux provided.

———

Like so many details of her life, the date of Sarah Baartman's death is not certain. It was sometime in the last days of December 1815 or the early days of January 1816. She likely died of tuberculosis or pneumonia.

In death, she was once again exploited. Some reports suggest that Reaux sold her body to Cuvier, while others say that the scientist was granted permission from the Parisian police to take possession of it. Either way, in January 1816, Cuvier meticulously dissected Baartman's body in the name of science. He began by making casts of the corpse so that his team could create a lifelike statue to study. He removed her brain and put it into a jar of embalming fluid. Then he turned his attention to her labia, that intimate part that in life she had kept so adamantly private. He molded them in wax and removed them to another jar of preservative for further inspection. After a complete dissection, he boiled all the flesh off of her bones.

Once Cuvier finished his dissection of Baartman, he added the parts of her body he'd saved—her bones, her brain, her labia, and the cast he'd made of her body—to his vast collection at the National Museum of Natural History, where they were exhibited in case 33.

In his autopsy report, Cuvier reduces Baartman to a specimen. He notes that her large bottom was made of fat, not muscle, and describes her breasts and areolas, providing measurements and descriptions of the colors. He also discusses her labial folds at length. The examination was a kind of molestation in the name of science. At the end of the report, he drew the conclusion that Baartman was "a closer relative of the great apes than of humans."

Standing in Cuvier's museum, looking into the case where
Baartman's remains had been exhibited, I found myself imagining the objects that had once been there. I'd seen photos of
them, and they were excruciating to look at—body parts in jars
displayed in large, wood-framed vitrines—the trappings of a
museum used to sanitize a history bloated with cruelty. But as I
thought more about my feelings of outrage, I realized that there
was another feeling there, too: a desire to distance myself and
my own time from the long-ago past. I wanted to believe that,
in my lifetime, curators and visitors would find the practice of
ogling Baartman's human remains barbaric and unthinkable. I
wanted to believe that the Londoners who paid an extra shilling
to poke Baartman with an umbrella were profoundly different from me and completely alien to the era I'm living in. And
while there are, of course, tremendous and meaningful differences between 1810 and 2020, the story of Sarah Baartman is
important not only as a troubling tale of a large-butted woman
who was mistreated in the early nineteenth century, but because
of the many ways her life, display, and dissection have remained
relevant across the centuries.

The white, Western understanding of women's butts
changed the moment Sarah Baartman came to England, and
it has never been the same since. The butt, and particularly the
large butt, became stubbornly associated with the exotic and the
erotic, associations that are never far away today. Baartman's
popularity, which was immense in her own time, grew, evolved,
and became distorted over many decades after her death. Even
when enough time had passed that most people no longer knew
her name, the legacy of her dissection and display lingered in
the ways that butts so often do: in jokes, suggestions, and visual
echoes.

Janell Hobson, professor of women's, gender, and sexuality studies at the State University of New York at Albany, has written extensively on Sarah Baartman, the history of Black women's beauty and bodies, and the meanings of Black women's butts in both the past and the present. Before trying to understand the long and complex legacy of Sarah Baartman's life, I ask her to first help me understand what, exactly, was going on in Europe in 1810 that made Sarah Baartman so incredibly popular.

According to Hobson, Baartman's display helped to bolster two of the biggest racial projects of the past two centuries: colonialism and the continuation of slavery. In both popular culture and the annals of science, Baartman was used as evidence that African people were more primitive than Europeans and therefore in need of Christian, European moral guidance. This would become one of the major justifications that European countries used in the colonization of Africa over the next two centuries.

Baartman's body was also used as evidence of the false belief that African women were inherently more sexual than white women, a premise that had become vitally important in Europe and the United States when she appeared in London in 1810. In the aftermath of the abolition of the slave trade in 1807, the many people who benefited from slavery on both sides of the Atlantic searched for a way to continue the practice of enslavement without bringing new enslaved people from Africa. "If you're cutting off the supply of captive Africans who are being transported to the Americas, but slavery is still happening in the Americas, now you need to [find a way to] perpetuate the next generation of slaves," Hobson explains. "In the Americas, laws required that any children that were born to enslaved women become enslaved. The law basically legitimized rape." Hobson explains that the display of Sarah Baartman as a hypersexual specimen—a point repeatedly made in scientific papers and in popular accounts through depictions and descriptions of her butt—offered a kind of evidence for the belief that Black women were, by their nature, sexual, a logic that many used to justify the rape of enslaved women. "This is how the Christian slave owners absolve themselves of any sexual violence," Hobson says.

And yet, although Baartman's body was being used to justify widespread racist viewpoints, most of those who came to ogle her in Piccadilly or at the Palais in Paris probably believed the show to be nothing more than a silly bit of spectacle, which made it easy for them to gawk, and laugh, at Baartman's body without fully considering the larger implications. "Folks were definitely being entertained," says Hobson. "But the show also perpetuated ideas around African savagery and primitive Black womanhood. [It] brings forth the tales that they already had about savage Africans running around naked on the continent. So when white people were looking at Sarah Baartman, they were projecting all of this stuff they'd already inculcated in the culture."

But Baartman's popularity was not confined to her own lifetime, nor was the racial ideology that had become attached to her image. Well after her death, the fetishization of Baartman's body remained stitched into the popular culture of the nineteenth and twentieth centuries. There were songs written and plays performed about her. Her likeness was featured on a deck of playing cards, and she was satirized in pantomime for the same crowds who had paid to see her perform in life. Over and over again, in pornographic novels and newspaper cartoons of the Victorian era, there are sexualized likenesses of large-butted Black women that closely resemble the images that Baartman's captors circulated of her in London and Paris. As Sander Gilman, a historian who has studied the story and legacy of Baartman, says, "Female sexuality [became] linked to the image of the buttocks, and the quintessential buttocks [were] those of the Hottentot."

Sometimes these images were explicitly of Baartman, but more often they portrayed the "Hottentot Venus," a term that first referred to Baartman but was later applied to other Khoe women brought to Europe to serve as colonial curiosities in her stead. Baartman had become a commercial entity, her individual identity stripped away, and the name that had been coined for her became a blanket term for others like her. An image from 1829, for example, depicts a large-butted, nude Black woman— labeled "Hottentot Venus"—displayed as an attraction at a ball given by the Duchess du Berry in Paris. In an engraving from 1850, a white man looks at a woman labeled "Hottentot Venus" through a telescope; the lens is trained on her large butt. Many of these women met similar fates as Baartman in death as well: in British, French, and even South African museums, scientists stripped Khoe women's corpses of their skin and stuffed them for display, emblems of the Indigenous South African. Baartman wasn't the only large-butted Khoe woman to be put on display in the dioramas and cabinets of curiosities that were the cornerstone of early anthropological museums. She was simply the first.

LEGACY

• •

As people were playing bridge with cards adorned with Baartman's likeness, scientists were continuing the work that Cuvier had begun with her autopsy, trying to scientifically reinscribe the ideas of racial difference that he had first codified.

Janell Hobson explains that, in the eighteenth century, scientists had used skin color as the fundamental way to determine difference between the races. But in the early nineteenth century, they began to shift from skin color to anatomy and body shape as a means to order humans and codify racial differences and hierarchies, and often used Baartman as evidence for this changing logic. The Khoe people were light skinned compared to people from equatorial Africa, which would have at one time suggested to European scientists and philosophers they were a higher order of African. And yet, the Khoe were often the people that nineteenth-century European scientists fixated on and determined to be the lowest in the racial order, using what they claimed to be a distinctly Khoe body feature (although this, too, is a dubious idea)—their butts—as evidence of what they believed was their place at the lowest end of the human hierarchy.

Cuvier's written autopsy report of Baartman's dissection—reprinted at least twice during his lifetime—was crucial to this new form of racial order and was widely cited as a source by other scientists. But there were at least seven other autopsies of

Khoe women written by major scientists in the nineteenth century, all of which were done to advance similar ideas. Scientists went into those dissections with a thesis they wanted to prove—that Khoe women were the lowest in the racial order—and they always claimed to prove it.

But it wasn't only the anatomists who were interested in the bodies, and butts, of Khoe women. In his 1853 book, *The Narrative of an Explorer in a Tropical South Africa*, a statistician named Francis Galton, who was deeply interested in heredity and race, reported his desperation to see a "Hottentot" woman naked so that he might "obtain accurate measurements of her shape." When the Khoe women he encountered on his trip to South Africa refused to be studied, Galton found a woman whom he described as "turning herself about to all points of the compass, as ladies who wish to be admired usually do," and measured the angles of the woman's body with a sextant from a few meters away. Then, despite her protests, he calculated her proportions—the largeness of her butt, the size of her head—using trigonometry.

Although it was primarily the butts of Khoe women that tantalized the public, it was Galton's interest in the cranium that ultimately became the cornerstone of a new field of study, which he called "eugenics," a word that literally means "well born." For much of the nineteenth century, scientists in both Europe and the United States measured and remeasured the skulls of people from around the world, attempting to find proof for a conclusion they already believed to be true: that white people of European descent were the most evolved species on the planet, and therefore the most intelligent and civilized.

Galton and other eugenicists not only asserted that white people were of a higher order of human than Black and Asian people; they were also profoundly interested in ordering people whom we would now consider to be white. These classifications

of whiteness were always in a state of flux through the nineteenth and early twentieth centuries in the United States, al-
though they generally followed a similar pattern: Northern
Europeans were considered to be a superior race than Southern
Europeans, Jews, and Irish people. Before the Civil War, books
like Sharon Turner's *The History of the Anglo-Saxons* and Ralph
Waldo Emerson's *English Traits* helped to define Englishness in
contrast to Irishness, an ethnicity that was situated just above
Black people, and sometimes considered partly Black, in the
United States during the mid-nineteenth century. That designation in the racial order only changed when a new wave of
immigrants from Southern and Eastern Europe arrived in the
United States and took their place in the hierarchy. In 1899,
economist William Z. Ripley published the enormously popular *Races of Europe*, which classified Europeans more broadly
than Emerson and Turner, organizing them into Teutonic,
Alpine, and Mediterranean categories, using cranial measurements, face and nose shape, skin and eye color, and height to
determine their place within the system. He also ranked them
in that order, placing Germans and Northern Europeans on top
and Southern Europeans at the bottom. As with all racial ordering systems, Ripley's made no scientific sense—Ripley himself
bemoaned the way that head shape, hair color, and height (his
three major racial traits) aren't reliably correlated—but these
discrepancies did little to dissuade Ripley or make his project
less popular.

These fluctuating racial rankings permeated American science, philosophy, and popular culture in the nineteenth century,
and body parts—whether the nose, the head, or the butt—were
always components of the systems used to determine what race
a person belonged to. Bodies had come to carry a significant
amount of racial meaning, and those meanings were cropping
up not only in scientific and intellectual circles, but also in the

pages of a new kind of publication aimed at women: fashion magazines. *Godey's Lady's Book*, consistently one of the most popular women's magazines in the nineteenth century, published its first issue in 1830. It was in this antebellum era that the first wave of Irish immigration was arriving by the boatload and the Second Great Awakening was inspiring a renewed fervor for both religion and self-discipline, historical events that would help to form the ideological backbone of the magazine. In 1836, *Godey's* hired an editor named Sarah Hale, and it was under Hale's tenure that, according to scholar Sabrina Strings, the perverse logic that equates thinness in women with morality, beauty, and whiteness first began to emerge. In the pages of *Godey's*, there were few conspicuous butts, which had become associated with Blackness, foreignness, and hypersexuality. In fact, largeness generally had become equated with Africanness. Instead, Hale offered images of thin, buttless women as an ideal of Anglo-Saxon Protestant beauty. According to Strings, in Hale's *Godey's*, the thin woman is morally disciplined and the woman who best embodies racial superiority.

But what, exactly, was up with this nineteenth-century obsession with the Black butt? Why did the butt become associated so potently with Black female sexuality? According to Sander Gilman, by the middle of the nineteenth century, the butt had become a proxy for female genitalia. That is, the butt of someone like Sarah Baartman implied hypersexuality because, for the scientists and gawking public of the nineteenth century, it was as if they were looking at a vulva. It was commonly assumed that the big butt of a Black woman implied that she had oversized genitalia, and such genitalia indicated both increased sexual appetite and a biological difference between a Black woman and a white woman. This association between vulva and butt may seem strange, because the two body parts are so different and have such radically different functions, but in the scientific literature of the era, these two most intimate parts of a woman's anatomy are consistently conflated. Rarely were Baartman's labia and her backside spoken of separately.

By the end of the nineteenth century, anthropologist Abele de Blasio advanced this association between large butts and hypersexuality even further when he published a series of studies on big-butted, white sex workers in an effort to establish a link between sex workers of any race and the women he called "Hottentots." He published images of white sex workers with large, high butts in profile that echoed the widely known images of Baartman, suggesting that any woman who is sexually deviant might have a big butt, and, therefore, a big butt was a sign of sexual deviance. According to de Blasio, for a woman to have a big butt, regardless of race, was indicative of an excessive sexual appetite.

In 1905, physician and reformer Havelock Ellis published volume 4 of his epic six-volume work *Studies in the Psychology of Sex*. Overall, the project was an attempt to write about human sexuality in a way that pushed beyond the taboos of the Victorian era. Ellis believed that sex was a healthy expression of love, discussed masturbation openly, and questioned taboos around homosexuality. Unfortunately, his views on butts weren't quite so enlightened. In this fourth volume, whose first appendix is the poetically titled "The Origins of the Kiss," he attempts to understand how each of the five senses is used in human attraction. For Ellis, there is an absolute, objective scale of beauty. Published after Darwin's *On the Origin of Species*, *Studies in the Psychology of Sex,* volume 4, foreshadows the arguments of the evolutionary psychologists of the late twentieth century by suggesting that butts and breasts are adaptive, sexually selected features: "Among most of the peoples of Europe, Asia, and Africa, the chief continents of the world, the large hips and buttocks of women are commonly regarded as an important feature of beauty." At the top is the European woman, who Ellis claims is the most beautiful and who is admired the most by all people on Earth. At the bottom of Ellis's beauty scale are Black people. Butts are the first, and "the most feminine" secondary sex characteristic that Ellis examines in a litany that includes small toes, large eye sockets, and broad middle incisor teeth. He points out that Europeans "frequently seek to attenuate rather than accentuate the protuberant lines of the feminine hip," while nearly everywhere else (besides Japan), "large hips and buttocks are regarded as a mark of beauty." He then gets himself into a tricky paradox. He says that large hips are necessary for birthing large-brained babies and that Europeans have the largest hips. But, according to Ellis, African people have large butts *because* they have small hips. He suggests that this is some form of aesthetic compensation for their small pelvises. Here, once again, are the strange maneuvers necessary for racial ordering to work. Ellis asserts that European women have big hips but flat butts, and African women have small hips but big butts. Despite the myriad counterexamples and dubious evidence, Ellis was intent on devising a way to demonstrate that Black people have smaller brains than white people, and he, like many scientists and thinkers in the nineteenth century, used butts to prove this point.

By the end of the nineteenth century, Galton's theory of eugenics had traveled to the United States, where it permeated both scientific and popular thought. Although today most people understand eugenics as a grotesque and cruel turn in global thought that led to mass genocide during World War II, in the early twentieth century, eugenics was wildly and pervasively popular. Mainstream scientists, politicians, and reformers across party lines openly supported it, including the first six presidents of the twentieth century. Nearly every biology department in the country, including at Stanford, Princeton, Harvard, and the University of Michigan, taught eugenics, and mainstream publications like the *New York Times* and the *Atlantic* regularly published articles that celebrated it.

Eugenicists sorted people, and bodies, into two basic categories: fit and unfit. They believed that problems like poverty and crime were not derived from systemic inequity, racism, or class disparity, but instead from bad genes: poor people bred more poor people, criminals made more criminals. The best way to end suffering, in their view, was to prevent the "unfit" from reproducing, and encouraging the "fit" to have more children.

In order to accomplish this goal, eugenicists had, by the end of the 1930s, created robust sterilization programs in thirty-two states and Puerto Rico, ultimately sterilizing more than sixty thousand people against their will because they were poor, disabled, mentally ill, or placed in the catchall category of "feebleminded." Although sterilization laws in the United States were often challenged in court, they were usually upheld as constitutional, including in the landmark 1927 Supreme Court decision *Buck v. Bell*. By the 1930s, the Nazis modeled their own eugenics program after the practices and policies in California, where more than twenty thousand people were sterilized. Even after the atrocities of World War II, sterilization programs in the United States continued for decades in many state hospitals, and as recently as 2010, women incarcerated in the California prison system were sterilized against their will. Although eugenics and the dubious science of racial classification, like the display of Sarah Baartman at Piccadilly, may seem to exist in a distant past, they actually powerfully live in the present, in the form of both contemporary sterilization programs and the theories and prejudices that undergird the way bodies are discussed and classified. As we will see, the ordering of bodies according to shape, size, skin color, and ability—the legacy of these nineteenth- and early twentieth-century racial projects—are woven into our understanding of what constitutes a body that is desirable, healthy, and, in some sense, correct.

As the racial scientists of the nineteenth century ordered and reordered humanity, Sarah Baartman's remains stood sealed inside case 33 at Cuvier's museum of natural history for more than a century. In 1889, they left the museum for six months, when they were displayed at the Esposition Universalle in Paris, a celebration of France that attracted thirty-two million visitors from around the world. In 1937, they were transferred to the Musée de l'Homme, where they remained on public display until 1982, when they were removed to the museum's back rooms following public protest. In 1994, Baartman's remains went on display a final time, for an exhibition at the Musée d'Orsay called *Ethnographic Sculpture in the 19th Century*, where the curators still used the language of Baartman's captors, describing her as the "Venus Hottentot." For more than 175 years after her death, well into living memory, visitors could gawk at Baartman's embalmed body parts at Paris's most vaunted institutions.

In the 1990s, after decades of relative obscurity, Sarah Baartman's story was becoming central to new histories of science, race, and the African diaspora thanks to the work of scholars like Sander Gilman and artists like Elizabeth Alexander and Suzan-Lori Parks. In South Africa, as apartheid was coming to an end, a lawyer and historian named Mansell Upham brought Baartman's story to the attention of the Griqua, an ethnic group who claimed Khoe heritage and therefore saw Baartman as one of their ancestors and her story as central to their own Indigenous identity. In 1995, the leaders of the Griqua approached Nelson Mandela and the French embassy to ask that Baartman's remains be repatriated to South Africa.

Mandela sent Professor Phillip Tobias—a paleoanthropologist and one of South Africa's most esteemed scientists—to Paris for negotiations. There he met with considerable opposition—the director of the Musée de l'Homme strenuously opposed the repatriation of Baartman's remains on two grounds: precedent (the museum had thousands of human bones and other remains in its collection from around the world and he did not want to return them all), and offense that the story of Baartman situated Cuvier, one of France's most celebrated scientists, as a racist, colonialist, and perpetrator of sexual assault.

The negotiations went on for six years, seemingly intractable, until French senator Nicolas About intervened and brought a bill to the National Assembly that required the museum to return Baartman's remains to South Africa. It passed unanimously in 2002, and in April of that year, they were finally returned to Hankey, South Africa, near the village where she is thought to have been born.

On August 9, 2002, more than seven thousand people gathered for a funeral service that included both Indigenous Khoe practices and Christian burial rites, an acknowledgment of Baartman's heritage as well as her conversion and baptism. Herbs were burned to purify the air, performers sang Christian hymns and played traditional Khoe music, and aloe wreaths were placed on Baartman's coffin. South African president Thabo Mbeki made a speech that situated Baartman as a symbol of the history of South Africa. "The story of Sarah Baartman is the story of the African people," he said. "It is the story of the loss of our ancient freedom." And then a pile of rocks was laid upon her grave, as was traditional for Khoe people in the eighteenth century, her life finally commemorated, as best it could be, on her own terms.

In the twenty years since, Baartman has become an important symbol in South Africa and as a part of the African diaspora.

In South Africa, there are regular debates about what the story of Sarah Baartman means and how she should be represented, including a decade-long struggle to remove a statue created upon her repatriation that many women found offensive. Recently, that statue was removed from the University of Cape Town, and a building that had been named after Cecil Rhodes was renamed to honor Sarah Baartman. But as activist, scholar, and artist Nomusa Makhubu explained to me when I asked her if the renaming of the building felt like a version of justice, "You can never say I've arrived because tomorrow some other right gets taken away: one step forward, two steps back. Justice is always a process."

Shape

BIGNESS

• •

I 've seen nearly every film and TV costume drama ever made about the nineteenth century: the ones about Queen Victoria, the ones where quirky small-town characters contend with the arrival of the railroad, the various Dickens and Eliot adaptations, all the versions of *Little Women*. My encyclopedic knowledge of period movies and shows has not only acquainted me with most of the BBC's character actors from the past fifty years but also provided an accidental fluency in the language of Victorian undergarments, those lacy, embellished bits of cotton and whalebone that so often serve as metaphors for what screenwriters imagine was happening to women in the nineteenth century. There are crinolines and petticoats, enormous and heavy, holding women down. There are plots that focus on the arrival of bloomers and the individuation of the lower limbs, suggesting freedom and rebellion. And then there are corsets, confining and controlling. You know a woman is finding liberation, or embracing her sexuality, when she loosens her corset's laces. But there is one Victorian undergarment I've never seen deliver a star turn: the bustle. The bustle—essentially a false butt designed to make a woman's backside look enormous using an accordion-like cage or puffy pillow tied to the waist—came to define the female silhouette of the late nineteenth century. The effect was that the bustled woman resembled a flouncy, adorned sofa. And although all parts of her actual anatomy were hidden, she actually looked like a person with a big butt.

When I conduct an internet image search of the contraption, the women who appear on my computer screen are clothed from chin to ankle in fringe and frills, buttoned up, and prudish. The outline of their bodies, however, is undeniably (to me at least) in some kind of visual conversation with the widely seen cartoons of Sarah Baartman from 1810.

Although there are whispers of a link between Baartman and the bustle in the historical record, there are no think pieces from 1870 that outline a connection, no quotes from the designers who first sketched the bustle describing how they were influenced by Baartman's physique. But as I have learned from my work as a museum curator, objects and clothes from the past speak to us differently than words do. In order to understand the popularity of the bustle, it is necessary to understand the ways that unspoken, barely conscious notions of bodies, gender, and race become inscribed in even the most mundane parts of our lives.

Documents and words convey the reported version of history: they say, *Here is what happened—and here is what the people who recorded history thought about what happened*. But objects and clothes communicate from another part of the mind. Like a dream or a joke or a slip of the tongue, the ways we make, use, and save objects reveal feelings and beliefs that otherwise go unsaid. "The existence of a man-made object is concrete evidence of the presence of human intelligence operating at the time of fabrication," says art historian and object expert Jules Prown. "Artifacts, then, can yield evidence of the patterns of mind of the society that fabricated them." In other words, someone intentionally made every object that exists, and even if the maker didn't realize what they were doing, they brought their culture, beliefs, and desires to the task.

I expected the archives of the Victoria & Albert Museum to be in the back rooms of the museum's red-bricked building in central London, where grand, arched doorways and vaulted, painted ceilings inspire a sense of reverence and awe. But once I arrived in the swampy summer London heat, I realized that the storage facilities for the V & A instead were housed in the posh western suburbs of the city, in a castle-sized building that was once the former headquarters of the Post Office Savings Bank. The V & A has one of the best garment collections in the world, and I'd come to look at their bustle collection to see if I could do what Jules Prown suggests is possible: peer into the unconscious of the past.

The receptionist at the front desk asked me to deposit my things in a small locker before directing me toward a long wooden bench. Other researchers—coiffed women in suit jackets—soon joined, waiting patiently for their turn to pass through the metal door that opened into vast reserves of bones and dolls and furniture, the overflow collection of the V & A, the British Museum, and London's Science Museum. One by one we left with our designated archivists, our locker keys attached to our wrists with rubber cords, like women at a spa on the way to a massage.

My assigned archivist, Saranella, introduced herself, and together, we rode an elevator to an expansive, high-ceilinged room filled with white floor-to-ceiling racks containing hundreds of still lifes, portraits in gilded frames, and shelves of objects wrapped in white, acid-free paper. Rows of mannequins stood haphazardly, their heads shrouded in white netting, their bodies cloaked with Tyvek, a plasticky white cloth that was used to protect the clothing from light and humidity. They looked like medieval maidens, covered and faceless, billowy and beautiful. A photograph pinned to each revealed the dress or petticoat stored beneath the synthetic covering.

When we arrived at my designated viewing space, Saranella directed me to three large tables covered in white archival paper where the garments I'd asked to view were laid out. There were no mannequins, only disembodied cloth lying flat and lifeless on the table. The poufs sagged, the fringe sat still.

The first bustle I inspected was a patterned maroon cushion with multiple stuffed oval lobes of varying size. It tied at the waist with simple white tape, and the pillows cascaded behind to create the desired gluteal lump. The second had a vaguely steampunk, S-and-M vibe. Made of now-rusty steel bands fastened together, it once would have opened and closed at a hinge to create the illusion of an almost triangular rear end. The third was made of stiffened white fabric that laced on the underside to create a pouf. The tighter the wearer cinched the laces, the more pert the butt became.

I'd come to the archive armed with a working knowledge of the basics: the first bustles, or proto-bustles, were small pads of cotton that women strapped to the small of the back to prevent the fabric from clinging to the body. They came to prominence during the Regency era—the period immortalized by Jane Austen—when dresses were relatively comfortable, Grecian-inspired shifts. Women wore only a few layers of petticoats, and most didn't even wear underwear, unless they were riding a horse. The bustle emerged as a way to keep fabric from getting stuck between the legs and creating what was, essentially, a wedgie.

The simplicity didn't last long—by the 1840s, women were wearing enormous bell-shaped skirts with an undergirding infrastructure of petticoats. Underneath a woman's taffeta dress, she would have worn layer upon layer of cotton skirts, heavy and hot, designed to puff out and show the luxurious, expansive fullness of her gown. Wearing lots of petticoats meant a woman could afford lots of petticoats—as is often the case in fashion, the skirts were a symbol of wealth. Eventually, women made the switch to crinolines—petticoats made of horsehair, whalebone, and, later, steel—which made clothing lighter and cooler, and allowed skirts to grow bigger. By the 1850s, skirts were so enormous that women often couldn't walk through doorways.

Enter the bustle. Popularized in 1868, it grew larger and more bulbous in the early 1880s. The simplest bustles were nothing more than pillows stuffed with cotton or horsehair buckled around the waist. Later, as materials advanced and manufacturers tried to find new ways to sell their product, bustles grew more complicated. Some utilized an accordion-style design that folded up beneath a woman as she sat down, others made use of a swollen mesh bolster or a complicated arrangement of springs. The undergarment transcended class—some women simply stuffed their dresses with newspapers (the London *Times* was said to be the best choice) or flounced their petticoats and pinned them up in the back, similar to the way many brides do today. Even little girls wore them.

The garments on the table in front of me at the V & A were examples of the bustle from different eras, and each seemed to present a different set of problems for the wearer. The pillowy one seemed like it might easily shift, its bulge drifting hipward to undermine the big-butted illusion. The bustle whose girth was created by stiffened fabric appeared delicate and easy to crush, and while the accordion bustle appeared sturdy, it threatened malfunction, leaving the wearer in the lurch if it refused to open or close.

In addition to the bustles themselves, I'd also asked to see an example of the dresses that a woman would have worn on top of them. The one that lay on the table before me was an expensive, bright purple creation, fussy and fancy, its skirt designed with ample room for a bustle. I found myself almost jealous—how often had I raged that no skirt or pair of pants in the world would accommodate a large butt? And yet, here were garments made entirely for that purpose, at least in a sense.

Eager to see how these objects might transform the shape of a body, I asked Saranella if it might be possible to put the bustles and dresses on a mannequin. Her eyes widened. "Oh no, oh no," she said. I realized she had misunderstood my question, thinking that I wanted to slip into one of the dresses myself—dresses that I had been forbidden to touch. The misunderstanding made me imagine my own body wrapped in one of the enormous dresses, a silk collar up to my chin and a silk hem down to my ankle, a cushiony protrusion tied to my rump. I thought of the hot, cumbersome material of all those skirts, the punitive straightness of a laced-up corset trapping my fleshy torso, the boning and caging and ties digging into my softest parts. I imagined having to reach down and pull on the accordion bustle to unfurl it when I stood up, grabbing at my butt as I rose up out of my chair. A woman must have been forever adjusting and poking around her backside, yanking at her bustle and doing battle with its various components. Even when she was seated, there'd be no rest in it.

Although the bustle is relatively under-studied by fashion historians compared to other nineteenth-century garments, there are various theories for why it became so popular. Some posit that it's nothing more than an extension of the corset, believing that women who wore them weren't interested in largeness, but rather smallness: a large bottom highlights a small middle, and it is of course a small middle that women most wanted. There is an assumption in this logic that women have always primarily wanted small waists, despite the fact that a small waist also can make a butt look bigger. Another theory suggests that we shouldn't think of the bustle as a butt enlarger so much as a streamlined crinoline—skirts had grown ridiculously large by 1870 and the bustle may have been a practical solution to a common problem: bunch all those skirts up in the back so a woman could successfully find her way through a door.

There are also materialist theories about the rise of the bustle. The first Industrial Revolution in the late eighteenth century had made fabric widely available, and by the 1870s and 1880s, the invention of the sewing machine made it much faster for women to make their own clothes, a development that greatly worried professional dressmakers. Not only could women sew dresses themselves, they also came to know just how much the materials cost, inviting them to wonder why they were paying vastly more than the cost of fabric to have a dress made. In a canny response, dressmakers decided to prove their worth, adding the complicated seams and flourishes that comprise a bustle. In that way, a bustle also became a sign of wealth. The more a lady resembled a sofa, the richer she appeared.

Another theory suggests that there is, in fact, no theory at all. "Everyone wants to know 'why,' but with fashion there is never a why," one fashion historian told me. "An idea starts out small, and then becomes exaggerated until it becomes absurd, at which point it fades away to be replaced by the next fad." The bell shape of a crinoline turns into the back fullness of a bustle turns into the tubular shapes of the 1920s. There are only so many shapes you can put on the human body, and when we collectively get sick of one, we move on to another.

To me, these popular explanations ignore the obvious: the bustle is, definitionally, about bigness. There must have been some appeal to the look on its own, separate from whatever effect it had on the appearance of the waist. Many people of the late nineteenth century must have liked seeing, and being, women adorned with large, enhanced backsides. To suggest that fashion is a cycle divorced from context is to suggest it exists outside of history. It is to suppose that somehow choosing what clothes you put on every day has nothing to do with the politics, science, or ideas about bodies that swirl around us all. How could fashion possibly be exempt?

The day after my trek to the bustle archives, I met Edwina Ehrman, a curator at the Victoria & Albert and an important fashion historian who has written extensively on the history of underwear. When I asked her for a theory of the bustle, Ehrman was eager to remind me of common misconceptions of the eighteenth and nineteenth centuries, a time often thought of as excessively modest, with rigid, closely policed rules about nudity and gender. She points out that many Victorians actually had a keen sense of each other's bodies. "They were living hugga-mugga with each other. They didn't have separate bathrooms," she said. There were no central sewage systems, most families didn't have private bedrooms, and women's underwear was typically crotchless, so the wearer could easily lift up her skirts to squat and pee. The truth of bodies was everywhere, a truth that so many of us now hide behind closed bedroom and bathroom doors.

Perhaps from living so close together, from having to hike up skirts to go to the bathroom, from witnessing others' bodies in all manner of undress, the Victorians knew all too intimately the functions and products of the butt and designed a garment that transformed it. "The bottom is associated with dirt, with feces, with excretion, associated with what in the past would have been called 'unnatural sex.' It's a complicated area," Ehrman explained. The bustle created what Ehrman calls a "mono-bum," a nonthreatening facsimile of a woman's backside that had no crack and idealized its shape and function, making it more erotic as it became sanitized—proudly conspicuous yet cleared of messy complications, and therefore more appealing.

Previously, during the Renaissance, underwear had been designed to provocatively intimate what was underneath, but during the Victorian era, the cage and corset themselves became the objects of desire, an exoskeleton built to supplant the body underneath. But if all that clothing takes the place of the woman, if her undergarments create a new layer of skin, then she is always simultaneously naked and clothed. Her body is both on top of and underneath the cages and cotton, and her body is on display. Or, at least, someone's body is on display.

"Bustles! What are bustles?" asks the cheeky anonymous writer of the *Irish Penny Journal* in late October 1840. "A bustle is an article used by the ladies to take from their form the character of the Venus of the Greeks, and impart to it that of the Venus of the Hottentots!"

I'd been looking for visual evidence of a link between Sarah Baartman and the bustle in the puffs and springs of the garments on display at the Victoria & Albert, but I was still on the hunt for a written connection when I found this article in an Irish periodical that was sold to the working classes.

When the article in the *Irish Penny Journal* appeared, it had been more than twenty years since the height of the Sarah Baartman craze, but there she was again in the pages of a newspaper, in the form of a joke. The article indicates an enduring popular awareness of Sarah Baartman. It also suggests a relationship between her body and the emerging fad of the bustle. But the connection, it turned out, had been made long before.

In 1814, when Baartman was still alive, a vaudevillian play called *The Hottentot Venus; or, The Hatred of Frenchwomen* was staged in Paris. The plot centers around a French nobleman, Adolphe, and his resolve to marry what he calls *une femme sauvage*. He would be content with an "Indian Squaw or a Hottentot girl," both of whom he is sure would please him in bed more than a refined Frenchwoman. Amelie, Adolphe's cousin, who has designs on marrying him, conspires to trick him by dressing up like a "Hottentot" woman, wearing a large padded bottom and imitating Khoe dances and songs. She performs for her cousin as though she is Sarah Baartman, applying a kind of modified, bodily blackface. The whole show is played for laughs, a satirical romp poking fun at the French aristocracy's persistent eroticization of the African female form. The large, Black butt initially elicits an animal desire, but the small, white butt is ultimately privileged and prized, even found to be more sexually appealing. By the end of the play, the ruse is discovered and all is put right—Adolphe no longer hates Frenchwomen, and he no longer desires the Black "Hottentot girl." The white woman triumphs over the Black woman as an object of desire, able to seduce her man with the help of a bustle and then cast it aside. Imperial and social order is restored.

In *The Hottentot Venus; or, The Hatred of Frenchwomen*, we see what may be the earliest suggestion of a link between the bustle and Sarah Baartman. The bustle is a prosthetic bottom, a cage that a woman can take on and off to transform from a "Venus of the Greeks" to a "Venus of the Hottentots." The connection is explicit, the goal clear: the white Frenchwoman can use the bustle to play in the stereotypes of sexuality that have come to be associated with African women. She can seduce her man and then cast aside the bustle that helped her to get the job done. The bustle is a prop of whiteness and Blackness both: it allows the Frenchwoman to mimic a body that she sees as undeniably Black and then reaffirm her whiteness by taking off her costume. It is a story we will see again and again.

Despite these and other cultural references, many fashion historians position the bustle as nothing more than a fashion item, a way to create a holistic silhouette rather than to enhance a specific body part, questioning the validity of the theory that the bustle was in part inspired by Sarah Baartman's body. For one thing, the bustle rose to the height of its popularity almost fifty years after her death. Why would it take so long for the connection to be made? But it's also true that Baartman's body was exhibited at the Museum of Natural History in Paris for the entirety of the nineteenth century and at the Paris exhibition in 1889, and she was not the only Khoe woman who was exhibited as the "Venus Hottentot"—many others were granted this designation and displayed throughout the nineteenth century. The idea of the big-butted Black woman with a very specific silhouette was deeply woven through the science and popular culture of the nineteenth century. There is also a question of why a late-nineteenth-century woman would have wanted to look like Sarah Baartman, whose silhouette had been used as the quintessential example of African as subhuman, immortalized in a museum vitrine. Her body, and especially her bottom, were displayed as proof that people of her tribe were of a lower order of animal than other humans on Earth. If this is the case, then why would it be a body white women would want to emulate?

And yet, white culture and fashion have both proved relentlessly adept at cherry-picking throughout the centuries, finding a way to poach the parts of other people's culture, histories, and bodies that suit them and leave behind the rest. This, too, is a recurring theme in the story of the butt. White culture is happy to take on "everything but the burden," as cultural critic Greg Tate calls it in his book by the same name. Take what you want and forget the rest. Enjoy, and poke fun at, the eroticism ascribed to the Black female body and discard the trauma of being cataloged as subhuman.

In a 1991 interview with critic Lisa Jones about the connection between Sarah Baartman's body and the bustle, poet Elizabeth Alexander explained it this way: "That which you are obsessed with, that you are afraid of, that you have to destroy, is the thing that you want more than anything." The white woman who wears a bustle can almost forget, or maybe never even consider, the body that hers has come to resemble, whose nudity she simulates. She thinks of it as fashion, or maybe her husband likes it. But this is a specific visual echo that she can strap on and take off—a dangerous and seductive bottom that is safely hidden and revealed at once. A bottom that represents the very thing her husband, her country, and even she is obsessed with and afraid of, and, consequently, desires more than anything.

Although Saranella didn't let me see one of the bustles on a mannequin, I knew where I could find one. In the dimly lit vitrines of the fashion galleries at the V & A, headless mannequins stood robed in seventeenth-century courtly dress and twentieth-century Chanel suits. In the section labeled "Couture & Commerce 1870–1910," a mannequin wore a beige dress with brick-colored flowers and a full bustle. The poufs were fully poufed, and the mannequin's rear protruded, high and large. A mirror stood behind the mannequin, so the museumgoer could see her dress and bustle from every angle. It really did look like an upholstered sofa. And it really did resemble the silhouette of Sarah Baartman.

Perhaps more than any other type of material culture, the things we put on our body speak explicitly to how we want to represent ourselves, how we want to be seen and understood. But sometimes we don't know exactly what we are communicating with the clothes we wear. It was mostly men who designed the poofs and pads and cages that nineteenth-century women buckled to their waists. It was mostly women who made them: in the sweatshops on New York's Lower East Side, in the cotton mills of Manchester, in the struggling dress shops burdened by the invention of the sewing machine. Enslaved people in the American South picked the cotton that stuffed the padding, miners in Pennsylvania chiseled out the iron that gave the steel bustle its shape. And women, lots of women, all kinds of women, wore them.

Those women might not have thought much about the meanings of their silhouette as they strolled down a London street in 1880, backside protruding, fringe swinging. But their bustles were communicating nonetheless, offering a message about modesty and control, and a visual joke about race, colonization, and the value that had been ascribed to the bodies of Black women. Sarah Baartman may have died a half century earlier, but the legacy of her life and death were being dragged ever forward. And although what constituted a fashionable silhouette—and a fashionable butt—would soon change dramatically, this unconscious commentary about femininity, whiteness, and control would long remain stitched into women's clothing.

SMALLNESS

• •

W hen Gordon Conway was living in Dallas during the
first decade of the twentieth century, she was young, rich,
popular, and chic. Her father, a lumber magnate, died in 1906
and left the twelve-year-old Gordon and her mother, Tommie,
a fortune and a mansion, which was soon filled with wealthy
and stylish men courting the elegant widow. Gordon loved to
draw, paint, go to the movies, and dance. She and her mother
were inseparable and at the center of Dallas's burgeoning sophisticated smart set. The pair wore flashy red dresses, owned
innumerable pairs of shoes, smoked cigarettes, danced the one-
step, and were regularly scolded by members of the religious,
conservative community surrounding them. They were both, in
their way, a new kind of woman, profoundly different from their
bustled Victorian foremothers. They were unrestrained and sophisticated, fun-loving and fashionable.

But Gordon and Tommie Conway looked very different
from one another. Tommie was a classic Belle Epoque beauty,
a woman whose pretty, curvaceous body and soft face were perfectly suited for the time in which she lived. As the stiff, cagelike
crust of the bustle and corset had loosened, the ideal feminine
look at the turn of the twentieth century came to be marked
by swooshy, soft lines. The look of the "Gibson girl"—named
for well-known illustrator Charles Gibson, who drew them

in popular magazines including *Harper's* and *Collier's*—was looser, permitted a greater freedom of movement than her Victorian counterpart's clothing, but still boasted plenty of curves. She had ample breasts, a full butt, and a large mop of hair piled into a loose chignon atop her head.

Gordon Conway, in contrast to her mother, was all angles. She was tall and thin, with a prominent chin, a wide smile, and a flash of red hair. Although she had a strong sense of style and she did her best with what she had, her immutable traits—her height, her bone structure, her skinny, coltish body—weren't the ones that Gibson was immortalizing in the magazines. As a child and teenager, she would cut her own face out of the family scrapbooks—a gesture of angst, perhaps, over the contrast between her own looks and her mother's. She knew her body wasn't the kind that many considered fashionable, even if her lifestyle very much was.

In the single biography dedicated to Gordon Conway's life, there are many anecdotes about parties, clothing, and love affairs. While she was traveling in Europe with Tommie, World War I broke out—a fact that the fun-loving women primarily considered an inconvenience, the cause of a premature end to their grand tour of teas, tennis, and gazing upon the works of the old masters. Plus, Gordon found that her many international boyfriends had all suddenly become inconveniently indisposed. In 1914, the Conways left a belligerent Europe by steamship, forced to take a route back to America through the North Atlantic—the same route taken by the *Titanic*—in order to avoid an ocean full of U-boats. When they disembarked in New York, it was as if the war was an easily forgotten dream. The United States was still years away from entering the conflict, and so Gordon and Tommie filled their days with cocktails at the Ritz, dinners at the Marie Antoinette, and dancing until the early morning hours on the roof of the Amsterdam.

But Gordon Conway wasn't a flibbertigibbet—or she wasn't exclusively a flibbertigibbet. She was also hardworking, reliable, and ambitious, and had set serious professional goals for herself. Busy as she was with her robust social life, nineteen-year-old Gordon had come to New York not only to party and drink, but also to join the ranks of the great magazine illustrators whose work she admired in the pages of *Vanity Fair* and *Harper's*. Gordon didn't just want to follow fashion, she wanted to change the definition of what was fashionable.

Within a year of arriving in the city, Gordon found a mentor in the form of artist and illustrator Heyworth Campbell, Condé Nast's first art director and a leader in the era's shift to make illustration a legitimate, essential, and lucrative part of editorial and advertising. Conway loved to draw, and she was good at it. She wanted to create fashion illustrations that would sell, but she was also eager to develop her own particular voice and style. Campbell encouraged her to do just that, helping her find work at defining publications like *Vogue*, *Harper's Bazaar*, and *Vanity Fair*, an unusual role for a woman at the time. Over the next fifteen years, Conway would create over 5,000 magazine drawings, mostly depicting young, fashionable women. She also designed graphics and costumes for 119 stage productions and 47 films. Gordon Conway's illustrations would become iconic, defining images of the era—the Gibson girls of their own age.

The look that evolved in Conway's work was daring and new, upending centuries of rules and preferences regarding fashion and femininity. The women in her drawings were buttless and lissome. Their bodies were often caught in gestures of action or repose—mid–dance step, or ready to serve a tennis ball, or slouched on a sofa or stool. But the bodies of Conway's women had no natural curves. Occasionally, she allowed a slight nip at the waist or a hint of a breast or butt—always pert and always tiny—but the women inhabiting her illustrations were, as a rule, lithe, thin, and white, much like the person who drew them. The choice to depict women's bodies this way was a bold one, and perhaps a way for Conway to reclaim the body that had caused her so much grief as a young woman by projecting it proudly into the world, literally drawing herself into the story of fashion.

But it wasn't just the bodies of the women in her illustrations that resembled Conway. They also dressed and behaved like her. They wore short dresses with drop waists and cloche hats, and bobbed their hair. They were out at night, dancing, listening to music, and blowing smoke rings. Gordon Conway's women weren't just society girls, they were flappers, an archetype in the process of being invented and codified in the 1910s by illustrators such as Conway and her colleague John Held Jr., fashion designers like Coco Chanel and Paul Poiret, and a new kind of urban, bourgeois young woman who spent her nights drinking gin rickeys at Harlem jazz clubs—or at least imagining herself doing so.

This burgeoning concept of what it looked like, even what it meant, to be an adult woman would result in a profound and lasting cultural shift, expressed perhaps most overtly through fashion. Once again, the curves (or lack thereof) on a woman's body were the screen on which definitions of femininity and sexuality were being projected; bodies had again taken on a potent metaphorical meaning. The nineteenth century was an era intrigued by, even obsessed with, big butts—in the 1800s, curves and bigness were central to what it meant to be a fashionable, feminine woman. But the twentieth century would offer a radical change. In a matter of a few short years, it was no longer curvaceous women gracing the pages of fashion magazines. Starting in the 1910s, a new silhouette began to appear, a silhouette that would have incredible staying power for at least another century. The buttless woman—rail-thin and glamorous—took hold with remarkable ferocity and resiliency, and has never really let go. As one scholar put it, "When the flapper raised her skirts above the knee and rolled her hose below it, the naked flesh of the lower limbs of respectable women was revealed for the first time since the fall of Rome; the connection of the two events was not seen as coincidental." Where once there had been curves, now there were angles; where once there had been bustles, now there was buttlessness; where once there had been domesticity and constraint, there was now nightlife and liberation. Or at least that's the way the story of the buttless woman is usually told—straight lines became synonymous with modernity and freedom.

The word *flapper* has at least two potential origins. One story suggests it was coined in the 1890s, first employed as British slang for a very young sex worker who looked like, and indeed often was, an underage girl. Another claim is that the word originated in England as a way to describe an awkward girl in her early teenage years whose body had not yet matured. This "girl who flapped" was supposed to require a particular kind of dress, with straight lines that covered her gawky, flapping limbs. From the very beginning, the flapper was, by definition, young, boyish, and lacking the bodily or behavioral characteristics usually ascribed to the mature woman. She was a perpetual adolescent yet was somehow always sexualized, a fact that underscores ever-shifting interpretations of women's bodies— in the nineteenth century, it was the curvaceous body that carried the implication of excess sexuality; in the early twentieth century, a body that was in many ways the opposite seemed to convey a similar meaning. The characteristics associated with the flapper were radically different from those associated with proper Victorian womanhood, and their popularity in the 1910s and '20s was the result of complex societal shifts in work, education, and sex.

At the end of the nineteenth century, the United States was becoming increasingly urban, thanks to surging immigration from overseas and steady migration away from rural farms and towns. Between 1860 and 1920, the number of people living in American cities rose from 6.2 to 54.3 million. Many of those migrants were women, who moved from their family homes to make their own living. Once settled in Chicago, New York, or San Francisco, they found themselves going out on dates with young men, away from the watchful parental gaze. Suddenly, there was new opportunity for unchaperoned romance and sexual experimentation.

Around the same time, the Nineteenth Amendment— ratified in 1920—gave many women the right to vote in the United States, and the idea that women could have a say in the realms of politics, education, and cultural life was becoming more widely, if unevenly, accepted. Even the question of how much women could, and should, move their bodies was changing—after decades of anxiety about middle-class and wealthy women overexerting themselves, popular books like *The Power and Beauty of Superb Womanhood* suggested that women should pursue exercise and sports to an "almost equal degree with man."

With these societal changes came a sartorial revolution. It began with Paul Poiret, a cranky and competitive designer trained at the renowned House of Worth—often considered the first couture house—where he had been assigned to create dresses for everyday use. By 1906, Poiret had opened his own house, churning out an entirely new kind of dress for women, one with a long, straight silhouette, a V-shaped neckline, and a bold, colorful palette. Most notably, he cast out Victorian underwear, making clear his particular disdain for the corset. "I waged war upon it," he said. "It divided its wearer into two distinct masses: on one side there was the bust and bosom, on the other, the whole behindward aspect, so that the lady looked as if she was hauling a trailer." Due largely to Poiret's forceful opposition, the bustle—and the silhouette that suggested a big butt—would more or less disappear from mainstream American fashion for a century.

Although Poiret's notions about the corset may have emerged, in part, because of the burgeoning urban culture of women working and dating, he didn't intend to liberate women: he also invented a garment known as a hobble skirt, which greatly restricted a woman's ability to move her legs, forcing her to take tiny steps as she walked, literally hobbling her. There was a bit of authoritarian sadism in Poiret's thinking about fashion. He saw himself as a sartorial innovator and believed the women of the world had to obey whatever he capriciously decided should come next in fashion. He believed it was he, as a leading representative of the idea of fashion itself, who was in control of women and how they looked, moved, and behaved. They may have been freed from the corset, but they now had Poiret to contend with.

It wasn't long before fashionable women had a new ruler: in 1910, Gabrielle "Coco" Chanel opened a millinery shop and, later, a boutique in Normandy that sold her signature style of clothing inspired by menswear—including pants, simple sweaters, and belted jackets. Gone completely were the puffed sleeves and ruffles of Victorian and Edwardian dress. Chanel's clothes were simple and modern and looked best on women who looked like her—skinny women who had few curves and barely any butt.

Chanel's designs grew and remained popular throughout the First World War in large part because they were so practical to wear while doing the sorts of jobs that women were asked to take on as men went off to battle. By the 1920s, Chanel employed three thousand people in her factories and stores, and her signature look—sometimes referred to as the "garçonne"—had found its way onto the bodies of women across Europe: hemlines rose, waists dropped, and corsets were abandoned. Whether nursing in a hospital or making bombs in a munitions factory, women embraced styles that allowed them a greater freedom of motion.

Of course, the young women who had left their farm towns to work in urban shops weren't wearing original Chanel garments, nor were the women who took on wartime factory work. They were wearing knockoffs. Ready-to-wear fashion was on the rise, and Chanel's dresses were far easier to replicate than Victorian garments, since they were based on simple patterns and made of cheap jersey. Catalogs from retailers like Sears, Roebuck brought these inexpensive fashions beyond the cities, and soon the flapper look could be spotted on main streets across the United States.

But popularity did not mean widespread acceptance. In the 1925 article "Flapper Jane" in the *New Republic*, writer Bruce Bliven offered an anxious, disapproving description of the flapper figure. "She is, for one thing, a very pretty girl," Bliven explains. "She is, frankly, heavily made up, not to imitate nature, but for an altogether artificial effect—pallor mortis, poisonously scarlet lips, richly ringed eyes—the latter looking not so much debauched (which is the intention) as diabetic." He added that Flapper Jane was known for "not wearing much." Her dress was "brief": "It is cut low where it might be high, and vice versa." Of course, Jane has a bob. She wears no corset, petticoat, brassiere, or stockings. She embodies what Bliven calls "the new nakedness." Others would describe those who embraced flapper style as "rectangle women." That is, the flapper had no waist, no hips, no breasts. Both the clothes and the body underneath were at their most attractive when they resisted the bodily signs of womanliness. These were the women Gordon Conway drew and the kind of woman Gordon Conway was. These were the girls who were kissing young men in speakeasies and who didn't seem to care about housewifery, or modesty, or decorum.

Although the unconscious, metaphorical associations of the bustle had at first seemed mysterious to me, the meaning of the rail-thin, curveless flapper physique feels easy to parse, in part because we still live in a landscape defined by it. For more than a century, the fashionable woman's body has been a slim body, a body enrobed in sleek, straight lines rather than grand, arching curves. There have of course been fleeting periods when a bit of a frill or va-va-voom has snuck into fashion, but never to a pre-twentieth-century degree. To be fashionable, to be beautiful—according to the standards of mass culture—is to be slim, sleek, and liberated, from marriage, from the rules of society, from the heaviness of the back of the body.

The look of the flapper is the look of a woman who, according to the usual narrative, has thrown off the shackles of Victorian mores and Victorian clothes. She is both unquestionably female and yet unconstrained by maternity or domesticity. She is also very much a woman in motion—it's no coincidence that the image of the flapper developed along with the popularization of motion pictures. All of a sudden, people could see style in action. Fashion historian Anne Hollander suggests that, prior to the invention of photography, the only way for a female body to take up visual space was through layers of fat and clothing. "But a body that is perceived to be about to move must apparently replace those layers with layers of possible space to move in," she says. "The thin female body, once considered visually meager and unsatisfying without the suggestive expansions of elaborate clothing, had become substantial, freighted with potential action."

But even if the typical story of the buttless, fashionable woman suggested liberation, there was, of course, quite a bit more going on. Valerie Steele, the director of the Museum at the Fashion Institute of Technology, argues that, throughout the 1920s, a complicated, paradoxical revolution transpired: women found themselves physically unbound from their corsets, but they began to experience a new kind of confinement: a pressure to reshape and distort their bodies, this time not from without, but from within. In order to achieve and maintain the new, fashionable silhouette, many women—those who didn't naturally look like Gordon Conway or Coco Chanel—had to diet or exercise. For Steele, there was, in fact, little freedom in the new look of the 1920s. Instead, it demanded masochistic self-control, or even self-harm.

Steele clearly has a point. After all, it was in the early decades of the twentieth century that plastic surgery was invented and popularized, offering a radical new option if a woman wanted a different silhouette and had money to burn. General anesthesia was rudimentary and still somewhat experimental; every surgery was dangerous. Yet, some women still elected to undergo a procedure, risking their lives in an effort to eliminate fat in the butt and hips and achieve a straight, slender shape.

In these same years, women's magazines began to endorse various, often dubious regimes in order to transform the body and accommodate the fashions depicted in their pages. In a study from 1912, researchers questioned ninety-nine women about their perceptions of their body: none of them were their desired weight, and most thought that they were too fat. These women weren't worried about their health, but instead about the way they looked, and, as one of the participants in the study said, the cure for these worries was "martyrdom." Bathroom scales, invented in 1917, became a popular way to monitor weight. A group called the "Slim Club" suggested that hips should "slope" and be no larger than a woman's shoulders. There were butter-milk diets, toast-and-hot-water diets, peanut-and-lettuce diets. Women were advised to take up chewing gum, or to eat gum-drops containing laxatives, or to smoke cigarettes, heavily and frequently.

But the look of the flapper wasn't only about sleek buttless-ness; it also incorporated elements of exoticism. Designers like Poiret drew heavily from what they perceived to be "Eastern" influences, a broad and vague category that encompassed every-where from Russia and the Ottoman Empire to Japan, India, and China. The "East" was a vast category for these designers—a category defined as everything that was not "West." In creating his looks, Poiret drew from the costumes of the Ballets Russes—which were themselves stylized versions of Ottoman and Arabic designs—and also heavily referenced an imagined idea of Japan. This Japonisme was part of a much larger mania for all things Japanese that emerged in the mid-nineteenth century after Western governments formed trade and diplomatic relationships with Japan. Moneyed Europeans held Japanese-themed balls, both the London International Exhibition in 1862 and the Paris Esposition Universalle in 1867 prominently featured Japanese art, and there was even a replica of a Japanese village installed in a London park. Many European artists—including Whistler, Monet, Proust, and Oscar Wilde—took inspiration from this boom in Japanese cultural products in both subject matter and technique, helping to create a Western aesthetic heavily influ-enced by Japanese style, one that helped usher Japanese aesthet-ics into the domains of high art and refined taste.

The Japonisme phenomenon ballooned further in the early twentieth century with the work of Poiret and, to some extent, Chanel. Both designers not only borrowed Japanese fabrics and patterns but were influenced by the way cloth was utilized in some traditional Asian garments. Rather than building on the highly tailored and embellished forms of dress that had been popular in the West since the Middle Ages, Poiret and Chanel took inspiration from the way that Indian saris and Japanese kimonos emphasized the "flat terrain of the cloth." In 1912, for example, Poiret offered an evening coat that directly referenced Japanese kimonos—a long, T-shaped garment that wrapped around the wearer and had large, open sleeves. It had no waist or even a tie (unlike a kimono, which ties with a sash called an obi), which meant that the garment hung on the wearer in long, unbending lines. When customers purchased and wore these garments, part of what they were signaling was a commitment to what Japanese aesthetics has come to represent—high culture, good taste, and modernity.

But there was another subtext to the adoption of Asian motifs in the fashions of the 1920s, particularly in the United States. By the turn of the twentieth century, East Asian women had been popularly construed as highly sexual, thanks, in part, to the Page Act of 1875, which had effectively prohibited the immigration of East Asian (and primarily Chinese) women to the United States because they were assumed to be sex workers. This association meant that by the 1920s, garments like Poiret's coat—inspired by those traditionally worn by East Asian women—carried with them such connotations of Asian femininity: another example of racialized hypersexuality conflated with signifiers of sophistication and taste.

As with almost all American cultural phenomena, the flapper was also formed by her relationship to (and distance from)

Blackness. Although the archetypal flapper—the kind depicted in Conway's illustrations—was a white woman, arguably one of the most famous flappers was Josephine Baker, a Black woman who possessed what was almost certainly the most famous butt of the 1920s. Born in 1906 in St. Louis, Baker was, by age fifteen, working as a vaudeville dancer in New York City. By nineteen she had left New York for Paris, where she later said she went "to find freedom."

In the midtwenties, Paris was a hub for Black American artists and intellectuals, many of whom understood the city as a place where they could meet and live among Black people from around the world and enjoy a level of tolerance and respect that was unavailable to them in the United States. World War I had brought 200,000 Black American soldiers to Europe to serve in segregated forces, as well as 500,000 French forces conscripted from the colonies, many from African countries including Senegal and the Sudan. These groups encountered each other during the war and after, fostering a sense of Paris as a place of Pan-African intermingling and cosmopolitanism. Nearly every major Harlem Renaissance figure—including Langston Hughes, Claude McKay, Jean Toomer, Sidney Bechet, Ada "Bricktop" Smith, Archibald Motley, and Nella Larsen—spent time in Paris in the 1920s, part of the reason the city would become a center for the Négritude movement in the 1930s.

But, of course, France was hardly free of racism. As many have pointed out, the paradox baked into the kind of "freedom" that Josephine Baker enjoyed was that it took place in the capital city of an empire that was actively subjugating millions of Black Africans. It was also a place where white intellectuals and artists were enthralled by what they called the "primitivism" of African art and culture and an exoticized conception of Black people. This interest in Blackness was common in white bohemian and flapper circles in the United States as well; in

New York City, flappers like Conway regularly went to Harlem nightclubs—a way of engaging with Black culture and rebelling through racial mixing.

It was in the Paris of Harlem Renaissance expats and modernist fantasies of primitivism that Josephine Baker's most famous performance, *La Revue Nègre*, opened to titillated crowds and massive popularity. No film footage survives of *La Revue Nègre*; we have only contemporaneous accounts of the performance to indicate what it was that intoxicated so many spectators in 1925. The performance, organized by a French music hall director to exhibit different modes of "African-ness," consisted of four acts. Although Baker appeared in the first act, it was when and how she emerged in the fourth that caused a sensation. Some said she came onstage completely nude (although she may have been dressed as if to appear nude), wearing only a pink flamingo feather. She was carried onto the stage on the back of her Black male dance partner and then slid down his body, or perhaps cartwheeled off of it, to present herself to the audience. Then, Baker danced. According to her memoir, everyone near the stage during rehearsals was enraptured: stagehands stared, the theater's typists peeped at her through a hole in the wall of the set, and the twenty people seated in the orchestra began spontaneously shaking their legs, electrified and transfixed by her movements. She danced the Charleston, a Black American vernacular dance that had originated in South Carolina. Baker described the dance, which was new to Paris, as "dancing with the hips, one on top of the other; one foot on top of the other; and getting your butt out and shaking your hands." In one account of the first performance, a man cried out, "What an ass!" Others were horrified. In his biography of his mother, Baker's adopted son Jean-Claude Baker described what he had heard about the moments immediately following the dance: "Some people in the audience scream for more, others rise, wrapping themselves in indignation and little furs, and stalk from the theater, muttering that jazz and blacks are going to destroy white civilization." Jean-Claude Baker described the chorus girls— young Black girls like Baker—as horrified for other reasons: "She had no self-respect, no shame in front of these crackers," a chorus girl named Lydia Jones told him. "And would you believe it, they loved her."

Critics went wild for the performance. But in their fervor, they trafficked in the racist stereotypes that had been applied for centuries when it came to Black women and butts. In *L'Art Vivant,* for example, André Levinson said that Baker had "the splendor of an ancient animal, until the movements of her behind and her grin of a benevolent cannibal make admiring spectators laugh." In her memoir, Baker explained why she thought her performance became a sensation. "We've been hiding our butts too much for a while now. It does exist, the butt. I don't know why we have to criticize it. It's true that there are butts that are so stupid, so pretentious, so insignificant, that they [are] only good to sit on."

"Like Stravinsky's *The Rite of Spring,*" is how dance scholar Brenda Dixon Gottschild describes the first performance of *La Revue Nègre* in the documentary *Josephine Baker: The First Black Superstar*. "It just set some people crazy. Some people thought it was the end of European civilization as they knew it. And the battlefield was Josephine Baker's bum." The performance created what the French called "Bakermanie," or Baker-mania: in the wake of *La Revue Nègre,* Baker became one of the most famous, and wealthy, women in France. Her image was used in advertising campaigns for cigarettes and hair pomade, and she became a muse to illustrators and photographers. There was even a Josephine Baker doll available for purchase.

La Revue Nègre was a bold statement, drawing from the long history of both Black American vernacular dance and the minstrel and vaudeville theater in which Baker had performed in the United States. It contained elements of the shimmy and the shake, and challenged traditional Western European ideas of dance. "All of these moves that in the European mode would have been considered awkward become beautiful, sexy, silly, and savvy at the same time," explains Dixon Gottschild. Later, as the performance evolved, Baker incorporated her famous banana skirt and, eventually, a pet cheetah who regularly made his way into the orchestra pit—elements that played into the idea of Baker as an exotic creature and added notes of vaudeville humor.

Baker's performances were complex, as are their legacy. Some have characterized her as a twentieth-century Sarah Baartman, another Black woman put on display for the titillation of fascinated, scandalized bourgeois white spectators. But she is often also criticized for exoticizing herself, knowingly participating in her own exploitation, playing into African stereotypes with her nudity, the banana skirt, and the cheetah. Others interpret *La Revue Nègre* as a means of reclaiming those stereotypes: Baker enthusiastically, and freely, participated in the performances and made lots of money doing it, and she surely understood that she was engaging with, and even subverting, stereotypes of Black femininity. She was also funny, and her performances always contained elements of humor and parody. From her early days as a chorus girl, she would add an element of knowingness by feigning being a bad dancer onstage for a laugh. She may have been sexualized and objectified by her largely white audience in Paris, but she also maintained significant control over what she was doing.

And so although the flapper was, in part, the buttless fantasy of Coco Chanel, and although many women in the 1920s used diets, exercise, and surgical procedures to minimize any hint of a curve, they were also sticking their butts out like

Josephine Baker and dancing the Charleston. Some of those women may have had butts that were, as Baker put it, "so stupid, so pretentious, so insignificant" that they were only good to sit on—a barely veiled dig against white people's discomfort around butts—but many of them were trying out, and trying on, the sexualized freedom that they imagined into the body of Josephine Baker and other women of color presumed to be more inherently sexual than white women. It was a relationship between Black and white femininity that was old, and one that would prove to endure.

The creation of a silhouette—whether the bulbousness of the bustle or the straight lines of the flapper—is both an aesthetic and a political gesture. As garments are designed and trends emerge, the curves of a woman's body—whether created by clothes, genetics, diet, or exercise—are transformed into metaphors that come to stand in for larger stories about gender, taste, and class. And although those meanings almost always remain unspoken, and even unconscious, like the butt itself, they exist nonetheless, made all the more powerful for remaining unuttered.

Norma

CREATION

· ·

The first dressing room I remember was at Hudson's, a Detroit-based department store where middle-class people in the town where I grew up went to get things that were "nice." It was the place where my mother bought me overalls and hair bows, where she bought herself high-heeled shoes displayed like pastries on wooden pedestals, and where we picked out cloth napkins for relatives who were getting married.

On those shopping trips, my mother would gather a pile of clothes, hunting and pecking her way through the various women's departments. We both loved this part. For me, the initial search on a shopping trip is when optimism is at its peak, the time when all the garments on offer might actually fit, when they still might actually look good. It is during the second act of the shopping experience when it all goes awry.

Despite its being a "nice" store, the dressing rooms at Hudson's were, in my mother's parlance, "jenky." The worn carpet was dirty; the dividers that created the stalls, flimsy; the ceilings, oppressively low. The lighting wasn't just unflattering but outright cruel. As a little girl, I sat without thought on the floor, exhausted in the same way I feel now after a trip to an art museum—overwhelmed by sense, but also overwhelmed, I realize now, by the store's manifestation of femininity: the puffs of perfume, the textures of raw silk and combed cotton, the fantasies that all that adult femaleness unleashed inside me. Sometimes I curled up on the stained brown carpet and just fell asleep.

Meanwhile my mother, always so neat and thoughtful, hung up her garments before changing out of her own clothes. She had once worked in a Hudson's, and so was aware of all the perpetual folding and steaming that the saleswomen had to do. She unfurled each pair of new pants, stepped inside them, and examined herself in the mirrors.

This was the part that was hard.

My mom rarely liked clothes once she wore them. The promise she'd seen in each garment on its hanger was dashed once she had buttoned and zipped it onto her body. The hem was revealed to be too long, the waist too wide; the material hugged her too tight. But her language, my language, our language, for what was wrong was never about the clothes, but instead was about ourselves. *I'm too short*, she'd say, or *My arms are too flabby*. And always, always: *My butt is too big*. In other words, *The clothes are not flawed. I am.*

It was something I soon came to understand and practice myself. Trying on clothes often feels like trying to jam your body into a template of someone else's—and most of the time, that is exactly what's happening. Bodies are bespoke, and most clothes made since the 1920s are mass-produced industrial products: when the pants don't fit, it's because the proportions of a body don't match up to the proportions that the clothing companies imagined for it.

In addition to all the other tacit work the fashion industry does to define what different body types mean, clothing offers a frank materialization of rightness. Pants are a physical object you can hold in your hands, reminding you that there are parts of your body that literally do not fit. For everything that reveals itself to be too big, or too small, there is the clear indication that somewhere there is a thing that is just right, a body that is in the middle, a body that is correct.

This middle thing is somehow both an ideal and an average, made perfect by not being too much of anything. But what is this middle thing, this normal thing? My mother always said her butt was too big. I often say the same thing. But "too big" compared to what?

Norma's butt is twenty-nine inches across, from hip bone to hip bone. It's round and pert and, because it's made of stone, alarmingly smooth. It is substantial, a handful, but no one would call it big. If it were made of flesh, it would fill out a swimsuit nicely, but I doubt it would elicit a long second look. Norma has the Goldilocks butt, the Goldilocks body. Everything about her, at least according to the people who designed her, is "just right."

In June 1945, Norma made her first appearance, at an exhibition hall at the American Museum of Natural History in New York. On the other end of the hall stood her male counterpart, Normman. The pair were representations of the "typical" reproductive human adult male and female, and were created by gynecologist Robert Latou Dickinson and artist Abram Belskie, who had previously collaborated on a series of sculptures for the 1939 New York World's Fair called *Birthing Series*, which displayed cross-sections of normal human development in utero.

If *Birthing Series* showed viewers what happened as a healthy fetus developed, Norma was the example of the body that could, and, according to her makers, should carry that fetus through a pregnancy. She was not voluptuous and she was not skinny. She was strong, robust, and capable of bearing many children—not too sexy, but clearly fertile. She wasn't one of Gordon Conway's flappers, nor was she a Gibson girl with soft, fleshy curves. She had slender, but present, hips. Her breasts seemed to be something of an afterthought, designed by a person who seemed to have never seen breasts in real life: two perky orbs that floated awkwardly on her chest. As her name suggests, Norma was not, in any real way, exceptional. She was *normal*.

But just what did that mean? The statue suggests a very specific concept of normal: she was white, heterosexual (Normman steadfastly stood by her at all times in the exhibition hall to reassure us of that), and able-bodied. She was a little dour, offering none of the seduction of classic statuary, and stood perfectly erect, arms by her sides, posed as if in a scientific drawing. She was appealing (as her name suggests) in her normal-ness— and that was the intent.

Norma and Normman were a project of American eugenics, the racial science invented by Francis Galton that had built on the work of Georges Cuvier and other nineteenth-century thinkers to create and enforce a hierarchy of human bodies. While one strain of eugenicists in the United States was working hard to eliminate the unfit through sterilization, others were busy encouraging the "right" people to have children. Those involved in this branch of eugenics—called positive eugenics—tried to make it as clear as possible which Americans they thought should be procreating. One popular strategy of positive eugenics was to host "better baby" competitions that awarded prizes to the most "eugenic" babies at state fairs across the Midwest—a vague distinction that encompassed health, robustness, and comportment with the eugenics ideas of human fitness. This was a way to show farmers—people eugenicists thought would understand the importance of making thoughtful breeding decisions—how to choose good mates. The contests were like a 4-H competition with children instead of pigs. The babies that eugenicists deemed the fittest were given a prize.

Norma and Normman were a kind of grown-up version of a better baby contest. They offered physical manifestations of what eugenicists thought the people of America should aspire to be. Standing in the halls of the most famous natural history museum in America, Norma and Normman exemplified to visitors what kinds of adult bodies, and people, were "fit." They were robust, fertile, able-bodied, and native-born white. The museum displayed them as singular objects, creations meant to codify the aesthetics of normality in the immediate aftermath of World War II, when normal was what many people very much aspired to be.

In the interests of maintaining a "scientific" approach, Belskie and Dickinson relied on data in the creation of Norma and Normman, rather than subjective preference. The specifications for Normman's creation had been easy enough to come by: during World War I, the military had measured every drafted US serviceman. There also was data from men who had volunteered to be measured at the Chicago World's Fair, as well as statistics from the early years of the Ivy League posture studies and insurance company physicals. They just had to be added up, divided, and *voilà*! The average American man.

Norma's creation, however, proved to be more difficult. Women didn't serve in the military at the time, and, at first, there seemed to be no large repository of measurements of the female population. But Belskie and Dickinson were living in an age of metrics, a time when it seemed that all things could and must be measured, managed, and known. Surely the female body was of interest to researchers somewhere.

In 1945, they finally found the data set they were looking for. Five years earlier, a group of researchers had measured thousands of American women at the USDA's Bureau of Home Economics, one of the only places where female scientists and statisticians could find a home in the first half of the twentieth century. The effort had been led by a chemist named Ruth O'Brien, who worked to find a way to create standard sizes for ready-made clothes. "There are no standards for garment sizes," O'Brien offered by way of explanation for her efforts, "and retailers and consumers are subjected to unnecessary expense and harassed by the difficulties involved in obtaining properly fitting clothing."

The study, funded by the Works Progress Administration and lasting for one year, sought to discover the girths, lengths, and heights of the American woman in all her difference. To do so, O'Brien sent government-employed measurers to Illinois, Maryland, Arkansas, New Jersey, North Carolina, and California. In municipalities across the country, "measuring squads," as she called them, recruited volunteers from local women's clubs. Each was asked to wear cotton measuring shorts and a not-too-tight-fitting bandeau bra and was invited to step onto a measuring platform, where they were weighed using a government-issued scale. Then, the measurer took fifty-eight additional measurements, including "sitting spread girth," "anterior crotch length," and "maximum thigh girth." The squads brought in fifteen thousand surveys, but O'Brien ultimately only used ten thousand. O'Brien discarded the other five thousand for one of three reasons: there had been a gross error, there were too many young people in the data set, or the volunteers weren't white. The truth was, O'Brien wasn't interested in data for all American women; she wanted data from all American-born white women. It was a criterion that she explicitly stated in her report but never fully explained—in fact, she encouraged the measuring squads to keep it hidden from groups of volunteers. "When it was found necessary, for the sake of good feelings within a group, to measure a few women other than the Caucasian race, this fact was entered under the remarks and the schedule later discarded," she wrote.

For the eugenicists constructing Norma, these exclusions were a feature, not a bug. After all, Norma was intended to be a composite of the *right kind* of American woman: a statue that defined femininity and made clear who should be reproducing and who should not. Harry L. Shapiro, the proud eugenicist and curator of physical anthropology at the American Museum of Natural History, was thrilled by the result. In his article about Norma and Normman, "A Portrait of the American People," which ran in the museum's magazine in 1945, he praised the statues for helping to codify the "White American"—a category of person he feared was in danger of being sullied and diminished through racial mixing. With delight, he explained how aesthetically impressive and well proportioned the White American was, how tall and long legged. The full text reads like an anthropological dating advertisement, as Norma and Normman are compared to people of other nationalities and from various historical periods: Shapiro declares them healthier, fitter, taller, less voluptuous, and more beautiful than the ancient Greeks, the Gibson girl, or the European.

Shapiro, who would go on to be the president of the American Eugenics Society, also emphasized how the average could be an ideal. "Norma and Normman, although they were designed to conform with the average adult before the onset of the ravages of age, exhibit a harmony of proportion that seems far indeed from the usual or the average." Their averageness was notable and, paradoxically, unique. Shapiro said, "Let us state it this way: the average American figure approaches a kind of perfection of bodily form and proportion; the average is excessively rare."

When I first read Shapiro's conflation of the word *normal* with *perfection*, I found it to be a bit of a stretch. Perfection, after all, suggests an apex rather than a middle, a singular kind of human who is, in some sense, above all others. The way I'd always understood it, a perfect human woman would be smarter, more beautiful, thinner, and more graceful than the rest. She'd be special, not typical.

And yet, Shapiro's formulation does make intuitive, if not actual, sense. I had often found my own body to be, in some small sense, *abnormal*. My large butt, my slightly crossed eye, and my poor performance in any and all sports always felt like defects when, in fact, they were characteristics of mine that were surely quite common. And yet, those characteristics never felt normal, because the notion of normal is not about averages or commonly occurring traits, but instead about an unattainable ideal.

Norma and Normman were on display at the American Museum of Natural History in New York for only a few weeks before traveling to the heartland. The director of the Cleveland Museum of Health, a man named Bruno Gebhard, purchased them, as well as *Birthing Series*, to display in the first health museum in the United States. There, they became a sensation.

Like Shapiro, Gebhard was a committed eugenicist: he had been the curator at the Deutsches Hygiene-Museum in Dresden from 1927 to 1935, overseeing exhibitions about the human body with an explicit eugenicist agenda. In the United States, he continued this work, albeit with a bit more subtlety. Norma and Normman were a prime example.

Once she arrived in Cleveland, Gebhard didn't want to celebrate Norma as fantasy; he wanted to find a version of her walking around in the world. He wanted to prove that his idea of normal could actually be a reality. If the "normal body" was something that seemed entirely out of reach, like a Venus or a fashion model, it wouldn't have served the ends of men like Gebhard and Shapiro, who aspired to bring about a world populated exclusively by Normas and Normmans. In order to attain their goal, eugenicists needed those they considered to be fit Americans to know that they, too, could be "normal." So, two months after the statues arrived in Cleveland, Gebhard announced a competition in collaboration with the Cleveland *Plain Dealer* to find a real-life Norma. It was a way to show the people of Cleveland who among them was the pinnacle of human perfection, and get some extra publicity for the museum's newest acquisitions.

For ten days in September 1945, the *Plain Dealer*'s health reporter, Josephine Robertson, churned out pages of Norma-focused content that encouraged female readers, explicitly and implicitly, to enter the contest, which, according to promotional materials, sought to "stimulate interest in physical fitness and the American type." She interviewed clergy, doctors, and educators about the "typical American girl," talked to artists about Norma's aesthetic qualities, and even asked physical fitness instructors how to achieve the Norma physique. The articles were a little bit corny but expressed the same sort of ideas that remain common in fashion magazines and lifestyle sections today: they were written to help to define normal, to explain why normal was beautiful, and to make clear who belonged inside the category of normal—the white, physically fit, able-bodied woman of specific proportion—and who did not.

The contest, like the fabrication of the statues themselves, happened at an opportune time: it had only been a month since the United States had dropped atomic bombs on Hiroshima and Nagasaki, and two weeks since Japan had officially surrendered. After four years of women taking on traditional male roles in factories and homes, there was a pressing need to clearly communicate the idea of the "normal woman" and to make that idea broadly legible. Normal was femme, but not too femme; normal was strong, but not too strong; normal meant having a butt, but only a little one. Normal meant leaving the factory behind, getting married to a GI, and joining in the effort to re-populate a world that had just lost millions.

All told, 3,864 women in the Cleveland area submitted their measurements to Gebhard and the *Plain Dealer*. The form published by the newspaper was simpler than those used by O'Brien's measuring squads, asking only for height, bust, waist, hips, thigh, calf, ankle, foot length, and weight measurements. Some women measured themselves at home, while others attended events around the city where it would be done for them. On the last day of the contest alone, approximately one thousand women were measured at the Cleveland Central YWCA.

The following day, the forty entrants whose proportions came closest to Norma's gathered at the YWCA for the final stage of competition. Like the contest itself, the scene was a little bit Miss America and a little bit science lab. The finalists were officially measured and judged by a panel that included a professor of anatomy at a local university, the head of physical education for girls at the Cleveland Board of Education, and another reporter at the *Plain Dealer*. Then, the panelists tabulated the measurements and tried to determine a winner. What they discovered should have been predictable all along: none of the contestants was a match for Norma. As Shapiro had said, the average is excessively rare.

The woman who came the closest was Martha Skidmore, a white twenty-three-year-old who sold tickets at the local Park Theater. In an article, Josephine Robertson described her as an almost cartoonish ideal of post–World War II femininity. When the war began, Skidmore had worked as a gauge grinder for the Parker Appliance Co., but by the time of publication, she had returned to her old job in order to make her position at the factory available for a returning vet. She was already married and was referred to as "Mrs. Skidmore" throughout the piece. She liked to swim, dance, and bowl, and thought "she was an average individual in her tastes and that nothing out of the ordinary had ever happened to her until the Norma search came along."

The idea of normal, it seems, always comes with some kind of agenda. In the case of Norma, the minds that collated her measurements were enthusiastic eugenicists, motivated by a desire to effectively eradicate insufficiently white, disabled, and queer people. They were openly attempting to engineer a race of perfectly normal Americans, equating full citizenship with having this decisively average, yet demonstrably unattainable, body. By codifying normal, the Norma boosters were also codifying abnormal, which is always the implicit project of the creation of an ideal.

But if the creation of Norma proves anything, it's that no body actually *is* normal. Despite all her rigorous measuring, Ruth O'Brien's study failed—even after measuring thousands of women and crunching and tabulating all the data, there were too many variables for her to create a meaningful set of recommendations for ready-to-wear clothes. Both Gebhard and O'Brien failed to find the superlative normal that they both craved, because creating something singular inevitably separates it from the group. Their projects couldn't work because bodies aren't standard. Some breasts bulge and some sag, some ankles are thick while others are thin, some people with wide shoulders have narrow hips. And some butts are big, while others are small.

Just as the exploitation and display of Sarah Baartman might feel like a relic of the distant past, it is tempting to think that we have outgrown Norma, that we have transcended the pernicious fantasy of an empirical and enforceable "normal."

But the truth is that while the material of normalcy is a moving target, the concept of "the normal" is extraordinarily durable, even if there are no curators and sculptors openly regulating it. It may not be staring us down in a museum of hygiene, but it is always lurking—in dressing rooms, in magazines, in the endless scroll of Instagram.

PROLIFERATION

• •

For all its power and staggering profits, the vast ready-to-wear fashion industry is a relatively new system, and the attempt to create standardized sizes is newer still. Until the nineteenth century, almost all clothing was made the way couture clothing is made now—individually, by hand, for a specific person. Before 1300, most clothing in Europe was not formfitting but loose and flowy, which allowed for sizing to be general and generous. A medieval belted tunic was easy to make fit, and most people only had one or two such garments for their entire adult lives. This relative sizelessness existed because the process of making clothing was arduous: not only did a person have to sew each garment by hand with a needle and thread, they also had to spin wool or other fibers in order to create the cloth for the garment. Each article of clothing had to be worn for many years and accommodate changes in height and girth.

In the late eighteenth century, the first Industrial Revolution simplified textile manufacturing and advanced weaving technology, which meant a great many more people could buy ready-made cloth, a truly monumental shift. The process of making clothing grew simpler and cheaper for the home tailor because a large part of the work was outsourced to low-wage laborers in textile mills. Wealthy women hired well-paid dressmakers to make adorned and elaborate garments, while low-paid seamstresses who worked out of their homes sewed precut garments into clothes for enslaved people in the South, miners in the West, and even New England gentlemen. In the 1850s, the invention of the mass-produced sewing machine further upended garment making: clothing became even cheaper, and more clothes than ever were being produced, although the wages of the seamstresses in home sweatshops did not markedly improve.

Like so many other technologies, the first standard garment sizes were developed by the military. Napoleon, ever the innovator, needed to fit thousands of men with uniforms and could not possibly fabricate each one individually. It was a problem that would also confront the British during the Crimean War and the Americans during the Civil War, and one they would all solve in more or less the same way. Military officials discovered that you could get a general sense of a man's proportions if you measured his chest, and so created a set of standard sizes extrapolated from that single measurement.

During peacetime in the nineteenth century, the military sizing system was utilized to make men's clothing for the burgeoning white-collar workers who required suits for everyday wear. The approach wasn't perfect, but it worked well enough, in part because men's bodies are less fleshy than women's, and the distribution of that flesh is more uniform (they are also spared the unpredictable bulbousness of breasts, fleshy butts, and pregnancy). Men's clothing became big business: by the 1890s, the garment district in New York was the single largest employer in the city. But, as would always be true in the garment industry, big profits did not mean fair wages. From the beginning of the nineteenth century, the people who actually made the garments were largely immigrants—first from Ireland, then Germany and Sweden, and, by the 1890s, Southern and Eastern Europe—and their working conditions and pay were almost universally abysmal.

For much of the same period, the garment industry did

not offer a comparable sizing system for women, despite the success and popularity of male ready-to-wear fashions (that is, clothing that could be bought in a shop and worn without alteration). That wasn't, however, for a lack of trying. Manufacturers knew there was a tremendous amount of money to be made if women could buy clothes off the rack; they just struggled to figure out how to make it work. The first attempts were half-measures: by the 1890s, women could purchase garments that were three-quarters of the way finished at a shop or in a catalog, which they could alter and fit to their bodies using their sewing machines, completing the last step of labor at home.

Then, in the early twentieth century, around the same time that Coco Chanel was busy pioneering simpler and more sporty styles, manufacturers started to produce fully finished clothing for women. At first, they tried to model their approach to women's sizes off of men's sizes, using a bust measurement as the basis of a woman's entire body size. This, obviously, did not work well. Breast size is in no way indicative of any other measurement on a woman's body: a woman with large hips can have small breasts; a woman with long legs can have big breasts. Soon, women who had ordered clothes through catalogs (a common practice at the time) were sending back their purchases in droves.

Following Ruth O'Brien's 1930s study, the fashion industry attempted to put her data into practice, but her system was impossible for manufacturers to use. Every size cost a tremendous amount to make because manufacturers had to create new dies to cut each size, and O'Brien's system suggested the need for twenty-seven sizes, a prohibitively expensive number. Then, in 1958, the National Bureau of Standards, a part of the federal government, reworked Ruth O'Brien's data and, combining it with sizing's relentless dedication to chest measurements, came up with a system similar to the one we use today. The numbers were derived from bust size and the assumed proportions of an

hourglass figure, and each size was indicated by a single number, in even intervals from 8 to 38. At first mandatory, this system became voluntary in 1970, and was ultimately abandoned
entirely in 1983, largely because it never really worked.

"Unless your clothes are made for you, they don't actually
fit you," Abigail Glaum-Lathbury tells me in one of our many
conversations about clothing size. An artist, fashion designer,
and professor at the School of the Art Institute of Chicago,
Glaum-Lathbury has done a tremendous amount of research
into the history of sizing and how it works now. She explains
that today, women's clothing sizes offer almost no information about how a garment actually fits. I've talked to Glaum-
Lathbury several times, in part because I find this fact baffling
but also intriguing. Although I've never purchased something
that feels right on my body, it's a revelation to learn that clothing designers and manufacturers don't actually expect their garments to fit. It isn't that they don't want to make clothes that fit
a variety of bodies, it's just that, even with advanced technology
and manufacturing, it is simply impossible.

Fit, after all, is determined by the distribution of flesh around
a body, Glaum-Lathbury explains, and flesh cannot be standardized. Even if two women have the exact same height and
circumference measurements, they don't necessarily share the
same flesh distribution over their bones. There is nowhere you
see this more, she says, than with breasts. Even if she and I had
the exact same measurements, our breasts might differ. "I might
have a wider rib cage than you," she told me, "or you might
have a broader shoulder than me, or my breasts might go further
out to the side and yours might be bigger and go forward." The
same could be said about butts—hip and waist measurements
don't speak to the distribution or shape of a woman's backside.
There's no uniformity in the panoply of butts, so uniform pants
sizes are completely unrealistic.

When designers create clothing, they usually start by fitting the clothes on mannequins—hard, fleshless, headless torsos and legs that approximate a body. Although they are practical for an early prototype, mannequins become less useful as the process continues. Garments must be worn by real humans in order to determine what happens when people sit down, or bend over, or have sensitive skin. And so, once a designer has a pretty good idea of what it is they are making, they bring in fit models, people who are used to help designers determine the fit of their clothes. If a designer happens to be designing women's pants, they often call on one in particular.

If you've worn women's jeans in the last decade, it's likely that you've stepped into a pair designed to fit the butt of Natasha Wagner, one of the fashion industry's most in-demand denim fit models. Wagner has worked with brands including 7 for All Mankind, Mother, Citizens of Humanity, Re/Done, Paige, Black Orchid, Vince, Proenza Schouler, Gap, Lucky Brand, Old Navy, and Levi's. *Vogue* described her as the woman whose "bottom is shaping the nation." Refinery29 describes her as having "the best butt in the business." Her job is to be the body that stands in for all the rest of us, a body that, like Norma, is simultaneously normal and ideal—the one that all the clothes actually fit.

Wagner grew up in LA and went to college at Cal State Long Beach, where she studied communications, joined a sorority, and worked as a waitress at Chili's. One Friday afternoon, one of her sorority sisters, who was working as a fit model, asked Wagner to ride with her to pick up her paycheck at her modeling agency, so she could take advantage of the carpool lane. When they arrived, an agent asked if she could measure Wagner. "They measured me and I didn't think much of it," she says. "And then they started calling me. It turned out I had the exact measurements they were looking for. I felt like I won the lottery."

Just what those measurements are, Wagner won't tell me.

When I talk to her on the phone, she speaks of them almost as if they're a trade secret. So instead, I ask her to describe her butt. She hesitates a bit before settling on "perfectly imperfect." Judging from photos online, Wagner is a leggy white woman with long blond hair and beachy highlights. She's thin and conventionally attractive. I find many images in varying degrees of close-up that show her butt in jeans. To me, it's actually pretty small compared to the general population, though certainly bigger than those of the waifish models of the 1990s—which, according to industry professionals, is the key to her appeal. "If you fit with someone who is too curvy (tiny waist, big butt), or with someone who has a straight body (no hips)," one designer who employs Wagner explained to *Vogue*, "you are limiting yourself to just a certain body type. . . . She has the best of both worlds where she's slim and she still has shape."

It is this perceived averageness that Wagner says makes her a good fit model. "If the company only has a budget for one model, they want someone who's not too big, not too small, not too tall, or too skinny," she told me. I'm immediately reminded of the idea of the "too" that dominated the conversations around Norma in 1945. Wagner's body is in many ways exceptional, even though it is being used as a template for the quintessentially normal.

When Wagner is approached about a job, the first step is an interview at the corporate offices of a clothing brand, where her measurements are taken. For this part of the process, she wears tight spandex, but occasionally, if she trusts the person doing the measuring, she will allow them to measure her in her undergarments behind a curtain. They measure her everywhere: the base of her neck, the width of her shoulders, her bust, her natural waist, her low hip, thigh, midthigh, and inseam. Then, they have her try on a few garments to determine if she is right for the brand.

Because there is no standardization across the garment in-dustry, each brand determines its own metrics, and therefore its own ideal customer. Many of us have learned this experien-tially: if you've ever tried on the same size in different brands, you know that there is little consistency from one to the next. According to Glaum-Lathbury, each brand markets itself to a specific kind of customer, which is communicated, in part, by its approach to sizing. If Natasha's measurements—lanky, tall, with a bit of a butt—align with the image or ideal that partic-ular brand is trying to sell, she's the right fit, regardless of how few women share her particular proportions. Garment makers are rarely in the business of making clothes that will work for actual people; instead, they cater to a fantasy of who the cus-tomer hopes to be.

After brand representatives meet with Wagner and decide to work with her, the designer provides a sketch of the garment to a pattern maker, who then creates a pattern in Natasha's size. Next, the brand fabricates a prototype from the pattern. In an ideal world, Wagner tries on two or three versions of the proto-type and offers recommendations. In each iteration, designers make micro-adjustments to match the garment more precisely to her body, and take Wagner's feedback about construction and feel. From experience, she knows that if belt loops aren't sewed into the yoke seam, they will rip out when people pull up their pants, and that pockets work best if they are a certain shape. Wagner says that when a company achieves the perfect fit, she can just feel it. "The back isn't pulling down. The waistband isn't chafing or cutting. It hugs you in all the right places."

After the initial patterns and instructions, the factory runs what's called a preproduction fit—a sample to make sure what it's making conforms to what the designers had in mind. Wag-ner usually tries on the preproduction fit and works with the designers to make any minor last-minute adjustments. Then, after the factory goes into production, Wagner tries on the garment for a final time to make sure it is acceptable to send out into the world.

Though Wagner provides the baseline "ideal," companies must be able to generate clothes in more than one size. To do this they each use slightly different mathematical formulas to make larger and smaller versions of the prototype. This process, called grading, is complex. Glaum-Lathbury explains that each size increase adds a proportionately larger amount of fabric, so the difference between a size 2 and a size 4 might be one inch of fabric, but the difference between a size 14 and a size 16 might be two and a half inches. That fabric doesn't all get added in the same place: the companies try to predict where flesh will be distributed as people get bigger. This means that a neck measurement may not change much at all, but the center front of a garment might add a full inch of fabric. In addition to circumference additions, there are also length additions, the assumption being that a woman who wears a size 4 is shorter than one who wears a size ten. So, as clothing sizes get bigger, it is less likely they will fit.

What baffles me about this—what has always baffled me—is how this method of sizing manages to work as a business model. The garment industry is one of the largest in the world—surely companies would make even more money if their products actually reliably fit their customers? Surely, there has to be a better, and more profitable, way.

Glaum-Lathbury explains that it isn't out of cruelty that our clothes don't fit, but rather due to necessity. "You have to remember, your clothes don't have anything to do with your body," she says. "Clothes are a series of questions related to the bottom line, not the correctness of the product." Because fashion is a volume business, the only way a company can make money is if they sell a huge amount of something, and there are a limited number of ways to make that process more efficient. Although a manufacturer can cut two hundred T-shirts at once, every single one of them has to be sewn by hand. There are no robots that can sew; every garment you have ever worn has been stitched by a human being sitting at a sewing machine. And although the widespread use of sweatshops and other unethical labor practices throughout the history of the garment industry has made this sewing as cheap as possible, it can't be made much cheaper. And so it is impossible to efficiently make clothes in as many sizes and variations as would be necessary for them to actually fit.

"In order for this system to work, our bodies have to be functionally interchangeable," Glaum-Lathbury explains. "Our bodies are a cog within a system." It's an issue she's experienced firsthand: when she had a small clothing line of her own, her goal was to create beautiful, well-made clothes out of lovely fabrics that fit well, but she often ended up making garments that didn't fit that well on a wide variety of bodies. Even though her goal was to make clothes that fit, she simply couldn't. It just wasn't economically viable.

"Our bodies are unruly," she reminds me, by way of explanation. It's a word that has stuck with me because it suggests our bodies are rebels—against sizes, against capitalism, against the enduring need to order and rank and control—an idea that appeals because it feels so deeply true. I slather on night cream, do squats, and try to stuff myself into a pair of pants that don't quite fit, but I still have wrinkles, cellulite, and a butt that feels like it is shaped incorrectly. My body constantly resists my efforts to control it.

But, of course, not everyone is trying to make their body fit. Not everyone is in search of normal. For some, the unruly nature of the body, and the myriad ways a body can be, are not only something to accept but are, in fact, something to revel in.

RESISTANCE

· ·

Like almost everything else I encountered at Icon in Astoria, Queens, the drink special was joyful, punny, and queer: customers shouted for a "Call Me by Your Rosé," a fruity drink that paid homage to the movie *Call Me by Your Name*. Two bartenders danced along to "I Touch Myself" by the Divinyls as they shook drinks beneath multicolored spotlights that flooded the brick walls. The room was festooned with rainbow flags.

I was there on a Sunday at seven forty-five p.m., but the place was packed. It was the first night of the Iconic drag competition, an eight-week-long live reality show in which New York–based drag queens came to perform for the Icon crown in front of a rotating panel of judges. That night, eleven drag queens would perform in individual, choreographed performances as well as in something called Drag Queen Roulette, where each contestant would have to create a performance on the spot to a song of the DJ's choosing.

Outside of the subway, Icon was one of the most diverse spaces I'd ever been to in New York City. There were myriad races, gender presentations, and class markers on display; gay-seeming couples cuddled next to straight-seeming couples, the middle-aged mingled with the young. I stood next to a woman with a buzz cut and a *Friends* baseball cap holding a femme-presenting woman by the waist. In front of us, a drag queen who wasn't performing that evening obstructed our view of the stage, her silver-sparkle heels and voluminous blond wig rendering her a full foot taller than me. I spent the evening triangulating my view through her mass of curls and the sea of phones held aloft to capture the event live on Instagram.

I went to Icon to see if I could find an antidote to the relentless emphasis on sameness and normalcy woven throughout the history of bodies and size, and to the regulation of gender that was so closely tied to Norma's creation and display. I really couldn't have come to a better place. The theme of the night, "Getting to Know You," was meant to be a vehicle for the performers to introduce themselves to the judges and the crowd, but in many ways it highlighted the underlying reality of any drag performance: each performer gets to be whatever version of themselves they want. The bodies that they created and presented all played with the impersonation of femininity, but each performer interpreted the brief a little differently. Some of the performers looked like characters in a sci-fi movie, donning iridescent skirts and bright blond wigs, and others looked almost old-fashioned, decked out in golden-age-Hollywood dresses and big, curly hair. Some seemed to wear no padding at all, achieving an androgynous, lithe look. Others appeared to have breasts; cleavage emerged from atop bustiers and sweetheart necklines. And some had large, voluptuous butts, created by foam padding strapped underneath ornate dresses and tight pantyhose, which produced a look that read as classically feminine, if there is even such a thing. Over the course of the evening, I took in a performance that imitated the structure and graphics of the video game *Mortal Kombat*, incorporating gymnastics and martial arts. There was a drag queen named Zeta 2K who performed fellatio on a long red balloon, popped it, and then hid it in her mouth for several minutes, only to slowly retrieve it as she wrapped herself in a blanket of stitched-together plastic trash. Another performer, Essence, smeared herself with neon-yellow body paint as she writhed on the ground.

I, of course, took a particular interest in the butts, and was surprised at the range of methods used by the drag queens to embellish, shape, and augment their backsides. There were bare butts highlighted with contouring makeup and unpadded butts that were pancake-flat beneath skirts and dresses. One performer looked like Mae West: her curves were stuffed to appear big and brassy. Another resembled J.Lo, her padding giving her the type of body that comes only with a particular alchemy of genetic luck and hours at the gym. At Icon, butts were something to play with openly, to dial large or small according to taste and personality. The butt, and the body, was a site of joy and disruption rather than a place of prescription. But how, I wondered, was this multiplicity achieved? Where did all of these glorious butts come from?

On a hot July day in 2019, Vinnie Cuccia stood in front of his apartment building in Brighton Beach, a historically Russian neighborhood in Brooklyn where he lived with Alex Bartlett, his partner in life and business. An effervescent man in his fifties, he smoked a cigarette in the courtyard, wearing wraparound sunglasses, slim-cut jeans, and a yellow PFLAG T-shirt. I approached the building as he finished his cigarette, and he told me about how much he loved living in this part of the city, an area where he and Bartlett could afford to live in a building with ocean views. Coney Island was a ten-minute stroll away, and the aquarium was even closer. "Our friends always ask us to go to Fire Island," he told me. "But we don't need to—here, we can go to the beach and come back home to go to the bathroom!"

Cuccia and I took the elevator up to the apartment where

he and Bartlett lived and worked. When he opened the door, we were greeted by human-sized stacks of ivory-colored foam cut into the shape of enormous, corpulent commas. An entire room was dedicated to these foam chunks, but that didn't stop them from spilling into the hallway. These materials were the basis of the business Cuccia and Bartlett co-owned: they are perhaps the world's foremost purveyors of butt and hip pads designed for use by drag queens, cross-dressers, and trans women. Several of the drag queens I had watched at Iconic used their product, as did contestants on *RuPaul's Drag Race* and other well-known drag queens across the globe.

Bartlett soon appeared to welcome me. Dressed in cut-off shorts and flip-flops, he showed me the bedroom that the couple had transformed into a workshop. Two assistants, both young women planning to pursue a career in fashion, stopped to say hello before resuming their work shaping the foam with electric saws. A shelf near the ceiling held bolts of brightly colored fabric that Bartlett fashioned into costumes, both for himself (he performed in drag as "Pepper") and for clients and friends who performed on Broadway and in clubs across the country.

When they opened the business—aptly named Planet Pepper—Bartlett had been doing drag for about twenty years. He had also been sewing costumes for himself and other drag queens out of his apartment. Cuccia didn't know anything about sewing but wanted to start a small business and had access to $15,000 from the New York State Commission for the Blind, which was offering start-up money for people with visual impairments (Cuccia is legally blind). The couple decided to use the money to start a costume shop—Cuccia would handle the business side of things and Bartlett would take the creative lead.

At first, Planet Pepper lost money—small fashion companies often run on thin margins and it is rare to turn a profit quickly—but soon the couple realized that there was an associated, and untapped, market: specialized padding for drag queens to wear under their elaborate outfits.

"I was making costumes for people that didn't have a feminine body, and they wanted to present in a feminine way," Bartlett explained. "They'd come in looking like dudes and we'd have to basically start with the body and then do the outfit. After a while I realized—there's nobody doing this. No one is really making hip pads for drag queens and other people who want to present that way."

Bartlett, who had grown up and then come of age as a drag queen in Virginia, had learned how to make and shape padding the way most drag queens had always learned: his drag mother had taught him how to cut up couch cushions, sculpt them into the desired shape, and stuff them strategically into pantyhose.

"You learn from the people you're around," Bartlett explained. "A friend of mine could see I wasn't padding and was like, 'It's time to start thinking about padding because you look like a boy in a dress.'" The first time he stepped onstage in padding, he recalled, was a magical, life-changing moment. "For drag queens, there is this sort of switch that goes off when you figure out your shape. You become a different person. When you have a body and fingernails and boobs, you walk in a different way, move in a different way. You command space differently."

In the eighties and nineties, the drag community, especially in New York City, dutifully reflected the fashion industry's ideas of what it meant to be feminine and beautiful. While performers in Virginia often crafted their appearance after Mae West and Marilyn Monroe—a look that requires a full backside—Bartlett realized when he arrived in New York City in 1992 that the style was "very androgynous, very rock 'n' roll," and therefore less padded. "Everybody wanted to be a supermodel, size zero, look like a boy in a dress," Cuccia added. Even with his visual impairment, Cuccia says he could always tell when he was talking to a drag queen in those days. "I looked right at her hips. They didn't move; they didn't sway." It took a while, but Planet Pepper eventually found a foothold in the community as styles and outlooks on drag began to evolve and change. "When people think about being a woman, it's all about the breasts and hair and face," Cuccia says. "But you put these hips on and this butt on, everything changes dramatically. A lot of people say, 'It changed my look, it changed my life.'"

Like many women, I, too, have worn undergarments in an effort to change my silhouette, but unlike Cuccia and Bartlett, for whom the creation of feminine shapes is an act of acceptance, liberation, and rebellion, my attempts to shape my body using padding and spandex have almost always been an exercise in restriction.

The first time I used underwear to conform to predetermined ideals of femininity was in middle school. Before I had any breasts to speak of, I bought bras with a bit of bulk added to the underside of the cup. I tried to strike a balance between a change that might get me noticed and a change that was noticeably false: I wanted to look a touch more developed than I actually was but was terrified that my deception would be discovered. A decade later, as a twenty-four-year-old bridesmaid, I discovered shapewear because I'd forgotten that I would need a slip to wear beneath a gossamer dress at the front of a church. As I steamed the bride's wedding gown in a Sunday school classroom, another bridesmaid rushed to a nearby mall and returned brandishing a tan spandex tube with bra cups attached at the top. It was from Victoria's Secret and was designed not only to prevent the congregation from seeing through my dress, but also to make me smaller. By the end of the night, my stomach ached—the price of creating a body that felt normal and feminine was an acidic feeling of constipation.

The desire to change the way my body looked was, for me, an attempt at coherence, an effort to match the outside of the body with the inside, to have the self that is seen in the world match some concept of the true self lurking beneath the surface. The padded bra and the body-constricting Spanx each offered an opportunity to more closely align with an ideal of the feminine, to put on a costume and perform a version of femme: I want bigness here and smallness there in order for the outside of my body to cohere to a gender template that I have inherited and internalized. I feel myself—or want to feel myself—as feminine, or adult, or poised. It is an ordering, of both the self and the world. For me, it is often a complicated, conflicting desire: I want to be seen on the outside as something close to who I feel myself to be on the inside, and yet I also want to be seen on the outside as normal, as feminine, as correct.

But femininity is not a singular experience, and the tools we have to communicate it are blunt. Simple, obvious signifiers—a big bosom, a full behind, a slimmed middle—create an illusion of gender that is uncomplicated and binary. A feminine outside suggests a tidy, feminine inside, even if the truth is much more fluid and complex. In many ways, this is the point: to make femininity simple, straightforward, and singular is a way to dodge its nuance. After all, there was no bra that could have communicated the way, at thirteen, I longed for the freedom of being a little girl at the same moment that I craved what I imagined was the agency of womanhood. There was no constipating girdle or flouncy dress that could have made visible the multiple expressions of gender I felt within me as I stood at the front of the church on the day of my friend's wedding. I was polished and lovely, and took pleasure in the fact that I seemed to be pulling off the poise of a cookie-cutter bridesmaid.

But I was also standing at the front of an evangelical church, trying to catch the eye of the beautiful butch woman who was my date to the ceremony, both of us squirming as we listened to the pastor assert that marriage was between one man and one woman. There was a betrayal in that moment: I was passing as a rom-com femme, but my gender and sexuality both remained disguised.

"One is not born, but rather becomes, woman," Simone de Beauvoir famously tells us in *The Second Sex*. One of the places one becomes a woman is in the aisles of a lingerie store, where the fantasy of another body feels dimly within reach. Beauvoir's sentiment echoes through the philosophy of gender in the twentieth and twenty-first centuries. We see it in the pages of Judith Butler's *Gender Trouble*, which situates gender as a construction and a performance, rather than as a stable fact. We might wear the accessories associated with what has been deemed "female" or "male," we may plump and pad and slim, but the internal self cannot be known by these external signifiers, and the contrast between the outside and the inside is often heightened by the performance. There is, in fact, no real internal self at all, according to Butler. The fantasy of a genuine self, a stable notion of "femininity," is an illusion. There is no normal, there is no feminine. Part of the reason why any singular expression of gender is discomfiting, why earnestly plumping myself up in the ultra-femme dress of the bridesmaid felt so hollow, is that it suggests singularity when there is really plurality. There is a tragedy in that discomfort, but also, maybe, an opportunity. Or, as RuPaul has said: "We're all born naked, and the rest is drag."

The product offered by Cuccia and Bartlett at Planet Pepper provides a different way to think about creating a body than what Belskie and Dickinson proffered with Norma, or what I can find in the aisles of a lingerie store. The creation of Norma was an attempt to define, and confine, femininity. When I wear

Spanx or make a futile attempt to fit into pants designed for Natasha Wagner's body, I feel the echoes of those constraints. I'm trying to conform my body to another person's notion of femininity, another person's idea of normal.

And yet, Bartlett and Cuccia find freedom in versions of these same garments. For them it is all about the joyfulness of expressing multiple modes of the self. "At some point, it becomes this abstract idea of what is male and female," says Bartlett. "We go back and forth over time. And for me, I was bored wearing jeans and black tees, and I wanted to wear fun, flashy clothes. I asked myself: Why can't I wear fabulous dresses? I found a space where I could do that. For me there is a magic in dressing up. I become even more of myself."

Fit

STEEL

· ·

In the first panel of a comic strip from 1994, a woman arrives for what appears to be a date wearing a leotard and sweatband. Her male companion wears a suit and tie and sits at a table with a white cloth draped on it. In the second panel, as she takes her seat, a sound resounds through the air: "*CLANG,*" reads the text in enormous bold letters. In the third panel, the date offers his opening line: "So how long have you had buns of steel?"

Thanks (in part) to its name, the fitness phenomenon *Buns of Steel* was ripe for parody in the late 1980s and early 1990s: it was spoofed on *Saturday Night Live*, discussed in Jay Leno's late-night monologues, and referenced in *Cathy* comics. After all, butts are funny, and the idea of having a butt of steel is both alluring and a little bit ridiculous. But *Buns of Steel* wasn't a joke, at least not entirely. Based on a workout regimen developed by fitness entrepreneur Greg Smithey, *Buns of Steel* was also a bestselling VHS exercise tape purchased all over the world by people who actually wanted to have metal-hard buns, a fact that spoke to a fundamental shift in expectations about how bodies should look and what they were for.

The butt (or at least the ass) has long been linguistically associated with hard work. Having a "fat ass" is equated with laziness and sloth, as in "get off your fat ass and get to work." To give a person a "kick in the ass" is to get them going, to make them go to work. To be a "hard-ass" is to be tough and uncompromising. A person can also "work their ass off," a phrase that makes a direct connection between a small butt and diligent labor. It's no surprise, then, that these connotations would all come together to form one of the most successful exercise programs in history during a period when commitment to gospels of entrepreneurship and self-creation in America was reaching new peaks—or that that program was invented by someone whose personal story so thoroughly embodied those principles of success.

———————

It took me six months to track Greg Smithey down. I wrote him repeated emails at an address I found on a website he made in 2008. I scoured the phone books of Anchorage and Las Vegas, where I knew he had once lived. I tried to locate his representatives and his relatives. I had all but given up, assuming he had disappeared into the netherworld of the once-famous, when one afternoon I received an email from Smithey saying he'd be happy to speak with me; his silence, he explained, had just been because he doesn't regularly check his inbox.

So I gave him a call. Once he started talking, he didn't stop for three days.

Some of the stories he told seemed dubious. He claimed that he was the "white boy" in the Wild Cherry song "Play That Funky Music" (he wasn't). He said he trained the Commodores and Miss Alaska at his aerobics studio in Anchorage (possible, but unlikely). He told me that he is a storm chaser and has been inside eight typhoons, and described a harrowing encounter with a grizzly bear that he survived by utilizing positive thinking and a big, toothy smile. Recognizing his tendency to self-mythologize and stretch the truth, it's important to take anything he says with a grain of salt. There is, however, one thing that is undeniably true about Greg Smithey: he invented one of the most successful fitness phenomena of the last forty years.

Smithey's interest in fitness began when he discovered pole vaulting at twelve years old. He was good at it—so good that, in 1969, he attended Idaho State on a track scholarship. There he excelled, eventually jumping a very respectable sixteen feet. After college, he decided he wanted to teach physical education and moved to Alaska, where he coached the Wasilla High School track team (he claims he trained Sarah Palin). He liked teaching and coaching, but he was a man with a bigger dream: he wanted to start his own aerobics studio and introduce a new fitness approach to the masses. After attending a life-changing motivational lecture by sound-bite optimist Zig Ziglar, Smithey quit his job, moved to Anchorage, and, in 1984, opened the Anchorage Alaska Hip-Hop Aerobics Club.

It turned out to be a bumpy transition. Smithey soon found himself in a financial hole, haggling with his landlord for a break on rent and trying to figure out how to attract enough aerobics students to make the business viable. "I was looking at total failure with my exercise studio and I got more angry and more frustrated," he says. He decided to channel that anger into intense workouts in his aerobics classes. "Specifically, I put together a workout that just burned their butts."

According to the website he maintains now, Smithey's classes were filled with wild antics. He brought a cassette tape and a long leather whip (just as a prop, he reassured me), and referred to himself as Dr. Buns, Professor of Bunology, Prince of Pain, Master of Masochism, and the Bunmaster. He taught his class with the lights dimmed, a spotlight on him, music cranked. In fifty minutes, he would guide the group through at least fifty different butt-related exercises, all the while shouting, "Beautiful

legs . . . beautiful legs . . . work those beautiful legs . . . and don't
forget to squeeze those cheeseburgers out of those thighs, and
that carrot cake . . . and those french fries!"

Smithey says that, at first, there were only five or six students in his class, but the number quickly grew to over forty
repeat attendees. "They were coming because I was causing
their butts to hurt so bad. And soon, they started coming in and
telling me all these wonderful stories about how their butts look
so good and their husbands love it." He tells me that his greatest moment of inspiration struck while talking to a group of
students after class. One of them said: "Wow, our buns feel like
steel." "We all kind of fell silent," he recalled. They recognized
genius when they heard it.

Smithey's timing with *Buns of Steel* turned out to be perfect.
Throughout the 1960s and '70s, the very notion of what exercise was, and who it was for, underwent a profound change. According to fitness historian and New School professor Natalia
Petrzela, booms in American fitness culture usually correspond
to rises in white-collar labor. As more people are employed in
desk jobs—in the 1920s and 1950s, for example—the people who
work those jobs become less active than those who have more
physically demanding jobs, a fact that often causes a lot of societal
angst. Anxiety about fitness (and its corollary—fatness) perme-
ates middle-class culture in these eras because fitness isn't ever
only about having a body that is useful or a body that is healthy.
Having a fit body seems to almost always mean something more.

Petrzela explains that, in the United States, the concept of
physical fitness is very often linked to patriotism because the
perceived physical health and capacity of a nation's citizens has
(until recently) been indicative of military might: if you have
a strong body, you are better prepared to fight in a war. In the

1950s, for example, there was much concern that the Cold War might turn hot and American men would not be prepared to fight if they were flabby from their *Mad Men*–style office jobs. "People were invested in this idea of America being a superpower," she says, "but there is this anxiety that comes with it, which is, *Oh my God, all of these things that make America great—cars and TVs and washing machines and frozen foods—are actually making America fat and unconditioned.*" It is because of this anxiety that the government initiated programs like the Presidential Physical Fitness Test, designed to promote physical strength and stamina in American children and set them along a lifelong path to vitality.

By the late 1970s, physical fitness would take on another layer of meaning. In response to the increased strength of organized labor over the previous two decades, as well as a new wave of governmental regulations that included the Environmental Protection Agency and Occupational Safety and Health Administration, many of America's wealthy and powerful embraced an economic philosophy that prized the unfettered free market, relentless privatization, and individual liberties. This neoliberal philosophy gradually gained wider purchase across class divides as its boosters promoted it as a remedy to the economic crises of the 1970s, and because it appealed to the persistent American mythos of the self-made man.

But neoliberalism wasn't just an economic philosophy; its tentacles would extend into nearly every part of American life. It conflated the free market with individual agency, had no use for collective modes of expression or action, and judged the worth of people primarily in terms of market value—ideas that, if taken seriously, would alter how people thought about themselves on nearly every level, including how they perceived their bodies. Although there is a long history of equating a slim body with self-control, in the 1970s, to be physically fit became an important way to demonstrate the values of discipline and self-creation. A fit body became a visual symbol of a hearty work ethic and the ability to control the self, crucial attributes in a country that had a renewed commitment to the idea that the individual controls their own destiny.

It was on the cusp of this boom of individualism that, in 1968, an air force physician named Kenneth Cooper published a book called *Aerobics*, which extolled the virtues of exercise that strengthened not only the limbs and torso, but also the muscles within the heart. Until that point, most Americans associated the concept of "the gym" with bodybuilding, an almost entirely male subculture that was considered deviant, the progeny of circus acts and freak shows. Bodybuilders were perceived as somehow both too feminine—often suspected to be homosexuals because they spent so much time around other men and cared about the way they looked—and too masculine, grotesquely muscled and projecting conspicuous strength. It was such an extreme that much of the general population had no interest in emulating it. The publication of Cooper's book, however, provided an alternative to building bulky muscle: it promoted exercise as a way to create the lean muscles of a long-distance runner or a dancer. It was a look that appealed to all genders, but particularly women—then, as now, the promises of aerobic exercise were strength and cardiovascular health, but also a way to achieve thinness while increasing and maintaining strength. But the strength associated with aerobic exercise remained within heteronormative limits, avoiding bulk or shapes that might signify masculinity (or lesbianism).

Like human language, aerobic dance—which built on the concepts Cooper presented in his book—emerged in multiple locations at the same time, and it was the primordial ooze out of which many forms of exercise evolved, from spin to barre to Buns of Steel. Judi Missett taught the first Jazzercise class at a

Chicago dance studio in 1969, while Jacki Sorensen taught a similar style of aerobic dancing at a local New Jersey YMCA the next year. The basics of both were remarkably similar: a woman situated herself in front of a group of people and demonstrated rapid, dancelike movements designed to increase heart rates and offered targeted instruction in strengthening specific areas of the body. A class of mostly women would watch and follow along. Class attendees and instructors were clad in tight-fitting, leotard-like garb and moving to upbeat pop music (often disco). Everyone left the class drenched in sweat.

Both Missett's and Sorensen's styles of aerobic dance proved to be enormously popular. Sorensen penned a book and went on a multicity tour, appearing on television and radio programs across the country; by 1981, she had certified more than four thousand teachers to lead aerobics classes. Missett wrote her own book, which sold over four hundred thousand copies, and had the insight to turn Jazzercise into a franchise business that allowed instructors to earn a share of their profits. Jazzercise spread to nearly every corner of the country.

There are a few possible reasons why aerobics became so popular so quickly. To start, both Missett and Sorensen were teaching middle-class, relatively conservative women with families who had at least a little bit of expendable income and free time, women who voted for Reagan and Nixon and made cookies for bake sales, who saw their femininity and vitality as a crucial contribution to the nation. Sorensen's husband was in the air force, and she often taught on base, which helped to spread her workout around the country as she moved from one city to the next.

Perhaps paradoxically, aerobics' rise in popularity was also fueled by the unfolding second-wave feminist movement, which challenged the conflation of femininity and weakness through efforts that included advocacy that led to the passage of Title IX in 1972, giving more women access to competitive sports. For decades, the gym had felt like a hostile place to many women, and a woman who wanted to exercise her body—a fundamental human need—likely would have felt lonely in that desire. To move around—to swim, lift, jump, and run—is a way to feel liberated and connected, a feeling that was hard for many women to access before aerobics came along. From a contemporary standpoint, it's difficult to imagine that pre-aerobics world, a world where regular exercise wasn't a part of most women's lives, where athletic bodies were considered suspect and masculine. "It really was a big deal . . . for women to get together and exert their bodies in this rigorous, athletic way," says Petrzela. "It was a big deal for hard, rigorous exercise to be part of what it is to be sexy and feminine."

Missett and Sorensen may have invented aerobics, but there is one person who will forever be credited with making it a global sensation—a woman who would embody its strange blend of leftist politics and conservative, neoliberal hobby.

Jane Fonda, the daughter of screen icon Henry Fonda, had become famous as a theater and comedy actress in the 1960s and then was crowned a sex symbol after playing the title role in the 1968 sci-fi spoof *Barbarella*. Later, she went on to have serious and award-winning roles in films like *Klute* and *Coming Home* but became equally notable for her deep involvement in the political left and the protests against the Vietnam War. In 1972, she made a controversial visit to see the damage American bombings had wrought on North Vietnam with her future husband, Students for a Democratic Society cofounder Tom Hayden, and was photographed sitting on top of a Vietcong antiaircraft gun emplacement. The image shocked many Americans as antipatriotic and earned her the derisive nickname "Hanoi Jane."

It was amid this deeply chaotic moment, when feminists were condemning her as a silly Hollywood sexpot and many

Americans were calling her a traitor, that Fonda began to pre-
pare for a new movie role. As part of her training, she began
studying aerobics with Gilda Marx, who, like Missett and Sorensen, taught high-energy dance classes designed to whip participants into peak condition. Fonda was hooked—she loved
the classes so much that she started teaching her own at a studio
in Beverly Hills, and gained a large and devoted following. In
1981, she published an instructional book about aerobics as part
of a fundraising effort for the Campaign for Economic Democracy, a radical organization promoting policies to redistribute
wealth and protect the environment. The proceeds from the
project, she announced, would go toward supporting the campaign's work. The book offered both instruction in aerobics and
hundreds of images of Fonda in a leotard, images that would be
instrumental in forming the basis for a new kind of body ideal.
On the cover, she sits on the floor of what appears to be a dance
studio, propped up on one elbow, legs sticking straight up in the
air, grabbing the heel of her pointed foot in a pose that reads as
both balletic and tough. Hers was a body that could *do* things,
a body that was flexible, powerful, undoubtedly thin, famously
desirable, and markedly buttless.

Jane Fonda's Workout Book was an instant bestseller and a
massive success. People across the country in search of a body
like Fonda's rushed to purchase what they saw as an instruction
manual telling them how to get it. Two million copies were sold
in the first two years, and the book was translated into fifty languages. In 1982, Simon & Schuster cut Fonda the largest royalty
check the publisher had ever written. And then came the real
moneymaker: VHS tapes.

In the early 1980s, most people didn't have a VCR—videotapes
were primarily the purview of film aficionados and pornography devotees. No one had ever made an at-home exercise video.
But Stuart Karl, of Karl Home Video, saw an opportunity for

wider distribution of Fonda's workout. His wife had given him the idea after she mentioned how gyms and aerobics studios still felt unfamiliar and unwelcoming to many women. Karl reached out to Fonda and convinced her to record her routine, just to see what would happen. She agreed, and they produced the first video for $50,000 ("a spit and a prayer," is how Fonda herself describes the production). The initial retail price was $59.95 per tape, which in turn became part of a larger investment, because most people also needed to purchase a VCR, an additional expense of hundreds of dollars.

Despite these economic hurdles, the tapes became a sensation, staying at the top of the video bestseller lists for three years and selling seventeen million copies. (They are still some of the bestselling home videos of all time.) It was a phenomenon that was popular across racial lines—fashion magazines targeted at Black women, like *Essence*, regularly ran features on aerobics, and many aerobics videos, including Fonda's, featured women of color following along in the background, even if the star was almost always white. As VHS tapes became cheaper, aerobics videos also became an accessible way to exercise for women who couldn't afford pricey gym memberships. By the end of the 1980s, Fonda had not only popularized aerobics around the world; she had also become a fitness icon and laid the groundwork for other instructors—like Greg Smithey—to do the same.

By 1987, Smithey was in deeper debt than ever, owing months of back rent, despite his consistently full classes. In a last-ditch attempt to turn a profit in the world of aerobics, he took a page from Jane Fonda's book and decided to record his own instructional workout video, using the butt-burning method he had popularized in Anchorage. He acquired some rent-to-own furniture and arranged fake palm trees inside a studio that he'd painted in tropical pastels. The night before the shoot, he invited students from his class to participate, offering to pay them in pizza and soft drinks. *The Original Buns of Steel* was shot in two takes.

In the video (which is available on YouTube), Smithey doesn't brandish a whip, only too-tight sweatpants, a low-cut tank top, and a sweatband. The production values are low—the lighting is garish, the picture is grainy, and the sound is tinny. The *Anchorage Daily News* later described it as having "an Alaska feel," a kind way of saying it was cheaply made. The students following along in the background are occasionally out of sync or hidden behind one another. Their outfits, however, are dazzling: metallic blue catsuits with bright purple leg warmers, mustard-yellow harem pants, a bright white leotard with a Floridian landscape emblazoned across the front paired with fuchsia leggings. Smithey is encouraging, almost sweet. "You know you've got a great body!" he chirps to the audience. "We gotta do the other leg now!" There is no Prince of Pain here, but the workout is actually pretty hard, if at times a little boring. There are endless variations on donkey kicks and leg raises. A generic soundtrack of smooth jazz plays incessantly in the background.

At first, the videos did not catch fire. In 1988, Smithey only sold 114 tapes, almost all of them in the Anchorage area. It wasn't enough. He was making preparations to close his studio—he could dodge his landlord no longer—and needed to make money to survive. In a last-ditch effort, he tried his luck at an aerobics conference in Anaheim, but he sold only one tape from his homemade booth, to Ellen DeGeneres's assistant (she was doing stand-up comedy at the event and wanted to use his tape as the subject of one of her jokes).

He finally stumbled upon his lucky break—though he didn't know it yet—when he met a videotape distributor named

Lee Spieker. Desperate for cash, Smithey sold Spieker the distribution rights to *The Original Buns of Steel* (though he wisely and crucially retained the copyright to the name), and eventually Spieker sold the tape to a distributor called the Maier Group. Soon after, Smithey disappeared to Guam to become what he calls "the Jimmy Buffett of PE teachers," while the Maier Group got to work on creating advertisements for their new property (in the late 1980s, customers primarily bought tapes from print ads and catalogs; major video chains were just starting to take off).

Even though most of the people in Smithey's classes were women—and the target audience was female—*Buns of Steel*'s cover and promotional materials prominently featured a picture of Smithey and his steely buns as a promise of what you would achieve if you worked out along with the video regularly. Soon Howard Maier, president of the Maier Group, noticed that the video was selling very well in San Francisco, a spike he assumed was thanks to the title as well as what they imagined to be Smithey's roguish appeal to gay men. In order to achieve greater mass-market interest, they decided that they needed a new strategy. They needed someone other than Smithey, someone who, like Jane Fonda, could give female consumers something to strive for. In 1988, Maier found just that in Tamilee Webb, a rising aerobics star who would become the face (and buns) of the "of Steel" franchise for the next ten years, and help make Maier and Smithey *very* rich.

Webb had an ideal pedigree. After earning a degree in physical education and exercise science from Chico State, she moved to San Diego and found herself in the heart of the early-eighties Southern California fitness craze. She started working at the Golden Door, one of the poshest spas in America and a celebrity hot spot. During her first week on the job, Webb trained Christie Brinkley and her mother. "Back then it was called a fat farm," she told me. "Now it's the Golden Door spa and resort. People pay ten thousand dollars a week to go there."

For the next three years, Webb worked at several different Golden Door locations, including a couple of tours on the Golden Door's cruise ship, where she spent her days off writing a book called *Tamilee Webb's Original Rubber Band Workout*, which would become a bestseller. By 1986, she was a fitness celebrity of sorts, going on international tours, teaching at aerobics conferences, and filling up classes in San Diego. But what she really wanted was to become a star in the booming world of fitness videos.

In 1988, Howard Maier reached out to Webb, hoping she might be willing to become the face, voice, and body of Smithey's workout regime. According to Webb, a mutual friend told Maier that he should hire her because "one—she knows what she's doing, and two—she's got a butt." As soon as Maier pitched her the project, Webb was in. "I loved training the butt and I thought: *That's a great name*," she says. As an adolescent, Webb had been teased for her "bubble butt," but now she hoped it would make her a star.

Webb diligently rehearsed for *Buns of Steel* in her living room, and after a few weeks, she flew to Denver. She remembers that the set seemed cheesy and low-budget, particularly in comparison to the other videos she'd starred in. The lighting was bad, the crew was sparse, there were no "backs"—the group of people following along in the background. But Webb was a professional; she put on her game face and got to work.

She stood alone on a gray carpeted platform, against a bleak white wall with glass blocks and a strangely empty shelf. The music was barely audible as she earnestly explained that she was demonstrating exercises based on "the latest research in sports physiology." Her blond hair was arranged high on her head in a half-ponytail, and she wore coral-colored fitness bikini bottoms with a sports bra, enormous bulky tennis shoes, and flesh-colored tights. Webb described the experience of shooting the tape as a lonely one, and it seems that way. There is something strangely melancholy about the whole thing—when you watch the tape, it looks like she's being held hostage in a *Golden Girls* prop warehouse.

Despite the awkward setup, the convergence of Tamilee Webb and the phrase "buns of steel" created a hit. "When I got my first royalty check, I was jumping up and down," she told me. It was for about $20,000. "Then I got the next one, and it was fifty grand. And then it just kept going up." People started recognizing her in public. At an airport, she bent over to pick something up and someone tapped her on her back and said, "Aren't you the *Buns of Steel* lady?" She was recognizable based on her butt alone.

Over the next decade, Webb hosted twenty-one more "of Steel" videos. And although her cut wasn't huge—"Remember, I'm just the talent," she told me—the videos sold at least ten million copies and, according to Webb, made seventeen million dollars for the Maier Group. Greg Smithey got a significant cut, too, as the owner of the "of Steel" name. "People love the name," he says. "I made a million dollars off of three words."

The at-home VHS workout eventually faded from mainstream prominence, thanks to the rise of gym culture, DVDs, and apps, but the legacy of *Buns of Steel* remains a potent reminder of the aspirational promise of fitness culture. *Buns of Steel* pledged to transform its practitioners into something superhuman, to turn imperfect, soft flesh to unyielding metal. The mainstream ideal had shifted yet again, from Norma's fertile, hearty shape to a pert, muscular, tight butt; a butt forged by thousands of reps of what Jane Fonda called "Rover's Revenge"; a butt made of steel.

When I was around ten or eleven, just as I was starting to understand my body to be something that might be assessed and judged
by other people, a friend and I put on the tights we wore for ballet
class and the swimsuits we wore to play tea party on the bottom
of the neighborhood pool and "did Jane" on the beige carpet in
her parents' basement. We giggled as we squatted and crunched,
but rarely did we finish the whole video before growing bored
and moving on to other games. It was like playing dress-up; we
were practicing what we saw our mothers do, what we understood to be one of the necessary rituals of grown-up femininity.
We did donkey kicks on towels and played with the spring-loaded
ThighMaster her mom had bought from Suzanne Somers on TV.

Soon, exercise was no longer a game. It was a necessity. I
was never any good at sports, and so, by seventh grade, I was
trying to train myself to be a runner in order to lose weight and
create the slim, fit body that the popular girls on the school soc-
cer team seemed to inhabit so effortlessly. And I never really
succeeded. I could run a few times around the block, but never
much more. I regularly told myself the incantations at the heart
of the neoliberal myth of exercise: that I lacked discipline, that I
was lazy, that my life would be better if I were thinner.

In the years since, I've often longed for the experience of
bodily freedom and mastery that some women feel when they
play team sports, or climb rocks, or run long distances. But
for me, exercise has often felt like a chore, an opportunity to
constantly fail. The sense of it as a requirement—an activity
that will transform my body into something smaller, something
more correct—makes me rebel against it and siphons off any
pleasure it might offer. Although I know exercise can be a way
to take care of myself, to feel strong and free, it always ends up
feeling like another form of self-critique.

This tension between the possibility and the reality of exercise is embedded in the story of aerobics itself—while some argued that aerobics offered an opportunity for women to strengthen and liberate their bodies, its rise ultimately did little to free women from the pressure to conform to a notion of an ideal body. Instead it simply swapped one bodily standard for another and made it every woman's individual responsibility to meet that standard. Aerobics allowed strength training to coexist with a sense of femininity, in part because it never fully challenged a gendered idea of the body. It always emphasized the creation of a body that conformed to conventional notions of femininity—instructors encouraged women to become strong while remaining lean, lithe, and sexually appealing to straight men. Large muscles, butch aesthetics, and big butts were nowhere to be found. The standards of beauty perpetuated by the rise of aerobics and fitness culture in the 1980s didn't so much open up possibilities for how a woman could look, but instead doubled the amount of work she had to do to meet an increasingly high bar. Just as when Paul Poiret and Coco Chanel rid fashion of the corset but demanded bodies controlled by diet, *Buns of Steel* just created another aesthetic mandate.

The fantasy of aerobics, and of exercise more generally, is often a fantasy of transformation and self-improvement: *I will work out to become the best version of myself, to be both the body that is controlled and the body that is doing the controlling*. It is a fantasy of both hyper-responsibility and hypnotic passivity, and each side of the binary is played out in the videos themselves. *Jane Fonda's Workout* and *Buns of Steel* are not dance videos; they don't offer techniques that will ultimately lead to artistic interpretation or self-expression. Instead, when you do the moves, you are following someone else's lead, mimicking them beat by beat in order to become more like them. Aerobics is, by and large, a submissive practice: you stay on your mat, inside your little rectangle, and do as you are told. In that way, aerobics has the consequence of reinforcing and rewarding compliance and uniformity. Even as it helps to cultivate bodily strength, it also teaches passivity and obedience—some of the oldest and most harmful feminine tropes.

The aerobics movement, then, was in the business of creating a new mode not only of fitness, but of femininity. In order to be a proper eighties woman, you needed to look like Jane Fonda or Tamilee Webb. And for women whose bodies could never look like Fonda's or Webb's—women who weren't white, thin, strong, or straight—the fitness revolution created yet another unattainable and oppressive ideal. And yet, despite the fact that the ideal of aerobic fitness was impossible for many, some women who knew that no amount of hard work would give them buns of steel found a way to take pleasure in other things aerobics had to offer.

JOY

• •

When I asked Rosezella Canty-Letsome to tell me the
story of her life, she started by saying, "I'm a coal miner's
daughter. But I'm not a millionaire." Canty-Letsome grew up
in the 1950s in Connellsville, a small railroad town in Western Pennsylvania, three hundred miles away from where Lo-
retta Lynn's father mined the same Appalachian coal seam.
Canty-Letsome's family was one of the few Black families in the
community, which was still segregated at the time. Her father
was active in the civil rights movement, and as a girl, she went to
demonstrations and picketed with him in front of stores where
Black people couldn't get jobs. As a teenager, she integrated the
workforce at the local five-and-dime, GC Murphy Company.

Canty-Letsome also grew up in a family of large women
who felt good about their bodies. "The family I came from had
hearty stock," she says. "My mother weighed two hundred fifty
pounds. My grandmother was five feet tall and five feet wide.
But there was no shame around that." They loved food, too.
"We would have ice cream or Jell-O or cake for dessert every
night. We were a big ice-cream family." Canty-Letsome was big
but says, "I was perfectly happy. I went to the prom. I did everything everybody else did."

After graduating as valedictorian of her high school class,
she went to Howard University to get a degree in elementary

education while simultaneously studying for a master's degree at Antioch. She was prepared for a life as a teacher, but her activist upbringing had also given way to a dream of becoming a lawyer. Though "at that time, it was very hard for Black people to get jobs as lawyers," she recalls, but she decided to try anyway. She graduated from Howard in 1969 and in 1970 started law school at Duquesne University in Pittsburgh, where she earned her degree. After working as one of the first Black lawyers at the FCC and getting a master of legal letters from Harvard, Canty-Letsome applied for a job teaching law at Golden Gate University in San Francisco. She showed up to the interview in a mink coat she'd bought at a thrift store.

Sitting in front of an all-white group of administrators, Canty-Letsome realized that they hadn't been expecting a large, accomplished Black woman in a fur coat and were noticeably on edge. Five people barraged her with questions in a tone she found belittling, and they seemed surprised that she could answer them capably. As the interview wore on, Canty-Letsome grew increasingly annoyed. Finally, the subject turned to the thesis she had written at Harvard on Puritan thinking in John Winthrop's concept of law in seventeenth-century New England. "Why did you pick that topic?" one of the interviewers asked her pointedly, suggesting, perhaps, that it was odd for a Black woman to write about such a deeply "white" subject.

"Because I wanted to see how you people think!" Canty-Letsome replied, exasperated. She got the job and relocated to Oakland to become the second Black law professor at the college.

Canty-Letsome had always been a large woman, but around this time, her doctors started telling her to lose weight, concerned that she was getting too heavy after giving birth to two daughters in two years. She responded to her doctor's advice with her usual attitude of action and self-assurance—"You got to take me where I am. This is me. So we gotta deal with this the way it is." She started working out with a friend at an outdoor exercise park, running from the parallel bars to the monkey bars and doing exercises at each stop. "That was always fun," she recalled, "but it was in Berkeley and I had two little kids. It was too far of a trip."

In search of an option a little closer to home, she thought she'd try an exercise tape. Like millions of other women, she bought *Jane Fonda's Workout* on VHS, and although she liked it, she felt it wasn't designed for bodies like hers. She had to modify activities to adjust for her limited range of motion and aerobic capacity, which was discouraging. But then she met Deb Burgard.

Burgard had also come to the Bay Area by way of Cambridge. She had earned her undergraduate degree from Harvard in 1980, and taken part in consciousness-raising groups and feminist organizations that focused their activist work on women's bodies, an interest that stemmed from her childhood in the suburbs of St. Louis.

There, she had grown up in a relatively traditional 1960s white, middle-class family: her father was a doctor and her mother was a schoolteacher. Like so many other women at the time, Burgard's mother tried numerous diet fads in order to make her body look like Twiggy's or Jacqueline Kennedy Onassis's. Her father was also preoccupied with his physical health and appearance.

Burgard describes herself as a chunky little kid but explains that she was powerfully built. She was strong and athletic, and often teased for it. "I was your worst nightmare for Red Rover," she recalls. She also loved to dance. Her father taught her to jitterbug as a child, and when her parents threw parties, Burgard would sneak downstairs after her bedtime and dance in her pajamas in the middle of the room in front of all the adults, who found her antics hilarious and charming.

Despite her love of physical movement, Burgard's parents worried about her weight. By the time she was thirteen, her mother had already taken her to a Weight Watchers meeting. Throughout her teenage years, she dieted repeatedly, losing weight and then putting it back on. Between her freshman and sophomore years of college, she lost thirty pounds. It was a goal she'd been working toward for years, but when she finally achieved it, Burgard realized that losing the weight had come at a huge cost. For the first time since she was a child, when she touched her hips, she could feel the bones protruding, a sign of the physique she'd long coveted. But she also felt dissociated from her body after months of eating too little. "I started thinking to myself: *What the fuck are you doing? Why are you doing this?*" Burgard recalls. She realized how privileged she was: she was studying at Harvard and had meaningful friendships and relationships. Any success she achieved and power she felt would be because of those things, not what the scale read. "It was a huge thing. I realized: *I'm not going to win this game and I want to play a game I can win.*"

In 1983, Burgard moved to the Bay Area with the mission of helping fat women find a way to feel as good as she had when she was dancing in her parents' living room. Along with several other women in the region, she began offering aerobics classes to fat women, a revolutionary idea that not only expanded the possibilities of who could participate in aerobics but fundamentally reimagined the purpose of it as a whole.

The principles of her class were simple: "You don't have any obligation to do exercise if you're a fat or higher-weight person. You don't have to exercise at all. But you absolutely have a *right* to exercise." The distinction between want and need, she explains, was crucial. "I wanted to flip the association of movement for fat people from punishment and atoning to basic human rights."

Burgard's classes were a carefully crafted combination of choreographed exercises, free-form dance, and strength movements, and the intended audience was specific. "I advertised the class as being for women over two hundred pounds because I wanted to be extremely clear that I wasn't talking about somebody who thinks their thighs are a little fat," Burgard explained to me. "I was really trying to make this a space for people who regularly experienced weight stigma in the world."

In *Great Shape*, a fitness guide for large women Burgard later cowrote with Pat Lyons, the authors explain why they choose to use the words *large* and *fat* rather than *obese* or *overweight*. "Our use of the word *fat* is an attempt to normalize its meaning, to detoxify the word by using it in a matter-of-fact, descriptive way." Like activists in other social movements, they intended to reclaim the words that had oppressed them and aspired to reimagine what was possible for people who often felt excluded from mainstream fitness culture. "We have found that some of the miseries we attributed to our weight were in fact miseries of lives without movement, lives without play, lives without deep breathing and zest," Lyons and Burgard say in *Great Shape*. "And lo and behold, movement, play, deep breathing, and zest could be ours *right now*!" Then they ask a crucial question: "Could physical activity be an end in itself?"

Burgard called her classes We Dance and held them at parks and recreation departments and dance studios in Oakland and North Berkeley throughout the mid-1980s. Some of the rooms felt like gymnasiums, and some had ballet barres and mirrors. Anywhere with a large, open floor big enough for a group of women to have some space to dance worked for her. One of the highlights of each class, she says, was when she would crank up the music—Earth, Wind and Fire; funk; R & B; and disco—and encourage everyone to groove. Sometimes she'd try the old-school dances from the fifties, like the stroll, the pony, the boogaloo, or the mashed potato, offering choreography. Then, breaking with the conventions of traditional aerobics, she'd encourage her class to make up their own steps.

When Canty-Letsome tried Burgard's class, she was excited: she had found a place where large women could exercise free from judgment. "The class was doable. It was low impact. It was great," she says. Unfortunately, though, she confronted the same challenges as before: she had two kids and a busy job and no time to travel to exercise.

Seeking a solution, Canty-Letsome invited a friend from Howard to her house, and together they did some of the modified exercises from Burgard's class. After a few of these DIY home aerobics classes, Canty-Letsome realized she wanted to offer a class like Burgard's to the women of Oakland and started to attend classes to learn how to be an exercise teacher. "Of course, no one in the class was heavy. It was only me," she recalls. Being the only Black woman in a room wasn't new, so it didn't bother her much to be the only heavy woman in an aerobics class full of skinny women either. "I've always known who I am," she says.

After getting certified to teach aerobics, Canty-Letsome bought insurance and found a space to teach twice a week at the Oakland YMCA, fitting classes around her responsibilities as a law professor. She made it work by bringing her young daughters to the YMCA with her, dressed in leotards and tights.

The class, which she called Light on Your Feet: An Exercise Class for Large, Lovely Ladies, started with warm-ups and then added exercises that targeted different body parts. There was stretching and floor work, but if a student couldn't get on the floor, Canty-Letsome told them to just do what they could. "Your body is telling you what you need to do," she advised, prioritizing comfort over complex acrobatics. "I wanted them to recognize they were in a safe space," she says. "You could say anything you wanted to say. You could moan and groan."

The environment of acceptance and openness led to a larger shift, Canty-Letsome noticed, in the racially diverse clientele that attended the workouts. Her students, she recalls, "started out hiding their bodies and wearing plain old sweatsuits," since much of the existing athletic wear didn't cater to fatter bodies. But eventually they began to make their own outfits, "showing up in pink and purple leotards, looking gorgeous." Her own favorite was a red-and-white-striped leotard with a belt, tights, and leg warmers. "The tights always matched everything," she recalled. Burgard remembers her fashion fondly, too. "I had lots of leotards, lots of unitards, and I would layer them. They were all different bright colors. I had these pants that cinched right under my knee. I looked like a jester."

Jenny Ellison, curator of sport and leisure at the Canadian Museum of History, says that Canty-Letsome's and Burgard's classes were part of a larger fat fitness movement in the 1980s that had iterations across North America, particularly along the West Coast. In Vancouver, a woman named Kate Partridge founded a group called Large as Life, offering aerobics classes, community, and fitness-based outings. A short-lived chain of fitness studios called Women at Large opened across the United States and southwest Canada. In the back of *Great Shape*, Burgard and Lyons list almost fifty different fitness classes for fat women, many with punny names like Ample Opportunity and Positively More.

According to Ellison, the politics of these classes were disparate: Some, like Burgard's, were overtly feminist. Others, like the Women at Large studios, tried to mainstream fat fitness by rendering it more girlish: "They had to wear ultra-feminine uniforms. They insisted on calling their patrons fluffy ladies."

Women came to the classes from different communities and for different reasons. Some felt excluded from fitness culture and wanted to find a way to participate; some wanted to prove that they could be both fat and fit at the same time. "Most of the women weren't dying to be thin," Ellison says. "There are people for whom 'buns of steel' is never going to happen. That was at the heart of their critique: that ideal was a lie, and it was not attainable for everyone."

Before long, both Light on Your Feet and We Dance attracted national media attention. Journalists from the *New York Times* and the *Houston Chronicle* covered the fat fitness phenomenon in the Bay Area, and Canty-Letsome even did a segment on *The Phil Donahue Show*. But most of the coverage positioned fat fitness as a strange phenomenon rather than a necessary corrective to the pervasive aerobics culture. They also largely shied away from reporting on the more radical aspects of what Burgard, Canty-Letsome, and other fat aerobics activists were offering: the idea that fat aerobics was not about losing weight but about enjoying movement as an end in itself.

The promise of *Buns of Steel* was that it could help you sculpt a butt that was strong, but the title suggested something even more—that the video could help create a butt that transcended the limitations of the flesh, that freed a person from the inescapable imperfections and indignities of the body. A butt of steel is not a human butt; it's a butt that is manufactured, a butt that is uniform. It is a butt honed and perfected. But as we've seen again and again, bodies cannot be made uniform. Flesh always resists.

Women like Burgard and Canty-Letsome made a movement out of this resistance. In a world where a fat butt connoted laziness and a lack of self-control, the women who did fat aerobics were proving that they, too, could be fit and in control, deliberately pushing back against the bullies who had told them to get off their lazy lard-asses. They were also saying: *This fat butt is a joyful butt, it is, in fact, a fit butt, and this joyful and fit butt is none of your business*. They were embracing the reality of a body and all of what bodies are capable of doing. Burgard describes it to me this way: "My whole witchery around this my entire life has been to just create spaces of joy and to channel this joy into the world so that people understand: This is your birthright. You get to feel joy in your body if you want to."

Bootylicious

KATE

. .

Besides my own, the butt I probably thought about the most in the 1990s was attached to Kate Moss. At five foot seven, she was considered short for a fashion model, but what she offered made up for it: a rail-thin body, chic androgyny, and an icy air of indifference. Discovered in 1988 at age fourteen, Moss quickly became an iconic and unrelenting presence in the visual culture of the nineties as the fashion industry shifted away from the tall, tan, strong models of the previous decade. Before the turn of the twenty-first century, she appeared on the cover of American *Vogue* six times and international editions of *Vogue* thirty-two times, and was the face of campaigns for Dior, Burberry, Chanel, Versace, Dolce & Gabbana, and, most famously, Calvin Klein. She had also become one of the highest-paid models in the industry.

Moss's gaunt physique and her bony, youthful look would become an archetype for mainstream body ideals in the media landscape of the 1990s, conveying an air of rebellion and bohemianism, a potent combination that made me long to look like her, even though I knew I never could. I imagined that if I had a body like hers, I'd be able to access spaces that felt beyond my reach: places of authenticity, dark glamour, and, of course, rock 'n' roll.

It was an association that I made because Calvin Klein wanted me to: in 1991, Moss shot her first campaign with the designer, sitting topless on the floor in a loose-fitting pair of blue jeans, so waifish that her spine protruded like the spiky vertebral plates of a stegosaurus. Her face was blank, her expression enigmatic, and she looked discomfitingly young. The ad made Moss the most visible emissary for the look that came to be known as "heroin chic," a corporatized version of a style that had its roots in the era's grunge music scene. Grunge was a raw, stripped-down, guitar-based response to the hyperconsumerism, conservative politics, and corporate dominance of the Reagan 1980s, and the resulting recession that had dramatically limited working- and middle-class opportunity in the United States. But grunge was also a look, a repudiation of conventional beauty standards that aestheticized and glamorized harsh working-class realities with tattered secondhand clothes, long and dirty hair, and gaunt, undernourished bodies. The grunge body, for both men and women, was androgynous and thin, and often unabashedly evoked IV drug use.

Despite the fact that the artists who hatched this aesthetic explicitly rejected bourgeois, corporate values (or at least seemed to at first), the corporations they condemned were tantalized by the opportunity to shift from the ultraglam, "built" era of Brooke Shields and Christie Brinkley and into something new. "I didn't want these girls . . . who had big bosoms," Calvin Klein explained in 2017. "They augment their bodies. They used artificial implants and things. I found that offensive. I found it really unattractive, unhealthy, and a bad message to send." Although the actual difference between the bodies of fashion models in the 1980s and those that interested Klein in the 1990s was nominal—both were unquestionably tall and thin, even if the new nineties look was less muscular and less traditionally feminine—Klein was on the hunt for the one thing fashion always seeks: novelty. And in the look of grunge, and the body of Kate Moss, he found it.

Of course, this was hardly the first time that skinniness and curvelessness had been associated with stylish rebellion. In the late nineteenth century, the sickly, tubercular body became linked with bohemianism and counterculture, as typified by Rimbaud and Keats. ("When I was young, I could not have accepted as a lyric poet anyone weighing more than ninety-nine pounds," said Romantic poet and critic Théophile Gautier.) In the 1920s, flappers had effaced their feminine curves to assert and represent a new type of sexual and political freedom. And although the flapper look was born of the optimism of the boom years of the twenties, the underlying symbolism that equated the thin, androgynous woman with rebellion and nonconformity persisted, an association that would wind its way through various other twentieth-century countercultural eruptions, including the beatniks, hippies, and punks, each of whose style would be quickly appropriated by mainstream fashion.

While fashion designers in the 1990s were enthusiastic about this willowy, enervated new look, middle-class white parents were wringing their hands: despite what Klein claimed, they saw nothing healthy about what seemed to be an endorsement of smack shooting and anorexia. The fact that the gaunt look was rapidly proliferating in the pages of *Vogue* and *Seventeen* prompted outcries from parents' groups and sparked headlines like "How Thin Is Too Thin?," "Heroin: A Model Way to Die," and "The Perfect Embodiment of Degraded Pop Culture." The fears were widespread enough that, in 1997, President Bill Clinton publicly decried "heroin chic" because it supposedly promoted drug use.

But that cautionary message was lost on their children, who made up the dominant consumer base of Calvin Klein and other brands that employed extremely thin models to sell their products. (In my own middle school, the hallways stank of CK

One, and a peek of the Calvin Klein logo on a pair of boxer shorts was the epitome of cool.) When Moss posed with Mark Wahlberg in a Calvin Klein underwear ad in 1992, it was a phenomenon. There he was, built and hunky; her, bony and fragile, standing topless in bleach-white "Calvins," as the underwear would come to be known. Her butt is to the camera—it's there, but like the rest of her, it's skeletal.

Kate Moss's was perhaps the most prevalent, most visible butt of the first half of the 1990s, but it wasn't much of a butt. It was a small lump on the back of an otherwise curveless white woman, whose overall lumplessness was an essential part of her appeal. At the time, it seemed as though a tiny, flat butt would remain the ideal and the goal for most women in America, as it had been for decades previous. What few (including myself) seemed to realize was that a reckoning of sorts was coming, and the dominance of waifish butts was, in fact, quite precarious. Ideas about beauty, bodies, and sexiness that had long been ignored by mainstream, white culture were just beginning to gain a foothold, a cultural shift that, over the next thirty years, would radically transform what many people thought a butt should look like.

MIX

. .

"O*h—my—God, Becky, look at her butt.*"

It's 1992, and Becky and her friend—two white women wielding jean jackets and Valley girl accents—are busy leering at a Black woman in a tight yellow dress as she slowly rotates on a raised platform through an arched doorway. The woman doesn't seem to know she's being watched as she bends over and rubs her hands along her butt and thighs.

Becky's friend sucks her teeth and continues:

"It is so big! She looks like one of those rap guys' girlfriends. Who understands those rap guys? They only talk to her because she looks like a total prostitute, 'kay?"

An infectious bass line drifts in over their conversation; the platform beneath the woman in the yellow dress begins to slowly spin.

"I mean, her butt is just so big. I can't believe it's just so round. It's like *out there*. I mean, gross!" The girls just can't fathom the size of this woman's butt; they can't believe anyone could find it attractive or how the woman herself could be comfortable displaying it in public. One of them summarizes their confusion and revulsion in four short words: "She's just so . . . Black."

Suddenly, Sir Mix-A-Lot appears in a leather jacket and fedora, standing atop a giant, disembodied, yellowy-gold butt that rises from the floor. His feet rest on the cheeks, his legs straddle the crack. Barely a breath passes between the conclusion of Becky's friend's monologue equating big butts with prostitution and Blackness and the man's enthusiastic, now-iconic retort: "I like big *butts* and I cannot lie!"

For the next four minutes, he raps with gusto as women in skintight gold outfits shake their butts at the camera, decapitated by the top of the frame. At one point, five dancing women are filmed from above as they stick their butts into the middle of a circle, mimicking a Busby Berkeley routine. Meanwhile, a DJ scratches a record with a small plastic butt covering the record spindle. Bananas, peaches, lemons, tangerines, and tomatoes flash on the screen, proudly unsubtle stand-ins for butts and breasts and penises.

Sir Mix-A-Lot has something to say in "Baby Got Back," and he's going to make sure the Beckys, as they have come to be called, and the world, hear it: he likes big butts, and he believes other men do, too. He is certainly not going to be dishonest about this fact. What the Beckys declare as "gross" about other women's bodies, and perhaps even their own, Sir Mix-A-Lot celebrates and proudly objectifies. Where they are horrified, Sir Mix-A-Lot is titillated.

Despite the video's visual puns and the song's bouncy beat, Sir Mix-A-Lot has always made it clear in interviews that "Baby Got Back" is not a novelty song and is not meant to be a joke. In fact, he wrote it with a message in mind, a message inspired by the experience of his girlfriend at the time, Amylia Dorsey-Rivas, a mixed-race woman with a big butt. "There was one event that was irritating the shit out of me," he told *Vulture* for their oral history of "Baby Got Back" in 2013. "Amy and I were at a hotel on tour, when we saw one of the Spuds MacKenzie ads for Budweiser during the Super Bowl. . . . These girls in the ad: each one was shaped like a stop sign, with big hair and straight up-and-down bird legs."

That stop-sign look, a holdover from the 1980s, struck Sir

Mix-A-Lot as ridiculous. "Unless you were in the hood," he says, "women who had curves—and I'm not talking about women who are shaped like me, with a gut, but women who ran five miles a day, with a washboard, six-pack stomach and a nice round, beautiful, supple ass—wore sweaters around their waist!" He didn't find the big-haired, bird-legged women on his television sexy, and neither did his friends. But they were the sort of women dominating the pop culture landscape of the period, and as a result, Dorsey-Rivas, an actress and voice artist, was having a hard time finding gigs. "Where I grew up, in the suburbs of Seattle, if you weren't built like Paris Hilton you weren't appreciated," she told *Vulture*. "You could have the highest cheekbones in the world, but if you were a little more broad at the beam, forget it." When Mix, as Dorsey-Rivas calls him, asked her why she couldn't seem to get work, she'd say: "Look behind me."

"I knew for a fact that many artists felt that if they didn't use a skinny-model-type woman in their video, then mainstream America would reject the song," Mix explains in the *Vulture* oral history. He wanted to change that. He wanted big-butted women to feel proud of what was behind them and be given opportunities to represent themselves in the media. He decided to write a song that championed what he saw as the bodies of Black women, a song that celebrated the part of Dorsey-Rivas's body that he liked the most. For Mix, it was just as much a political statement as it was a personal one.

From the start, the people involved in producing the song and video for "Baby Got Back" interpreted it differently: some found it hilarious, others uncomfortable and objectifying, still others empowering. Dorsey-Rivas was enlisted to voice the spoken-word opening of the song, impersonating the voices of white women who found butts like hers "gross." She liked the song, she told *Vulture*, and even found it profound, an opportunity to be seen. "People said ['Baby Got Back'] was degrading," she said. "But I would say there's not one thing degrading about that song to anyone who felt like me." The video's director, Adam Bernstein—best known for his work with the Beastie Boys, the B-52s, and They Might Be Giants—initially felt otherwise: "When I heard the song for the first time, I thought it objectified women," he said. "But it made me laugh."

These differences were reflected in the video's costume design: Mix wanted the dancers to be dressed more sporty than sexy, but when he arrived on set, he saw the woman on the pedestal dressed in a blond wig, tiger shorts, and gold chains. "This song is called 'Baby Got Back,' not 'Baby's a Ho,'" he angrily told Bernstein. As Dan Charnas, VP of A&R at Def American Recordings, explained, "The girls in the video were cast by people who didn't quite understand what they were engaged in culturally." It seemed that many of the white people involved couldn't reconcile the idea that women with big butts could be desirable without being grotesquely sexualized.

The video production also confronted another one of the inevitable obstacles when discussing butts: they needed to make sure it was clear they were talking about the cheeks and not the hole. The song wasn't about anal sex or the taboos around feces, an important distinction. When Mix came to the set dressed in a brown suit and suggested that he rise up out of the crack of the fifty-foot gold butt, he was quickly talked out of both notions.

When the completed "Baby Got Back" video was submitted to MTV, the standards and practices department decided against airing it, citing a new station policy forbidding the broadcast of music videos that showed women's body parts without also showing their faces. The channel had decided that it would no longer cut women up into pieces with the camera, and it pushed for a very low standard of visual feminism: make sure women are rendered as whole people, literally. They didn't need to be represented as people with hopes and dreams and careers. Just heads.

As Patti Galluzzi, MTV's senior vice president of music and talent at the time, explained to *Vulture*, "We were trying to move away from MTV's recent past, when videos showing slices of pie would drop into a girl's lap, like in Warrant's 'Cherry Pie,' were shown around the clock." Those videos, she noted, were sexual and sexist, and both conservative groups like Tipper Gore's Parents Music Resource Center and feminist organizations like Women Against Pornography had pushed MTV to stop airing that content. It was a nominal gain for a certain kind of feminism that MTV was being proactive in their response, but there was some question as to whether "Baby Got Back" was disqualified from broadcast due to sexism and objectification of women, or whether it was simply too butt-forward and Black-forward. According to Sir Mix-A-Lot, the song and video were doing something different from what Warrant was doing with "Cherry Pie." Mix saw himself as critiquing objectification and challenging dominant, white beauty standards. Most rock videos were blatantly sexist, but "Baby Got Back" was, according to its creator, about that sexism, or at least about racism. Celebrating the curvy Black female form, Mix thought, shouldn't be lumped in with the worst offenders of early nineties pop culture misogyny.

Despite Mix's intended political message about changing beauty standards, the video shows that Mix certainly wasn't interested in erasing them. The women on-screen weren't exclusively stop signs, but they were still exclusively *something*. They were hourglasses—"little in the middle but she got much back"—women who were encouraged to maintain their bodies by "do[ing] side bends or sit-ups," even as they were praised for having a specific repository of fat. In the song, Mix is still dictating what constitutes a "correct" body, even if he is slightly altering the definition, and he is also reinforcing the stereotype that Black women definitionally have big butts, something that is, of course, not true.

And then, there is the woman Becky is shaming, standing on the literal pedestal at the beginning of the video. Her face is never clearly shown; her physical existence is defined by her backside. It's as though she is a sculpture on display at a museum or a showroom—an uncomfortable, and likely unconscious, callback to Sarah Baartman's display in both life and death. Although there is much that is different in this gesture of exhibition—perhaps most notably, Mix is trying to demystify the big butt and make it acceptable and admirable rather than freakish—it is still literally objectifying a Black woman. And, as is so often the case, the only way a woman's body can be seen as normal, or allowed, is if it is first brought into the realm of male desire. Mix aggressively sexualizes the butt, asserting that this body part that mainstream white culture has deemed "gross" is actually a good thing—not because all bodies are beautiful or even acceptable, but rather because "when a girl walks in with an itty-bitty waist and a round thing in your face, you get sprung." In the song, women's bodies exist for the visual pleasure of men, and it is men who are declaring what is allowed and what is attractive.

"That video does not pass the Bechdel Test," ethnomusicologist Dr. Kyra D. Gaunt, assistant professor of music and theatre at the State University of New York at Albany, told me without hesitation, referencing the popular metric that examines female representation in films. She sees the song and video as playing in racist, fetishizing stereotypes, despite Sir Mix-A-Lot's insistence that the song is empowering. Although some women see it that way, for Gaunt, the sort of power the song is offering to women is not one she's interested in. At best, she says, "Baby Got Back" is presenting what she calls "empowered misogyny" where spectacle and fetish are substituted for political power.

To explain, she points out that the early nineties was a terrible time for Black women interested in gaining actual political or economic power. She's right: Anita Hill testified in Congress in 1991, where she was grilled by a group of white men about her experience with sexual harassment, their questions and the accompanying media coverage often playing into stereotypes of the oversexed Black woman. Politicians in the 1990s were also busily creating policy—like the 1996 welfare reform bill—that disproportionately harmed Black women and trafficked in racist stereotypes about "welfare queens." That same year, Black women were paid on average 34 percent less than white men, and throughout the decade, Black women were experiencing intimate partner violence at a rate 35 percent higher than white women. For Gaunt, whatever "empowerment" was on offer in a video like "Baby Got Back" did little to grapple with the structural racism deployed against the women it purported to celebrate.

But ethnomusicologist Christopher Smith, author of the book *Dancing Revolution*, suggests that those who read the video as exclusively objectifying may be missing something, too. He identifies the dancing in "Baby Got Back" as part of a tradition in hip-hop videos of the period (and West Coast crunk specifically) that used the dancers to telegraph "a powerfully physical, visible, and independent expression of the rhythm track," unlike the dead-eyed gyrating dolls in videos like "Cherry Pie." They were asked to freestyle at several points in the song, he notes, offering up their own improvisational choreography, which indicates individual agency. For Smith, the dancers are not mere adornments but are at the very core of what "Baby Got Back" is. Their butts are uninhibited, unrestrained, no bustle or girdle in sight to control them.

In 1992, Mix had a conversation with Galluzzi at a radio conference in Seattle, hoping to convince her that his video shouldn't be included in her network's ban on controversial content, telling her "that he felt the message of the song is that all women are constantly bombarded with images of super-thin models on TV and in magazines, and . . . that women and young girls need to hear that not everyone feels that way." That idea spoke directly to Galluzzi, who, although white, was a curvy woman herself. "I had back and front, then and now," she says. And so she went to MTV and made a case to the higher-ups. They relented and allowed the video to be played after nine p.m.

"Baby Got Back" was (and is) many things—silly, weird, catchy, a little bit embarrassing. It's easy to dance to and undeniably funny. Despite Mix's protestation, most people think of it as a novelty song, likely because the word *butt* is featured so prominently and frequently. It isn't particularly aggressive or obscene, instead deploying a warm, goofy jollity to convey its message. Mix shouts *butt* over and over again, and although he uses plenty of other euphemisms—*back* and *booty* most prominent among them—his use of the word *butt* makes the song feel childish, like a joke a second grader would tell. The song seems to invite you into its world to laugh, sing, and dance along with it. At weddings, bar mitzvahs, and high school dances across the country, white boys and Beckys would shout joyfully along, not realizing, perhaps, that they are the villains of the song's world.

It was also very, very popular. In 1992, "Baby Got Back" was number one on the *Billboard* Hot 100 for five weeks, and it stayed on the charts for seven months. That year, it was the second-bestselling record, surpassed only by one of the bestselling songs of all time, Whitney Houston's "I Will Always Love You." After three months, it went double platinum. In 1992, it won a Grammy for best solo rap performance. To date, the song has earned more than one hundred million dollars.

I was still in elementary school when "Baby Got Back" came out, which meant by the time I was dressing up for school dances, the song was a fixture of Midwestern public high school

DJ sets. As I stood on the edge of the linoleum-floored cafeteria at a succession of homecomings and Sadie Hawkinses, the lights would dim, and the first chords would fill me with dread, as well as those iconic first words: *Oh—my—God, Becky, look at her butt.* Even though I had a big butt, I knew, on some level, the song wasn't about me. I even knew that the song was making fun of the tiny-butted white women who adorned the covers of my copies of *YM* and *Seventeen* magazines. But I still felt humiliated because it called so much attention to the difference between the way I looked and the way that I wanted to look. Whatever larger messages Mix was trying to communicate had not meaningfully penetrated the walls of my high school. He may have liked big butts, but all that mattered to me was that I did not—and neither, it seemed, did anyone else I knew.

"It seems like a benign joke," Kyra Gaunt says. "Just like every dumb-blonde or twerking joke seems benign." And yet, it is these kinds of jokes that form our stereotypes and our ideas of ourselves. They sneak into our unconscious mind, because we aren't ever invited to think very hard about them. "All novelty songs turn on these kinds of stereotypes as far as I can tell. They turn on something that has a serious valence, and then we make light. We can fool ourselves into thinking that we are thinking and talking about something seriously, but we're not." In describing the insidious ways a song like "Baby Got Back" can cause harm, Gaunt points to the most famous part of the song: the beginning, where the two Beckys call the big-butted woman "gross" and a "prostitute." "Everybody has committed it to memory," she says, "but as [the listener] parrots that positionality, you train your mind to tolerate it."

In high school, we would all stand on the dance floor, waiting for the beat, and chant along with a Valley girl accent: "She looks like a total prostitute . . . I mean, gross . . . She's just so Black." And although we were mocking, although we were goofing around, although "it's just a song; it's just a joke," as we said those words out loud, we inscribed them in our minds, infected ourselves with or reinforced those stereotypes. Gaunt calls it a type of epigenetics, a way that we unconsciously encode racist ideas about Black women in our minds. What potentially makes it worse, she says, is that while this is happening, the song is positioning itself as something with a positive message, and the listener can believe that they are actually doing something good by listening to it. "You get to feel like you're supporting a Black rapper who is trying to do something for Black women. But nobody ever asked Black women what they thought."

Of course, "Baby Got Back" is not the only song about butts. It wasn't even the only song about butts that was popular in 1992. That same year, Wreckx-n-Effect released "Rump Shaker," which climbed to number two on the *Billboard* Hot 100. (It, too, was thwarted by the mighty power of Whitney Houston's "I Will Always Love You," which stayed at the number one position for a record fourteen weeks.) The video was made up almost entirely of Black women dancing in bikinis on Virginia Beach. Sometimes one of them played a saxophone, but the focus was gyrating bodies and, not surprisingly, shaking rumps. Once again, the video was banned by MTV.

"Rumps ain't dirty," Teddy Riley, who cowrote and produced the single, told the *Los Angeles Times* in 1992. He recalled being frustrated that other artists, like Prince, were allowed to sing about so-called dirty things in their videos and faced no consequences from MTV, yet butt-related videos were verboten. "We don't make them dirty. They're just shaking a little. It's harmless fun, paying respect to females and not making fun of them," he explained. "It's something about the behinds that gets people riled up."

The album that got people *really* riled up was 2 Live Crew's

As Nasty as They Wanna Be, one of the most controversial records of the late 1980s and early 1990s, and another butt-focused endeavor: the cover featured four women in string bikinis on the beach, butts facing the camera, faces turned away, appearing basically nude. Throughout their career, 2 Live Crew recorded a lot of music about butts, including the 1990 song "Face Down Ass Up." They were part of the hip-hop subgenre of Miami bass, also called "booty music," which paired deep, resonant bass sounds with hissy cymbals and plentiful butt-oriented lyrical content.

2 Live Crew was proudly bawdy, even crass. The hit single off *As Nasty as They Wanna Be* was "Me So Horny," a song that sampled a line of dialogue spoken by a Vietnamese sex worker character in the film *Full Metal Jacket*, turning it into a chanted, repeating chorus. The song featured lines like "Put your lips on my dick, and suck my asshole, too / I'm a freak in heat, a dog without warning / My appetite is sex, 'cause me so horny."

It is perhaps not shocking, then, that when the album came out in 1989, conservative groups went ballistic. Although Tipper Gore and the Parents Music Resource Center had successfully lobbied the music industry to apply parental advisory stickers on albums with violent or "offensive" lyrical content, it was clear by the early nineties that a mere sticker wasn't going to deter young people from buying controversial records. Despite being banned by most radio stations, *As Nasty as They Wanna Be* sold extremely well, climbing to number thirteen on the *Billboard* weekly charts. In several states, retailers were prosecuted for selling the record because it was deemed "obscene," and members of the band were arrested after performing their songs in Florida.

The subsequent trial was an enactment of the tension in the 1990s between free speech and vulgarity, as well as the growing anxiety in white, middle-class communities about the popularity

of Black culture among white youth. A wide array of music critics testified on behalf of 2 Live Crew, and lauded historian and
professor Henry Louis Gates Jr. wrote an op-ed in the *New York
Times* that pointed to the fundamental misunderstanding at the
heart of the charges. "2 Live Crew is engaged in heavy-handed
parody, turning the stereotypes of black and white American
culture on their heads. These young artists are acting out, to
lively dance music, a parodic exaggeration of the age-old stereotypes of the oversexed black female and male. Their exuberant
use of hyperbole (phantasmagoric sexual organs, for example)
undermines—for anyone fluent in black cultural codes—a too
literal-minded hearing of the lyrics."

Despite this defense, Gates doesn't give the lewdness of
2 Live Crew's music a complete pass. "Much more troubling
than its so-called obscenity is the group's overt sexism," he
added, before asking that the listener put 2 Live Crew's sexism
into context, saying that it might cancel itself out because it is
working in extreme hyperbole. But he also cautioned that "we
must not allow ourselves to sentimentalize street culture: the
appreciation of verbal virtuosity does not lessen one's obligation
to critique bigotry in all of its pernicious forms."

The butt anthems delivered by 2 Live Crew, as well as
"Baby Got Back," "Rump Shaker," and even LL Cool J's "Big
Ole Butt"—an earlier butt-themed single that didn't climb as
high on the charts—were not only musical experiences but visual ones. MTV was at the height of its influence in the late
1980s, and although hip-hop music had not originally been part
of the station's purview (they called themselves a rock station),
Michael Jackson and Run-DMC had respectively broken the
color and hip-hop line that had made MTV a de facto white
station in its early years. In 1988, the channel began to broadcast
Yo! MTV Raps, a countdown show that featured hip-hop videos.
It performed extraordinarily well, jumping two Nielsen points

in the first week and soon the show was on every afternoon, playing the country's most popular hip-hop songs.

Yo! MTV Raps helped geographically disparate hip-hop artists hear and see one another's work and be in creative conversation with one another. The show also built the audience for hip-hop and became a vehicle for hip-hop style. As Snoop Dogg said in an interview for the book *MTV Uncensored*, "It put us on the same page as rock 'n' roll and music in general . . . it was a place where everybody could come, unite, everybody wanted to show their new videos." Rapper and VJ Ed Lover elaborated: "*Yo! MTV Raps* was responsible for bringing hip-hop to the masses. If you were from Compton, California, you could understand what was going on in New York and vice versa."

Because MTV had built its core audience in white suburbs across America, when *Yo! MTV Raps* became a hit, it also had the effect of exposing white audiences to hip-hop in a way that was unprecedented, a fact that made some parents anxious and contributed to lawsuits like the one against 2 Live Crew. Conservative groups feared that the frank sexuality, pervasive sexism, and perceived obscenity of hip-hop music and visual culture would corrupt white youth, concerns that were ostensibly based around sexual language and imagery but often had racial undertones. They were afraid Sir Mix-A-Lot might get exactly what he was after: that the jiggling Black butts in music videos might actually become appealing to white youth.

JENNIFER

• •

In 1998, mainstream America discovered Jennifer Lopez's butt. It was as if the white men of America had never seen an ass before or noticed that human women—their wives, perhaps, or mothers, or sisters—frequently have bulges and curves below the waist. Or maybe they had all been repressing their thoughts and feelings and finally, finally, they felt that they could speak.

Jennifer Lopez got her start in the entertainment industry in 1991, doing bounce grooves and splits as a Fly Girl with a voluminous mop of curly hair and a smear of mauve lipstick on the sketch comedy show *In Living Color*. It was a big break for the young dancer and actress, but Lopez's ambition was bigger. By the late nineties, she was trying to become a rare figure in American culture: the multimedia megastar. She wanted to be the lead in major Hollywood films as well as a platinum-selling recording artist—Julia Roberts and Mariah Carey in one. And she could—she would—do it. But first, she'd need to answer a lot of questions about her body.

It started in the Spanish-language media, when Lopez made her first star turn as Tejano superstar Selena Quintanilla in the 1997 film *Selena*. Quintanilla had been celebrated for her curves, her body representative of an ideal that many saw as emblematic of femininity in Latin and South America. There had been some controversy when director Gregory Nava cast Lopez, who is of Puerto Rican descent, in the role (Quintanilla was Mexican American, and fans and members of her community were protective of that distinction), but he justified the choice with an argument about body type. "If you're raised in this country, since childhood, you're given this image of beauty," he said. "And if you're *pocha*—Mexican American—it's not you. So you're made to feel bad about the way you look or the way your body is, having big hips or whatever, from when you're a kid." As scholar Frances Negrón-Muntaner explained in her 1997 article "Jennifer's Butt," Lopez and Nava were expressing what they thought it meant to be Latina through the body and curves rather than political activism, language, geography, or class.

When *Selena* was released, Lopez approached questions about her own body with a smile, perhaps in an attempt to assuage concerns that she hadn't been right for the role. She often told stories about how the costume designers she worked with before *Selena* had tried to find ways to disguise her butt, when she wanted to celebrate it. "*Todo eso es tuyo?*" one interviewer asked her—"Is that all yours?" Lopez replied with glee, "*Todo eso mío*" ("It's all mine"). It would become a refrain throughout her career: *Is that butt real?* It was a question the press had asked Selena, too. In both cases, the star's butt seemed to be separate from her own body, an entity that needed special consideration.

In 1998, Lopez, and her butt, reached a broad new audience when she played Karen Sisco in Steven Soderbergh's film *Out of Sight.* The film was a big deal—Soderbergh's first box-office hit in nine years, since *Sex, Lies, and Videotape* had been released to critical acclaim and financial success in 1989. In *Out of Sight*, Lopez starred opposite George Clooney, an actor who had spent the previous four years playing heartthrob Doug Ross on *ER* and who had been recently named the sexiest man alive by *People* magazine. *Out of Sight* was a mainstream movie, and it had a wide release. To promote it, the stars made all the usual appearances on late-night talk shows and granted interviews with major magazines.

Like the Beckys in the intro to "Baby Got Back," interviewers who talked to and about Lopez seemed unable to help themselves. *It's just SO BIG!*, they seemed to say, their hand to their mouth, embarrassed and excited. But the press in 1997 didn't parrot the Beckys' other lines from "Baby Got Back"—when Jennifer Lopez's butt was acknowledged or interrogated, there wasn't a sense that it was considered gross or offensive. Instead, when she talked to men, there was a feeling of surprising acceptance and of barely disguised desire. *Premiere* declared "Jennifer Lopez's ass" to be the "feminine asset" that was currently "in" in Hollywood, replacing "Sharon Stone's crotch." *Saturday Night Live* had guest star Lucy Lawless don an enormous false butt and impersonate Lopez in a sketch. Jay Leno twirled her onstage and encouraged the audience to ogle her backside. *Time* magazine ran an interview with Lopez that opened with the question "What's the deal with your booty?" "It's big," she replied.

What else could she say? The question is a strange one and doesn't so much demand an answer as reveal something about the person asking the question. "What's the deal with your booty?" seems to beg the rejoinder: "What's the deal with your interest in her booty? Why are you so obsessed?"

For the next twenty-five years, Lopez would be subjected to endless inquiries and innuendos about her butt. Magazines announced on their covers that they knew the secrets of her workout routine, and paparazzi scrambled to get both candid and red-carpet photos that captured as much of her behind as possible. In 2000, when she wore a revealing green jungle-print dress to the Grammys, Google programmers Huican Zhu and Susan Wojcicki invented the website's image search to accommodate the sudden uptick in users trying to locate photographs of the dress, and the body within. For years, rumors swirled that she'd insured her butt ($27 million is the figure quoted most often) and that hers was the titular "back" of Sir Mix-A-Lot's anthem. In a 2016 "Carpool Karaoke" segment, she finally clarified to James Corden that the former was untrue—and that she wouldn't even know how such insurance would work. In the beginning, Lopez laughed at the questions, refusing to be humiliated by them. Her butt, she made clear, was a natural part of her body, an attribute that made her distinct. In her "Jenny from the Block" video, she had her then boyfriend Ben Affleck literally kiss her ass, in a playful nod to the world's obsession with it. Still, the narrative quickly became repetitive and reductive, especially as Lopez began to achieve that multimedia megastar level she'd been chasing. By the time she was on "Carpool Karaoke," she seemed more exasperated than amused. *Are we really still talking about this?*

The butt obsession that accompanied Lopez's rise to fame was a touchstone in a significant, decade-long transition in mainstream American culture. Though the butt had to some extent "broken through" into wider attention and discourse via hiphop and butt-oriented exercise regimes, in the early nineties, popular print and electronic media still rarely engaged with it in a straightforward way. They often relied on euphemisms like *derrière* and generally only talked about the butt as something to be hidden, trained, controlled.

But by the end of the 1990s, in the wake of Jennifer Lopez's rise to fame, women's butts had become a frequent part of the conversation in magazines like *Cosmopolitan* and *Seventeen*—publications whose business was to communicate to women what was normal and what was beautiful. By the early aughts, they were running articles asking "Are Butts the New Boobs?" and others with titles like "Bootylicious: Guys Talk Tail" that attempted to make sense of an apparent shift in the bodily ideal for women. In the years immediately following Jennifer Lopez's crossover from *Selena* to Soderbergh and beyond, there would be an abundant new crop of popular songs about butts (with less public backlash), such as Sisqó's "Thong Song" and "My Humps" by the Black Eyed Peas. Department stores even began to display mannequins with bigger butts.

It's no coincidence that as this change was occurring, the United States was in the midst of a significant demographic shift: the country was in the process of becoming less white. In the 1990s, the population of Black people increased in the US by 15.6 percent, the population of Asians and Pacific Islanders increased by 46.3 percent, and the population of Hispanics (the designation used by the US census) increased by 57.9 percent. Although white people continued to outnumber all other racial categories by a significant margin, the percentage of people of color was growing, a trend that would continue through 2010 and is projected to continue through at least 2050, when statisticians predict that the Hispanic population will make up 30 percent of the population of the United States and white people will become a minority. As a consequence of these changes, the very definition of mainstream American culture had been thrown into question.

"Mainstream" has always been a slippery concept. To be mainstream is to *not* be alternative, eccentric, subcultural, deviant, or an outsider. It is a center defined by its periphery, a term that feels clear but actually isn't at all. Sometimes *mainstream* is a euphemism for *white*, sometimes a synonym for *popular* or *square* or *highly consumed*. Often, it's all of these things at once.

The changing demography of the United States certainly didn't lead to a widespread embrace of all facets of nonwhite culture, but it did mean that corporate America became increasingly interested in targeting the growing population of nonwhite consumers. In Hollywood, the financial successes of films like *House Party*, *Boyz n the Hood*, and later *Waiting to Exhale* proved to entertainment executives that Black audiences could and would turn out in large numbers for stories that represented people like them. "The black population is younger, and is growing faster than other segments of the U.S. population, other than Latinos," Ken Smikle, the publisher of *Target Market News*, a Chicago-based publication that tracked Black consumer patterns, told the *New York Times* in 1991. "So our future numbers look even better to studios, because young people buy the bulk of movie tickets." Black characters on television also multiplied in the 1990s—reaching nearly 17 percent—particularly in the early years of the decade when shows like *The Fresh Prince of Bel-Air* and *Hangin' with Mr. Cooper* aired in prime time (even if, as studies have shown, the female Black and Latinx characters often played into long-held stereotypes of hypersexuality and underachievement). As the decade progressed, that number diminished, hovering between 10 and 14 percent for the last half of the 1990s, though it remained a significant percentage and one that paralleled the actual Black population of the United States. Hollywood had a more difficult time targeting Latino audiences, a tremendously diverse ethnic group that, according to market research, was less likely than Black audiences to see a film primarily because of a star's racial identity. In the 2000s, after the census revealed just how much the US Latino population was growing, major corporations increased their efforts to target this demographic group, as well as other ethnic minorities. General Mills, Tide, and Honda all produced ads targeting Latinos, and McDonald's and Adidas created advertising campaigns that targeted Black audiences, as well as the increasing number of white people interested in hip-hop culture.

Although these demographic shifts were changing the face

of mainstream America, there was another, simultaneous shift
occurring that would have a profound effect on body ideals over
the next thirty years: white audiences were ravenously consuming hip-hop music, fashion, and culture. Research from 2000
suggests that as much as 70 percent of consumers of rap and
hip-hop records in the late 1990s were white. Some scholars,
including noted hip-hop feminist Tricia Rose, have argued that
those numbers don't take into account bootleg music and music
shared among friends, strategies of consumption that were popular in Black communities, a fact that might skew the numbers. But it is undoubtedly true that white audiences were an
essential component of hip-hop's rise to dominance in popular
music, and that hip-hop was increasingly important and interesting to young, white men in particular.

But why were young white men so interested in engaging
with a culture that seemingly had so little to do with most of
their lives? Hip-hop had its origins in the Bronx and spread
across the United States as a cultural form that expressed the
angst, rage, joy, and politics of the Black and Latinx experience
in a country that had systematically oppressed these groups for
centuries. This was a history and experience that the white people buying up to 70 percent of hip-hop records weren't typically
a part of.

In 2000, *MTV News* correspondent Chris Connelly offered
a succinct answer: "When they write the history of popular culture in the 20th century, they can sum it up in one sentence,
which is: 'White kids wanting to be as cool as Black kids.'" In
2019, Wesley Morris expressed it a different way when writing
about white interest in Black music: "This is the music of a
people who have survived, who not only won't stop but also
can't be stopped . . . music whose promise and possibility, whose
rawness, humor and carnality call out to everybody—to other
black people, to kids in working class England and middle-class

Indonesia. If freedom's ringing, who on Earth wouldn't also want to rock the bell?"

Since the Jazz Age, the phenomenon of young white people being drawn in droves to Black cultural products, particularly Black music, as well as the patina of coolness and authenticity those cultural products seemed to provide, had been a constant in American life. In the eighties and nineties, hip-hop assumed the mantle as the latest in a string of popular musical forms— following the jazz, blues, rock 'n' roll, soul, and funk of previous generations—that originated in Black communities and were then embraced with great and often predatory enthusiasm by eager white people. Of course, it is not only Black culture that is routinely appropriated by dominant groups in the United States, although the appropriation of Black culture by white people has been foundational to American popular culture and music. This same appropriative gesture—taking the parts of a culture that feel thrilling, subversive, or sexual without any acknowledgment of the broader cultural, political, or sociological context—happens with nearly every nonwhite culture, including Indigenous, Japanese, Indian, and many, many others.

But just what is it that white people are looking for when they "play in the dark," as Toni Morrison once characterized this type of idolatry and mimicry? Perhaps the most straightforward, and commonly given, answer to that question is that white people desire a sense of cultural identity. For many white people, whiteness itself does not provide a structuring force of selfhood, because most white people generally don't see whiteness as anything at all. It is the norm, the middle, the thing against which everything else forms—the mainstream. Whiteness is neutral, so boring and so normal that it cannot be a quality that generates identity, and it cannot offer the kind of distinction, individuation, or rebelliousness that many young people seek as they separate from their families and parents in adolescence and beyond.

And for those who do conceive of whiteness as an identity, it is often an uncomfortable one. It is the identity of the oppressor. Whiteness seems, by its history and perhaps very nature, cruel. Because whiteness, like Blackness, is a specious category—one constructed for no reason other than to create and maintain a racial hierarchy—to identify as white is to admit complicity in that construction. And so, for those uncomfortable with their whiteness, it is tempting to look to other cultures for a sense of identity and belonging.

In his crucial book on the topic of cultural appropriation, *Love and Theft*, scholar Eric Lott investigates this behavior through an examination of minstrel shows, the immensely popular nineteenth-and-early-twentieth-century performances where white people performed stereotypes of Blackness in blackface. Minstrel shows have long been seen as one of the primordial moments—and often the most vivid enactment—of the kind of appropriative gesture that has proved to be such a lasting part of American popular culture. According to Lott, the audiences at minstrel shows—mostly working-class white people in large urban centers like New York City—were doing two things at once: identifying with a rebellious, libidinal stereotype of Blackness and feeling superior, flattered, and assuaged by hateful stereotypes that cast Black people as stupid and child-like. The shows were a way for white people to see themselves as adjacent to the parts of Blackness that they saw as exciting and freeing, while simultaneously reinforcing their own white-ness. They could, as Morrison says, "play in the dark," but they would never remain there. They would always return to their own position as separate, and superior to, Black people.

For Lott and many other cultural historians, this doubleness is always at work when white people become interested in adopting and interpreting Black cultural forms. When Elvis played "That's All Right," a song written by Black blues singer Arthur "Big Boy" Crudup, white audiences interpreted him as rebellious, free, and sexy. But they never saw him as Black. Not only was his whiteness never in question, it was actually reinforced by the way he situated himself in relation to Blackness. He smuggled in the excitement, danger, and eroticism commonly associated with Blackness but kept it safely packaged in familiar, nonthreatening whiteness—his fans could have their cake and eat it, too. The "thrills" of Blackness, without the fear or guilt.

The appropriation of hip-hop by white people in the nineties, however, seemed to operate differently than it had with rock 'n' roll (or blues, or jazz, etc.). Although the Beastie Boys were a huge success, most white rappers, such as Vanilla Ice and Marky Mark, had little staying power compared to Black artists like Jay-Z and the Wu-Tang Clan. Unlike the generations before them, white teenagers in the nineties directed their interest and their dollars toward the Black performers who exuded (or appeared to exude) authenticity, resulting in a cultural consumption pattern Cornel West called "the Afro-Americanization of white youth." Beyond just absorbing the music, white kids fashioned themselves to look like and sound like the hip-hop stars they idolized on MTV, adopting distinctly urban Black American idioms and visual codes in an effort to be cool, to create identity, and, as Wesley Morris suggests, to be adjacent to the feeling of freedom, joy, rawness, and humor that had always been part of Black music. And for white men, specifically, hip-hop offered a way to grapple with masculinity. As cultural critic Greg Tate put it in his 2003 book *Everything but the Burden*, "[African American musical forms] have become the theme musics of a young, white, middle-class male majority—due largely to that demographic's investment in the tragic-magical displays of virility exhibited by America's ultimate outsider, the Black male."

Along with this larger adoption of hip-hop culture, cultural historian Janell Hobson explains, came a deep appreciation for and attention to women's butts. Butts, according to Hobson, have always been an important element of African American vernacular dance, and this is one of the major reasons that they have become a focus of African American beauty ideals and are prominently featured in the aesthetics of hip-hop. "In Black cultures, in terms of our dance expressions," she explains, "we tend to do more hip-shaking, booty-shaking kind of dances, and that definitely redirects the gaze." Although Hobson sees echoes of Sarah Baartman's display and white people's obsession with her body, she notes a crucial difference between interest in Baartman in Georgian London and white interest in hip-hop and the butt in the 1990s. "What we see in terms of the preference for big butts," she says, "that's coming from Black male desire. Straight-up, point-blank. It's only through Black males and their gaze that white men are starting to take notice."

But what, then, can be made of the frenzied focus on Jennifer Lopez's butt? She is not a Black woman, but rather a Puerto Rican woman who, at the time of her crossover success, was playing racially ambiguous roles (her race isn't mentioned in *Out of Sight*, and Italian American actor Dennis Farina plays her father). There is no doubt that the press understood her as Latina—she had come to fame dancing on a hip-hop television show and played a Tejano music icon, and many journalists who wrote about *Out of Sight* acknowledged her ethnicity. Her ethnic identity was often provided as a handy explanation for why she had, and enjoyed having, a large butt. But some, like journalist Teresa Wiltz, wondered if the fact that she was light skinned was an essential part of the mainstream acceptance of her body, something that had allowed white people to feel comfortable enough to express their desire. "Perhaps," she posited in a 1998 article, "her racially nebulous features, her cafe au lait complexion with an extra helping of cream, make her palatable to the masses."

Desire is, of course, complex, and it is perhaps too simple to say that white men writ large began to desire women with big butts—or openly admit to that desire—because they were consuming and absorbing hip-hop culture. Desire is both a societal force and an individual experience, something that is shaped by the world around us and idiosyncratic within each one of us. But it is undoubtedly true that the culture we consume can form what we see as desirable, and also grant us permission to access and express desires that have previously gone unacknowledged or unexplored. Whether this large-scale consumption of hip-hop in the late 1990s and early 2000s created a desire or unleashed it, the way women's butts were situated with respect to white male desire was undergoing a major transformation.

KIM

• •

The story that Beyoncé Knowles often tells about the 2001
Destiny's Child hit "Bootylicious" is that, when she wrote
the lyrics, the press had been giving her a hard time about her
recent weight gain, and she wanted to push back. "I wrote that
song because I was getting bigger and bigger and I just wanted
to talk about it," Knowles told *Newsweek* in 2002. "I like to eat
and that's a problem in this industry. I'm still probably twice as
big as any of the other actresses out there, and that's a constant
grind that I really hate to have to worry about."

The idea that Beyoncé was, in any sense, "big" is illustra-
tive of the contradictions around body image in the late 1990s
and 2000s. Although in the years following Jennifer Lopez's
rise to fame there was a growing enthusiasm for "curves" in the
media, this change was not so much a wholesale embrace of
the vast spectrum of human morphology as it was a new way
to scrutinize women's bodies. Just as corsets had been replaced
with cabbage diets in the 1920s, the newfound enthusiasm for
larger, more shapely butts in the late 1990s certainly did not
mean that women were suddenly free from pressures around
diet, weight, or fitness. Instead, gossip magazines continued
to give Beyoncé—a woman who was unquestionably thin—a
hard time about eating too many french fries.

"Bootylicious" was the second single off Destiny's Child's

third album, *Survivor*, and reached number one on the *Bill-board* Hot 100. The album was generally well reviewed and publicly embraced, in part for its celebration of curvier shapes and sizes. But it was also criticized for mixing what was referred to in articles as "G-rated fun" with an adult sexuality that might negatively influence younger fans. This gripe overlooked the album's determination to showcase women who were both sexy and in control, invoking a new brand of early-aughts feminism.

"Bootylicious" was a prime example: the song is written from the perspective of a woman out at a club, in the process of seducing (presumably) a man. The woman doubts he can handle just how sexy and confident she is—and it is her booty, her jelly, that is the source (or at least a source) of her power. "I don't think you're ready for this jelly," she sings, ". . . 'cause my body too bootylicious for ya, babe." It will take quite a man to handle the awesomeness of what she has to offer, and tonight's contender might not be up to the task.

In the years since the release of "Bootylicious," many have lauded it as a body-positive feminist anthem. It seems to be saying: *I love and respect myself how I am, and there is no doubt in my mind that you should love and respect me, too, or at least find me sexy. The thing that some might find shameful—my jelly, my booty—I forthrightly proclaim to be my most significant asset and a source of pride.*

And yet, there actually wasn't that much jelly in the video, or so some critics pointed out. There are a few larger dancers in the video's intro and then scattered throughout, but the women of Destiny's Child are thin, even if they do have and clearly draw attention to their shapely butts. But, to some extent, that may be the point. Even Beyoncé, whose body did not deviate radically from the ideals of the time, was ridiculed by the press. So stringent and narrow were expectations that there seemed to be no way a human woman could ever be free from criticism about her body. And so Beyoncé offered a novel, exuberant response: she celebrates those parts of her that have been deemed incorrect and unruly, and declares them to be sexy.

But an embrace of curves wasn't the only thing communicated about Black women's bodies in the video. Several of the costumes referenced the attire of pimps and sex workers from the 1970s, which, as scholar Aisha Durham points out, is a pattern in many of Destiny's Child's other songs and videos—"Nasty Girl," for example, traffics in the idea that big-butted Black women are typically lower class and sexually promiscuous. Not all butts, it seemed, were empowered.

For the past twenty years, scholars and journalists have debated whether or not Beyoncé is truly a feminist, and, if so, what kind. Is she complicit in the objectification of women or is she complicating that objectification? Is she asserting agency over her sexuality and celebrating her body or is she "offering her body up as commodity fetish," as one scholar put it? Is she subverting the patriarchy or, as bell hooks suggested in 2016, staying "within a conventional stereotypical framework" of Black femininity? In 2001, these conversations were in their nascent stages, and "Bootylicious" and its video were central to them. Like Sir Mix-A-Lot, Destiny's Child celebrated butts and curves, but "Bootylicious," unlike "Baby Got Back," was performed and created by the possessors of the butts under discussion—a group of Black women who wrote the music, owned the songs, and had control over their image, including the clothes they wore, which were primarily designed by Beyoncé's mother, Tina Lawson. Like Jennifer Lopez, they were proud of their bodies, but they were actively driving the conversation around them, rather than slogging through endless questions by titillated and scandalized journalists. Granted, it's perhaps an anemic kind of feminism that is situated mostly in the realm of beauty and sex—moving the needle only in terms of how much fat is acceptable and attractive on a woman's body isn't exactly upending the patriarchy—but it was something.

Much of the media attention around the song focused on the word *bootylicious* itself. What exactly did it mean? The term *bootylicious* first appeared in a song in 1992, when Snoop Dogg used it pejoratively, but it caught fire after Destiny's Child's single was released. It wasn't necessarily, or exclusively, a reference to the butt, but instead something more broadly, and vaguely, empowering. After all, *booty* means both the butt specifically and sex in general, and so the word could be about *the* booty or about a person's capacity to *get* booty. In 2003, when Oprah asked her to define it, Beyoncé said she thought it meant "beautiful, bountiful, and bounceable," a definition that was pleasantly alliterative but did little to clarify the issue. The following year, it was added to *The Oxford English Dictionary*, defined as "esp. of a woman, often with reference to the buttocks: sexually attractive, sexy; shapely." Via this "official" designation, a positive meaning around the butt was documented for the present and future masses: it was a desirable thing to have shapely buttocks. The word sounded far more fun, and far less pretentious, than its older counterpart *callipygian*, and the fact that the word had become widespread enough to find its way into the august and hardly cutting-edge *OED* suggested a meaningful shift: bootylicious—the song, the word, and the concept—was becoming a cultural force.

While bootyliciousness marked a sort of progress, the 2000s remained by and large a period of extreme fat anxiety within the popular media. The same programs and magazines celebrating curves and offering new ways to create just the right amount of butt cleavage in low-rise jeans were simultaneously encouraging liposuction and endlessly printing retouched images of impossibly thin celebrities. Alicia Silverstone and Drew Barrymore—as well as Beyoncé—were consistently ridiculed for being fat, even though they were thinner by far than most American women, and at the same time paparazzi photos made hefty sums catching them (and many others) in moments when they looked less than red-carpet ready. The fashion industry had moved on from the quasi-bohemian, waifish look popularized by Kate Moss but continued to glorify extremely thin bodies, including those of Calista Flockhart, Jennifer Aniston, Jennifer Love Hewitt, and the cast of *Sex and the City*. Runway models became so consistently, unnervingly thin in the 2000s that several European countries passed laws banning the hiring of models under a certain weight. But the fashion world embraced digital photo-editing technologies like Photoshop to make sure their models appeared adequately emaciated in print, if they couldn't be in life. It was a practice that was near universal, and would come to define media and beauty standards for years to come.

Although she wasn't a model (or at least she wasn't *only* a model), heiress Paris Hilton, slight in body but ravenous in her desire for attention, came to typify this other, non-bootylicious brand of early-aughts sexiness. Born into the Hilton hotel fortune, she was white and she was sassy, and she had protruding hip bones; a performative, high-octave, sexy baby voice; and an aggressively conventional, California-blond presentation that felt like a throwback to eighties, pre-grunge style. Hilton's rise to fame came in part due to famous friends and a graphic sex tape that an ex-boyfriend released to the media and then to home video, which quickly became a media sensation and sold extremely well. She was, as was often said at the time, "famous for being famous," the prototype for a new kind of celebrity, widely photographed by the tabloids as she shopped Rodeo

Drive and enjoyed bottle service at the Viper Room. In 2003, she brought her personal brand of faux-naivete into living rooms across America with the reality show *The Simple Life*, which documented the adventures of Hilton and fellow celebrity off-spring Nicole Richie as they abandoned their gilded existences to live and work with families in rural America. She was ridiculous in many ways—somehow she managed to trademark the phrase "That's hot"—but she was also living a life coveted by many, and doing so in a body envied by many women. If Moss aestheticized poverty and addiction, Hilton's look physicalized bottomless, unearned wealth.

Ironically, it was via the rise of Paris Hilton—and her inner circle—that one of the most famous and culturally influential butts of the modern celebrity era emerged. Kim Kardashian was, at first, a minor member of Paris Hilton's entourage of wealthy, chaotic women, which also included Britney Spears and Lindsay Lohan. Like Hilton, she came from great privilege: she grew up down the street from the Beverly Hills Hotel in a mansion with a Bentley in the driveway. Her fourteenth birthday party was hosted by Michael Jackson at Neverland Ranch.

Kardashian's father, Robert, was a successful attorney and businessman, now perhaps best known for being one of O. J. Simpson's closest friends and a member of his legal team during his infamous 1995 murder trial. He was also Armenian, an ethnic category that had been legally declared white by the Supreme Court following a 1925 immigration case. However, due to a long history of discrimination, both abroad and within the United States, many Armenian Americans do not identify as white today. Throughout her career, Kardashian would use her mixed-race identity (Kim's mother, Kris Jenner, is white) to situate herself as both white and nonwhite at the same time, enjoying the privileges of whiteness and strategically setting herself outside of whiteness when it suited her, pointing to her Armenian heritage as the reason for her so-called exotic or vixen looks: her dark hair, olive skin, and, of course, large butt.

In the 1990s, Robert Kardashian and Kris Jenner divorced after having four children—Kim, her sisters Kourtney and Khloe, and her brother, Robert Jr. Kris Jenner then married Olympic champion decathlete Caitlyn Jenner, who also had four kids from previous marriages. The couple went on to have two children of their own and to raise the whole brood together in a massive mansion in Calabasas, an affluent suburb of Los Angeles.

Kim Kardashian and Paris Hilton had been friends since they were little girls. In the early 2000s, Kardashian started working as Hilton's personal stylist, dressing her in purple velour sweatsuits and Louis Vuitton bags. But Kardashian was more Hilton's sorority sister than her employee, and they spent much of the early 2000s posing together for tabloid photographers on Australian beaches and outside of LA nightclubs, creating a compelling visual contrast—the stick-thin, bleached-blond superstar and the curvy, dark-haired sidekick.

Soon, though, Kardashian herself began to find her way into the headlines. In March 2007 (in what many speculated was an *All About Eve*–esque power play), Vivid Entertainment released a homemade, forty-one-minute video depicting Kardashian having sex and "goofing around" (as Page Six later put it) with her ex-boyfriend Ray J, the singer, actor, and younger brother of R & B star Brandy. Like Hilton before her, Kardashian's private erotic escapades made for endless tabloid fodder, and her newfound, ostensibly accidental celebrity helped thrust nearly her entire family into the spotlight.

In Kim's first scene of the first episode of *Keeping Up with the Kardashians*, the E! reality TV show that premiered just a few months after the release of the Kim and Ray J sex tape, Kris Jenner teases her daughter about the size of her butt. "She's got a little junk in the trunk," Jenner remarks snarkily as Kim heads to the fridge for a snack. "She could use a little cardio!" It was a fateful way to inaugurate what was to become one of the most popular reality shows to ever air on television. In the first season, the family spends a tremendous amount of time contending with the release of and fallout from Kim's sex tape, which her mother/manager (*momager* was Kris Jenner's preferred title) views as both a personal disappointment and a professional opportunity. After much hemming and hawing, Kim eventually agrees to capitalize on the moment and pose for a nude photo spread in *Playboy*.

The show was quickly picked up for a second season (it would go on to air a total of twenty) and was the number one show in its time slot for women eighteen to thirty-four, a coveted demographic for advertisers. Kardashian was propelled to a new level of fame: she was the most googled person in 2008 and became a fixture in tabloids, where her butt was nearly always mentioned. When she joined the cast of *Dancing with the Stars* in 2008, *OK!* magazine reassured their readers that her training wouldn't affect her shape. "Make no butts about it," the tabloid reported, "Kim plans to keep those curves." *Cosmopolitan* described her as an entrepreneur and asked, "So what if she's made bank off her butt?" She regularly denied persistent rumors that she padded her butt or had implants (she would eventually go so far as to have her butt X-rayed on an episode of *KUWTK* to prove she hadn't). In general, media stories about Kardashian seemed to suggest that her big butt was a good thing, something to be desired, although some weren't so sure; "It's a badonka-don't!" declared *Us Weekly* in 2008. In April 2008, Paris Hilton weighed in, calling in to a Las Vegas morning radio show and making it clear that she wouldn't want to have a butt like Kim's. To her, it looked like "cottage cheese stuffed in a trash bag." In 2009, Kardashian spoke to *News of the World* about the exposure and debate, echoing (intentionally or not) the words of Jennifer Lopez from a decade earlier: "There's constant interest in my bottom! The paparazzi always want 'butt' shots; girls come up to me and grab it and people ask to squeeze it. I sometimes think: 'Everyone's got a butt, why do you care about mine?'"

It was a valid question, with more than one answer. To some extent, Kardashian's body was garnering attention due to the larger cultural moment, one marked by increasing and long-overdue calls for body positivity following decades of body shaming in popular media. The push for more realistic and healthy representations of women's bodies took a number of forms, including a campaign by trade groups in the UK and the United States to limit how much magazines could digitally alter a model's appearance, as well as an effort by France's National Assembly to criminalize the promotion of "excessive thinness." In 2006, model and talk show host Tyra Banks, sick of reading cruel, punny headlines about her body—such as "Thigh-ra Banks," "America's Next Top Waddle," and "Tyra Porkchops"—dedicated an episode of her popular daytime show to defiantly addressing her critics: "I have something to say to all of you that have something nasty to say about me or other women who are built like me. Women whose names you know, women whose names you don't, women who've been picked on, women whose husbands put them down, women at work or girls in school. I have one thing to say to you: Kiss my fat ass." She appeared on the cover of *People* magazine the next month under the defiant headline "You Call This Fat?"

The Kardashians were clever in how they navigated this

growing cultural conversation. They weren't exactly radical in their body positivity—there was near constant emphasis on maintaining or modifying their looks in the show—but they also weren't stick thin, often portraying themselves as struggling with their weight and bodies in relatable ways, or as relatable as incredibly wealthy and famous people can be. Kim often spoke on *KUWTK* about wanting to change the way her body looked, but also about her enjoyment of sweets and hatred of exercise. Even as the Kardashian sisters were shown constantly eating salads—to the point where their salad consumption was turned into a popular meme—they also prominently displayed cookies in glass jars on their kitchen counters, implying a willingness to indulge. In one 2009 *Cosmopolitan* profile of Kim, the writer said Kim was out of breath after a long hike and described her as "digging into dessert—crepes with strawberries, bananas, and whipped cream." These behaviors, according to the article, contributed to her appeal: "Sure, men think she's hot. But women think of her as a refreshingly real alternative to skeletal fame-bots."

Another reason everyone seemed to care so much about Kim's butt was that *she* never stopped talking about it, displaying it, and capitalizing on it. The entire Kardashian family, but primarily Kim, created a cottage industry out of promoting their shapes. In the two-minute trailer for her 2009 workout video series *Fit in Your Jeans by Friday*, she mentions her butt or her curves ten times. (Never mind that her butt, she continued to claim, was a product of nature, not surgery or exercise.) The family talked about butts and bodies constantly on their reality show, and when, in 2010, Kim released her first perfume—imaginatively named "Kim Kardashian"—its tagline was "a voluptuous new scent."

And then, in 2012, Kim signed up for Instagram, a space where she immediately found a large audience, and one that has continued to grow—as of 2021, she is the sixth-most-followed person, ahead of both Beyoncé and Jennifer Lopez (three of her sisters occupy spots in the top twelve). The social media platform, launched in 2010, offered a simulacrum of truth similar to that of reality television, as well as a digital space for Kardashian to interact directly with her fans, inviting a quasi-participatory intimacy in a life that many already knew well from five seasons of *KUWTK*. Instagram turned out to be the ideal place for Kardashian to show off—and monetize—the part of her body for which she'd become so well-known. Instagram's community guidelines banned nudity in photos posted on the app, but, until 2015, the guidelines about butt cheeks were vague. This gave users relatively free rein to post nude or nearly nude images of butts and meant that the most explicit sexual images on Instagram were butt shots. Although Kardashian didn't post fully nude images of her butt, she often posted revealing pictures of herself in a skimpy bikini or a tight dress, striking a pose that would become one of her signatures: butt and back to the camera, with Kim peeking over her shoulder, a position reminiscent of the *Venus Callipyge*. Those posts received tens of thousands of likes (a good result in 2012), which in turn made them appear more often in subscribers' feeds, thanks to an algorithm designed to promote popular posts and boost imagery with similar content. It was a feedback loop: the popularity of her butt made her butt—and butts in general—more popular on the site. And, because Kardashian used Instagram as a platform to promote her brand, the popularity of her butt made both Kardashian and Instagram a fortune.

By the mid-2010s, the Kardashian sisters were using more and more extreme means to fashion and mold their looks, including lip fillers and waist trainers, and were suspected of utilizing surgical enhancements to maintain and create the sorts of voluptuous figures that they helped popularize (something they regularly denied). After promoting a certain look—whether it was a tiny waist or a bee-stung lip—they would then introduce Kardashian-branded products that promised to help women achieve a similar result through makeup, body care, and shapewear. The Kardashians set the trend and flooded the market, using their faces and bodies as their own best advertisements.

The mania for Kim Kardashian's butt only increased in subsequent years, reaching a new peak in November 2014, when she appeared on the cover of *Paper* magazine. The photographs for the cover and inside spread were taken by the French photographer Jean-Paul Goude, who had famously worked with Jamaican model, musician, and actress Grace Jones in the 1970s, and who had been regularly criticized for objectifying and reinforcing stereotypes of Black women's bodies. The magazine, and accompanying online article, promised to "break the internet" via provocative images of Kardashian and her butt: in one, a clothed Kardashian stands in profile with a champagne glass balancing on her butt and a rainbow of champagne cascading up and over her head to fill it. In another, Kardashian stands nude, her butt facing the camera, her skin shellacked in a lustrous glaze, as she peeks over her shoulder.

Paper got what it was asking for: the day after its publication, the article accounted for 1 percent of all online web traffic in the United States, and the images stirred up a huge amount of controversy. The image of Karadashian in profile, in particular, reminded many commentators of the posters and legacy of Sarah Baartman from 1810. It was, in some ways, a strange comparison: although Kardashian's big-butted silhouette did echo Baartman's, her circumstances and personal history could not have been more different. It

was this distance that rendered the image uncomfortable—
here was a privileged non-Black woman using her butt to
play in Blackness, breaking the internet (and the bank) in
the process.

It was hardly the only time that Kim made aesthetic
choices that smacked of appropriation, or worse: in 2018,
and again in 2020, she wore Fulani braids, calling them "Bo
Derek" braids. In 2017, she was accused of wearing blackface
thanks to skin-darkening makeup. In 2019, she named her
shapewear line Kimono (with no apparent regard for the fact
that a kimono is a traditional Japanese garment) before changing it to Skims because of the backlash. It seemed that a part of
Kardashian's brand was provocative racial performance, and
although she was often called out, and occasionally made a
change so as to "not offend anyone," she never offered a meaningful apology or experienced a professional reckoning. Instead, the Kardashians implicitly and explicitly justified their
constant use of Black aesthetics to create and maintain their
brand. Some have even suggested that the Kardashian sisters'
friendships with Black women and relationships with Black
men (and interracial children) usefully provided what critic
Allison P. Davis called a "cultural cover for their appropriation."

In a way, twenty years after the release of "Baby Got Back,"
Sir Mix-A-Lot's dream had come true: big butts were more
visible and openly desired than they had ever been. But Kim
Kardashian proved that any progress was extremely limited:
a world where sex symbols are known primarily for their big
butts did not prove to be a place where all bodies were accepted,
and it certainly wasn't a place where Black women could find
greater power or appreciation, or even the opportunity to become beauty icons themselves. Instead, the most famous big-
butted woman in the world was an extremely wealthy woman

who wasn't quite white but also was very much not Black, a set of facts that she would use to her advantage. Over the next ten years, Kardashian would continue to use her butt to regularly, and unabashedly, appropriate elements of Black culture, and continue to make a huge amount of money while doing it. And she wouldn't be the only one.

Motion

TWERK

• •

If you search YouTube for instructional videos on how to twerk, you'll find millions of results: there are routines filmed by amateurs on phones in bedrooms and apartment hallways; there are videos with decent production values and backup dancers released by dance studios; there are a number in Russian and other Eastern European languages; and there is one in which three professional ballerinas learn the moves ("start in second position," their instructor begins). Some of the best tutorials, though, are the work of Big Freedia, an artist and self-identified queen diva who has been central to the world of twerk and bounce (the musical form most associated with twerking) for more than two decades. In *How to Bounce Like the Queen of New Orleans*, which promises twerk instruction for beginners, Freedia stands tall, with long black hair and a full face of tasteful makeup, wearing green stretchy pants, a colorful striped shirt, and black sneakers. Two students stand just behind her, dressed in long black pants and black T-shirts, ready to learn some of the essential moves of the form: "exercise," "rock the boat," and "mixing." She begins with a simple piece of advice for novices: "If your booty ain't movin', you ain't doing it right!"

After the students have tried out the first two techniques—

which both require placing one's feet at a forty-five-degree angle, bending over, and rocking the hips from side to side at increasing speed—Freedia transitions into mixing, which she describes as moving "like a mixing bowl—your butt goes round and round." It's all in the hips and back; the feet don't move at all. Freedia shows her students how to perform each of the techniques bent over, with their hands against a wall, or with their arms in the air. Although these gestures are undeniably sexy, in the video they read as more joyful than seductive. As hips shake side to side and butts begin to bounce, smiles appear on the students' faces.

Freedia, who identifies as a gay man and uses all pronouns, has been twerking and performing and dancing to bounce music since the 1990s, helping to popularize the dance over the last decade through "twerkshops," a TV show, and videos like *How to Bounce Like the Queen*. But Big Freedia isn't only a twerk evangelist, she's also an educator, dispensing information about the history of bounce and the roots of twerk as part of a mission to correct misunderstandings and misinterpretations that have emerged over the last decade about what twerk is, what it means, and where it comes from. Freedia's work makes it clear that the popular version of twerk often neglects the history of the dance, which has always been associated with resistance, joy, and, yes, sex, but is often presented as something trendy, more overtly sexual, and less complex.

In order to understand twerk, you need to know about Congo Square. Located in an open, inviting area in the Tremé neighborhood of New Orleans, Congo Square is a large, tree-lined space paved with cobblestones arranged in concentric circles and dotted with bronze statues. The statues—which depict second-line parades, Mardi Gras Indians, and women dancing—are monuments to what is perhaps the most important three acres in the cultural history of the United States.

Even before the arrival of Europeans, the land that would become Congo Square was a ceremonial ground for the Muscogee, a place where Indigenous people gathered to dance and sing. By the eighteenth century, New Orleans had become a port city, a gateway to the Caribbean and a crucial geographical anchor in the transatlantic slave trade. The French had colonized Louisiana and brought the institution of slavery with them. They also brought a set of laws called the Code Noir that regulated enslaved people, which consisted of fifty-five articles that made Roman Catholicism compulsory, regulated marriage and ownership of children, and codified allowable punishment. Because of the Roman Catholic requirement, the code also mandated that slave owners provide enslaved people with a day of rest on Sundays. Consequently, it was on Sundays when Congo Square became an epicenter for the creation, celebration, and mixing of Black, Caribbean, and Indigenous cultural forms. It was the place where the drum kit was first assembled, and where music and dance from across the African diaspora had the space to thrive and evolve into new, unique forms such as jazz, second lines, and eventually, twerk. Wynton Marsalis once declared that "every strand of American music comes directly from Congo Square."

In the eighteenth century, the square was festive, vibrant, and loud. The dancers wore feathers, bells, shells, and pelts and moved to the music of marimbas, flutes, banjos, and violins. Women faced away from the audience and shook their butts side to side, in a dance likely inspired by the mapouka, a celebratory festival dance from the Côte d'Ivoire that was colloquially known as *la danse du fessier*: the dance of the behind. The dance was part of a spiritual practice, a way to encounter and celebrate God. They also danced the bamboula, a frantic feat of endurance accompanied by banjos and drums, and the calinda, a combination dance and martial art that made graceful use of a long stick, and a hybrid call-and-response form called the Congo, an inspiration for many contemporary forms.

The gatherings, as one might expect, soon became a concern for the city's ruling white population. Congo Square represented not only the continuation of cultural identities colonialism had tried to suppress, but also the power of a community structure and bond. If enslaved people could come together to dance, they could also come together to revolt, even beyond New Orleans. These types of dances and celebrations, after all, happened not only in Congo Square—they were part of an artistic resistance across the colonies, pushing back against European notions of meekness and modesty. According to scholar Elizabeth Pérez, "The authorities intuited what many scholars now argue: that bodies remember." In both their overt African identity and their overt sensuality, butt-oriented dances were a form of defiance against slave owners and the culture they represented, a defiance that would remain a part of such dancing through the centuries.

In 1817, the city government of New Orleans—which had by this time become a part of the United States—enforced new restrictions mandating that gatherings of enslaved people could take place only in the square, and only on Sunday afternoons. As slave laws in the United States became increasingly strict and draconian, the gatherings at Congo Square withered and died, only to gradually be resurrected over a century later, in the 1910s and '20s.

In the beginning of the twentieth century, Mardi Gras was the most important day of the year in New Orleans, marked by raucous parades attended by costumed revelers flowing throughout the city. According to Kim Marie Vaz, professor of education at Xavier University of Louisiana, this tradition of dress-up, or masking, offered the Black people of New Orleans a way to transgress the social order, forge a collective identity, and assert their humanity in the face of constant persecution and marginalization and persistent, dire poverty.

Most of those who donned costumes, however, were men, most notably New Orleans Black Indians who wore feathered headdresses and other Indigenous clothing. Women, and specifically those who worked in brothels and dance halls, however, were excluded from masking, because of their gender and occupation. Tired of being left out, in the 1910s a group of these women, who called themselves the Baby Dolls, decided to join second-line parades, wearing short dresses, frilly shorts, bonnets, bloomers, and parasols. It was a performance at once childlike and sexy, and was one possible inspiration for Josephine Baker's contemporaneous performances in Paris. The Baby Dolls wore dresses far shorter than was considered acceptable at the time, and in the parades, they danced popular and provocative dances, like the shimmy, the shake, and bucking, all of which put their butts at the center of the action. Merline Kimble, a granddaughter of a Baby Doll, later confirmed that the dancing "was an activist thing," describing the clothing choices and insistence on "having a ball" as a rebellion against "what was put on women during the time."

Another thread in the evolution of twerk comes from Jamaica in the years after World War II, when reggae began to evolve rapidly, ultimately sprouting new forms such as dub, and from dub, dancehall. Each of those genres utilized enormous sound systems assembled by DJs in the dance halls of Kings-ton, informal spaces where poor and working-class Jamaicans who were unwelcome in the city's tonier nightclubs could dance freely. Dancehall was a combination of reggae, dub, and electronic music, and was a reflection of what it meant to be Jamaican: the lyrics were often delivered in local patois and spoke to issues of injustice. This music, and the butt-centric dance moves it inspired, would travel to the United States along with a wave of Jamaican immigrants in the sixties and seventies, where it would become a fundamental ingredient in the creation of hip-hop. By the 1980s, hip-hop had spread across the United States, including to New Orleans, where local musicians and dancers, deeply influenced by the cultural history of the city, would in turn create bounce, a high-energy, call-and-response-based music with heavy bass and a rapid beat.

Although undoubtedly used colloquially for some time prior, the first known public use of the word *twerk* as a verb appears in the lyrics of the first bounce hit, "Do the Jubilee All," released by New Orleans rapper DJ Jubilee in 1993. The music video has a homemade feel, showcasing everyday men and women twerking alongside a marching band. There are moments when DJ Jubilee points approvingly to a shaking butt, but the video doesn't sexualize the butt to the degree found in other butt-forward videos of the era, from artists like Sir Mix-A-Lot and 2 Live Crew. Instead, we see iconic New Orleans metal balconies, tuba players on a football field, and Jubilee sporting his signature style—a white T-shirt and khaki shorts. In this primordial twerking video, the dance move is less about sex and much more about the city where it origi-nated.

After "Jubilee," twerk began cropping up in the lyrics of mainstream pop hits, like the Ying Yang Twins' "Whistle While

You Twurk" and Destiny's Child's "Jumpin', Jumpin'." Still, it remained mostly a New Orleans phenomenon, evolving and expanding rapidly through the many subcultures and communities of the city. The queer community, in particular, came to embrace the style after a drag queen named Katey Red performed a bounce set at a local club in 1998. In the early 2000s, she and Big Freedia became well-known in the New Orleans scene for raunchy, stylish lyrics that openly engaged with queer themes, and for their enthusiastic use of twerk in their shows, leading to the formation of a subgenre of bounce called sissy bounce. "A lot of people think bounce is simply a booty-shaking dance from the ghetto," Big Freedia says. "But bounce is as shallow or deep as you want to make it. The groin area has extraordinary power. Moving it at lightning speed is more than sexual; it's also deeply intimate and transformative. For us sissies, who lived under such constant oppression—the violence, poverty, and homophobia—bounce is our way to transmute that pain into joy."

It wasn't until 2005, after Hurricane Katrina hit, that bounce emerged from the region in a major way. The devastation of the hurricane and its aftermath was brutal and cruel, leaving more than 1,800 people dead, 80 percent of the city underwater, and 1.2 million displaced. The mass diaspora that resulted brought the city's subcultures to new parts of the country, and all of a sudden Katey Red, Big Freedia, and other bounce artists found themselves performing in clubs in Houston, Nashville, and Atlanta. New audiences were being exposed to bounce and twerk for the first time, and the rise of shareable videos on sites like YouTube brought even wider awareness. A group of dancers from Atlanta called Twerk Team gained significant popularity on the site, prompting girls and women of color to upload clips of themselves twerking joyfully in their bedrooms and living rooms.

Twerk had gone national but still had not hit its peak popularity. That moment would come almost a decade later, nearly three centuries after the French first brought enslaved people to New Orleans, in a pop culture frenzy instigated by a young white woman trying to show the world she was no longer a child.

MILEY

. .

Destiny Hope Cyrus was born in 1992 in Franklin, Tennessee. Although she would later claim normal, if not exactly humble, beginnings, from the start there was more than a whiff of Nashville fame about her, and a good bit of money and opportunity—her father was a successful country singer with a recent *Billboard* crossover hit, "Achy Breaky Heart." As an infant, the story goes, Destiny Hope grinned so often, her parents nicknamed her Smiley. Eventually, it was shortened to Miley. The name stuck.

Growing up, Miley Cyrus was, at least according to her public image, a good American girl. She was baptized and went to church on Sundays. She wore a purity ring. Dolly Parton was her godmother. And when she was twelve years old, she got a job playing a good American girl on television.

Hannah Montana premiered on the Disney Channel in 2006 and followed Miley Stewart, a "typical" middle school girl by day who, on nights and weekends, transforms into famous pop singer Hannah Montana (the simple act of donning a blond wig rendering her unrecognizable to family and friends). As silly as the premise might have been, the majority of the show focused on typical growing pains—crushes, homework, identity, and the everyday embarrassments of being a preteen—and presented a complicated blend of fiction and reality. The real-life Miley Cyrus and her TV alter egos were presented as Christian, goofy, wholesome, and entirely nonthreatening to the parents of America. Both Miley Cyrus and Miley Stewart have a country-music-singer father who helps write her songs and manage her career, and they both happen to be Billy Ray Cyrus, who also played Robby Ray Stewart on the show. The songs that Miley-as-Miley-as-Hannah performed on the show became pop hits and resulted in an album that, in 2007, Miley-as-Miley-as-Hannah went on tour to promote, and in 2009 Disney released *Hannah Montana: The Movie*. On a branding level, it was genius, a nearly perfect symbiosis that invested young fans in two characters for the price of one and motivated them to devote time and money across numerous platforms. The problem, of course, was that one of the people was real, and, eventually, she would come to want what all previous Disney tween stars wanted: to grow up.

The final season of *Hannah Montana* aired in 2011, with Miley making the decision to go off to college with her best friend instead of shooting a film as Hannah. The real-life Cyrus was eighteen, coming off a massive hit single under her own name, "Party in the USA," and it wasn't clear what she could or should do next. She released more music, but the albums didn't sell well, at least by her standards. She acted in several films but received consistently terrible reviews, and some were financial flops (the Nicholas Sparks adaptation *The Last Song*, released amid tabloid coverage of her romance with her costar Liam Hemsworth, was a notable exception). In 2010, she was caught on camera smoking salvia from a bong—typical teen behavior, but also a clear affront to her straitlaced image. If she was going to successfully transition out of her Hannah Montana persona and establish herself as a different kind of performer and star, it seemed Cyrus needed to do something bold. And fast. That's where things got complicated.

In a documentary made by MTV about the rollout of her 2013 album *Bangerz*, Cyrus describes that year in her life as "not a transition" but a "movement," a classification she was so committed to that the documentary itself is called *Miley: The Movement*. The word is a clear reference to the shift from one state (childhood) to another (adulthood) but is perhaps also an attempt to position herself as a leader and inspiration to legions of her fans about to go through the same change. Her album contained songs with more adult themes and had been created in collaboration with well-respected producers such as Pharrell and Mike Willy instead of the Disney machine.

In the publicity, music videos, lyrics, and overall aesthetics of her new album, Cyrus had made clear that her more mature brand would not only feel "urban" but also weave in Black cultural forms and sounds. The cookie-cutter Hannah Montana lyrics of her past ("Life's what you make it, so let's make it rock") turned into statements of defiance that evoked hip-hop vernacular ("You ain't with it, could've said that / Why you tripping, let me hit that"), and her look transformed from jeans and sparkly tank tops to gold grills and garments that left her nearly nude. A line was being drawn, it seemed, between her previous, squeaky-clean innocence and her new, unabashed rebellion and foray into nonwhite culture. This radical shift was put clearly on display for millions at the 2013 MTV Video Music Awards, in one of the most controversial live performances of the 2010s.

It started with a giant space teddy bear sitting on the stage of Brooklyn's Barclays Center. The bear was brown and several stories tall and had a face that looked like it had been designed by the engineers of the starship *Enterprise*, composed entirely of flashing lights. The bear's torso popped open and out stepped Cyrus, wearing a silver leotard emblazoned with another teddy bear's face (magenta ears covered her breasts). Two bright blond pigtails sprouted from her otherwise buzzed head. She clung to the side of the bear's open torso and stuck out her tongue. A male voice, manipulated to sound spacey, began to chant, "Twerk twerk twerk twerk it out," as Cyrus dismounted the bear. A long line of dancers dressed in pink teddy bear costumes then populated the stage, proceeding to dance around Cyrus as she sang the first lyrics of her new single, "We Can't Stop," her own body gyrating smoothly to the music. And then, a group of four Black women—the only Black women to appear during the performance, and the only women not fashion-model thin—appeared onstage wearing tight stretch pants and huge stuffed teddy bears affixed to their backs. They began to shake their butts, their oversized accessories bouncing to the rhythm.

Cyrus herself was lithe and waifish, her butt and breasts both small. And yet she, too, determinedly shook her butt (she was, she would say later, twerking). In an effort perhaps to hammer home the point of the whole exercise, Cyrus greedily grabbed the butt of one of the bear-laden, big-butted Black dancers as she belted the lyric "Doing whatever we want."

Shortly after this moment, "We Can't Stop" transitioned into the opening chords of a massive summer hit, Robin Thicke's "Blurred Lines" (a song also produced by Pharrell, which would soon be embroiled in controversy over its apparent endorsement of rape culture and use of uncredited elements of Marvin Gaye's "Got to Give It Up"). As Cyrus ripped off her silver teddy bear leotard to reveal a flesh-colored latex bikini and began to prance, Thicke himself emerged, wearing a referee-striped suit. Cyrus appeared all but naked, but she did have a prop: a white foam finger, the type you'd hold up at a football game to signify "We're number one!" For the next three minutes, Cyrus danced athletically and provocatively: bending over and shaking her butt (more in the manner of an animal shaking off bathwater than a practiced twerker), strutting all around and repeatedly rubbing the foam finger in her crotch.

Taken as a whole, it was a weird spectacle. Cyrus doesn't seem quite comfortable, as though she's making up many of the dance moves as she goes along. She is goofy and gawky in her efforts to communicate, *I'm no longer a child, no longer Hannah Montana*. But even she seems less than 100 percent convinced.

That evening was likely the first time that many viewers at home—particularly white viewers—had heard the word *twerk* or seen the movement itself, but the performance suggested little of its rich history or technical strength. Cyrus's dance was an anemic interpretation, and the twerkers hired as backup dancers hadn't been able to show the full range of their skill, thanks to the teddy bears strapped to their bodies.

Cyrus would later say that the performance was meant to be "obviously funny," but for weeks after the VMAs, the media was ablaze with aghast commentary and a disproportionate amount of outrage. The *Los Angeles Times* reported that reactions to Cyrus's new path veered between "disgust and sadness," while singer Kelly Clarkson tweeted in response to the performance: "2 words . . . #pitchystrippers." *The View* cohost Sherri Shepherd told Jay Leno that Cyrus was "going to hell in a twerking handbasket," and *Morning Joe* coanchor Mika Brzezinski called the whole affair "really, really disturbing." The man who invented the foam finger expressed anger and shame, and the director of the Parents Television Council stated, "MTV has once again succeeded in marketing sexually charged messages to young children using former child stars and condom commercials—while falsely rating this program as appropriate for kids as young as fourteen. This is unacceptable."

Of all the day-after critics, Brooke Shields, who had played Hannah Montana's deceased mother on the show, had perhaps the most apt word to describe it: *desperate*. Cyrus was trying to prove that she was grown-up but seemed to be playacting the part more than living it. If the performance was harmful to tween girls, it was because it was such a strange, awkward performance of sexuality, and any attempt to replicate it would likely result in humiliation.

The media reaction was, surely, precisely what Cyrus intended. Within a matter of minutes, she had severed herself once and for all from her Hannah Montana alter ego and announced herself as an unapologetically sexual being. Her butt, and the butts of the women she hired to dance with her, were apparently a crucial part of "the movement," and Cyrus later doubled down on this during her tour, attaching a large prosthetic butt to her waist and using it as part of her choreography when she took the show on tour. The crude sculpted pad made her petite derrière appear enormous and comical, bursting through a silver thong. The butt was also removable, which was yet another way she asserted her whiteness and privilege—just like women who wore bustles in the nineteenth century, Cyrus could make a choice to be aligned with Blackness or not in any given moment. She was using a prop to "play" in Blackness, manipulating it for her own ends. Cyrus was adopting and exploiting a form of dance that had long been popular in poor and working-class Black communities and simultaneously playing into the stereotype of the hypersexual Black woman, all in an effort to declare to the world that she was no longer a child.

In the weeks following the VMAs, Cyrus's response to all the charges leveled against her was essentially: *I'm young, I'm having fun. Stop taking it all so seriously*, dismissing the belief that she had a responsibility as a public figure and role model, while still encouraging fans to become part of the "the movement." In the documentary, she offers a justification for her behavior during the *Bangerz* era: "I live in America. The land of the free. And I feel like if you can't express yourself, you aren't very free." It isn't entirely clear what she means when she says this, because it is readily apparent that Cyrus *could* express herself.

She did whatever she wanted (as the "We Can't Stop" lyric suggests) on one of the biggest stages in the world. She endured criticism, but it certainly appeared that stirring up controversy was what she'd been hoping for. A few years later, in a 2017 *Billboard* magazine profile, she offered another response: "It's mind-boggling to me that there was even a controversy about me having black dancers . . . People said I was taking advantage of black culture. That wasn't true. Those were the dancers I liked!" In other words: she couldn't have done something racist, she says, because she actually *liked* her Black dancers.

Shortly after Cyrus's twerk debacle, the most mainstream and white of cultural outlets—publications like *Vogue* and the *New York Times*—fully threw themselves into the butt business, publishing articles like "Starting from the Bottom: Experts Weigh in on the Cultural Obsession with the Butt" and "For Posteriors' Sake," which both outlined and attempted to explain what they described as a new interest in the butt across American culture. Butts had become so pervasive, so visible, and so interesting to white people that they could no longer be ignored as a cultural, or economic, phenomenon. The issue, as many writers of color noted, was they had already been one for quite some time—it just had not been regularly covered in the pages of *Vogue*. As writers like Allison P. Davis pointed out, any "discovery" of the butt wasn't so different from Columbus's "discovery" of America. The butt had always been there, even if white people had failed to notice for decades.

THE YEAR OF THE BUTT

• •

Cyrus's performance was one of the most notorious butt-related moments leading up to the very butty year of 2014, which many pop culture media outlets came to call "the Year of the Butt." It was a period when an interest in butts seemed to suddenly be everywhere: in magazines (such as Kardashian's now-legendary *Paper* cover), on Instagram, on the *Billboard* charts, and in the offices and operating rooms of the nation's plastic surgeons, where the frequency of the cosmetic surgery procedure known as the Brazilian butt lift had undergone a massive spike.

For almost every major plastic surgery procedure, the American Society of Plastic Surgeons makes public both recent and historical data, but the organization didn't even start to record statistics about butt augmentation until 2012. That year 8,654 butt augmentation procedures were performed; by 2014 the number reached 11,505, a 33 percent increase in just two years. The Brazilian butt lift—or BBL, as it was more commonly called—was developed in the 1990s as an alternative to silicone implants, previously the only other option for butt augmentation. During the procedure, a surgeon uses liposuction to remove fat from the patient's stomach, lower back, and thighs and injects it into the butt. Although a BBL creates a more "natural" look, it can be a dangerous approach, especially when performed by an inexperienced surgeon, because of how easy it is to inadvertently inject fat into the major blood vessels running from the legs to the torso and lungs, which can cause a fatal embolism. The American Society of Plastic Surgeons issued a warning in 2018 about the dangers of BBLs, citing a death rate of one in three thousand—a rate "far greater than any other cosmetic surgery"—but still the number of BBLs performed has continued to steadily grow—in 2019, more than 28,000 were performed, up 16.5 percent from the year before.

The BBL may be the most extreme way for women to alter their butts, but it is hardly the only way. By 2014, many of the moves from the *Buns of Steel* video had found their way into women's magazines offering tips for toning, tightening, and lifting the butt. Some magazines promised the keys to unlocking the look of Kim Kardashian's bulbous, round butt, while others offered exercises to sculpt a ballet dancer's petite and muscular backside, and still others instructed readers on how to achieve something akin to the slight but highly coveted silhouette Pippa Middleton had displayed to the world at her sister's royal wedding to Prince William.

The variations were likely due to a larger conundrum facing wide-circulation women's magazines: for decades they'd been cultivating, and profiting from, fat phobia, but now they had to contend with the emergence of a new, fleshier body ideal. After so many years and so much ink dedicated to the "melting away" of fat, the only way editors knew how to engage with the desire for a big butt was to make it something earned through endless exercise and dietary regimes, a blend of flesh and muscle that could only be achieved through hard work, self-sacrifice, and a healthy amount of shame.

Butts had also become a shareable commodity thanks to social media, which helped to dramatically amplify all the other changes that were afoot. In 2013, a Long Islander named Jen Selter first coined the term *belfie*, a portmanteau of *butt* and *selfie* that, despite its name, was less about an individual's documentation of their own butt—many belfies had to be taken by other people, because of the challenging contortion required to photograph one's own backside—and more about a very specific photographic pose that centered the butt in an Instagrammable image and featured a coy over-the-shoulder peek. It's a pose Kim Kardashian had been modeling and perfecting for years (the promotional image from the first season of *KUWTK* is an excellent example) and a look that is both sweet and sexy. It also puts a face to the butt, disrupting the anonymity that is so often a part of rear-end appreciation. When she coined the term, Selter was a rising fitness star who boasted a shapely, if small, white butt and a fitness column in the *New York Post* called "Kicking Butt," in which she promised to help women exercise their way to a comely rear. But, for Selter, there emerged another, more direct route to monetizing her commitment to a quality butt: she began posting her belfies on Instagram, which quickly turned out to be lucrative—according to Selter, every belfie she posted drew five thousand new Instagram followers, which then translated to significant income in promotions and fitness clients. "Anyone who works hard could be where I am," she told *Elle* magazine in 2013. You could take Selter's meaning in two ways: hard work can earn you a good butt, but it can also turn you into a millionaire.

The music industry also was cashing in on the Year of the Butt thanks to a string of hits. Jennifer Lopez released the anthem "Booty," a collaboration with fellow proudly callipygian pop star Iggy Azalea. Beyoncé, the woman who had introduced the world to the word *bootylicious* a decade before, released her eponymous album, whose music videos prominently featured her barely clad butt, accompanied by a slew of music videos and televised performances that featured butt-forward dancing and posing. And white singer-songwriter Meghan Trainor offered up "All About That Bass," a reference to her own big butt, featuring lyrics that were ostensibly body-positive, like "I won't be no stick-figure, silicone Barbie doll" and "Every inch of you is perfect from the bottom to the top."

That August, Nicki Minaj released "Anaconda," a song that directly referenced and sampled "Baby Got Back" and foregrounded Minaj's butt in both the music video and the lyrics ("He say don't like 'em boney, he want something he can grab"). In sampling "Baby Got Back," Minaj nodded to the lineage of butts in mainstream hip-hop, but she was also asserting her control over the narrative of the big-butted Black woman. She was not a headless gyrating body, as were the women of "Baby Got Back," but instead the creator of the music, the controller of the image, and the maker of the money. If there was exploitation, it was self-exploitation, and a choice Minaj herself was making.

The butt song was a lucrative subgenre to be operating within, but for the original New Orleans bounce performers Katey Red and Big Freedia—people who in many senses built twerk into the very thing Miley Cyrus and others would later commodify—financial success and recognition came slower, and with not nearly as much of a bang. Katey Red started recording an album in 1998, but it wasn't until 2011 that the album and music video were finally released; she has never achieved widespread mainstream fame or name recognition, despite her crucial role in the history of bounce and twerk. Big Freedia fared better. In 2013, she starred in her own reality show on the Fuse network, *Big Freedia: Queen of Bounce*. She also became an ambassador for twerk's history and cultural significance, a go-to spokesperson who teaches twerkshops at universities and published a memoir. But Freedia would always be cast as the person correcting the popular narrative rather than as the one who drove it. As Nicki Minaj said in September 2013, during the aftermath of Cyrus's VMA performance, "If a white girl does something that seems to be Black, then Black people think, *Oh, she's embracing our culture*, so they kinda ride with it. Then white people think, *Oh, she must be cool! She doin' sumpin' Black*. So it's weird! But if a Black person do a Black thang? It ain't that poppin'."

RECLAMATION

· ·

Kelechi Okafor, one of the most popular twerk instructors in the United Kingdom, was born in Nigeria in 1986. She moved to London when she was five, settling in a neighborhood called Peckham, in Southeast London, home to a growing Nigerian immigrant community in the 1990s, which she referred to growing up as Little Lagos. "It was almost like we never really left Nigeria," she says. "We would go to the same markets. I heard Yoruba being spoken all around." When I talked to Okafor, she explained that dancing was an essential part of her upbringing. "I would naturally dance at every party I'd go to. I would always, always dance."

When she was sixteen, Okafor attended a performing arts school, where she studied musical theater. It was there that she began to attend formal ballet, tap, and jazz dance classes, and where she began to recognize that something about her appearance and dancing ability set her apart.

Okafor felt discouraged at every turn: her ballet teacher instructed her to buy pink tights for ballet, ignoring the fact that they did not match her skin tone. A career advisor told her that as a Black person, the most she could really expect from musical theater jobs was "a nice best-friend role." When she would add vocal runs to a song in class, she would be reprimanded and told, "Sing it just as we've given it." When a white woman did the same, Okafor noticed, she'd be praised for adding something creative and quirky. "I started to understand what wasn't allowed for me but made sense if other people did it who weren't Black."

After high school, she went to Liverpool Hope University to study drama and law. It was her first time away from home and the first time she had the space and freedom to explore what dance meant to her. "For the three years that I was in Liverpool," she says, "I pretty much ran it when it came to the nightlife." She was well-known in the clubs and became what she calls a "mini-celebrity" because of what she was capable of on the dance floor. "It was just very free," she says when I ask her what her moves were like. "I was butt and hip focused. I was able to really engage the sacral region."

After university, in 2008, Okafor moved to Atlanta, a city where she didn't know anyone, but she did know that it was the home of her favorite performer, Ciara. "I knew that we were destined to be best friends," she says, laughing. She never met Ciara, but she did end up working in artist management for six months, mostly with rappers. Many of those artists performed at strip clubs, or went to strip clubs following their performances, and often they brought Okafor along with them. It was there that she was first introduced to pole dancing, and immediately fell in love with it. "Respectability politics shrouds sex work and pole dancing, but all I saw was really, really raw unadulterated power," she says.

In 2009, Okafor returned to the UK and worked in a call center while looking for work as an actor and studying to become a personal trainer. A few years later, she decided to take pole dancing lessons, and within a few months she had made her way through all the levels available at a local dance studio. Before long, she was asked to teach classes herself, which quickly became popular in part because she brought with her a knowledge of physiology and anatomy and helped her students to understand how the dances worked with their bodies. In 2014, the white owners of the studio asked her if she might teach twerk. "I thought, *Why? Is that a thing [that you think] Black people do?*" She told them she wasn't sure if her moves were twerking, per se, but agreed to demonstrate how she danced in the Liverpool clubs. Impressed, they immediately asked if she would teach her moves as a class, just as soon as she shadowed one of their existing twerk classes. "I went to this class," she recalled, "and I was horrified." There were only two people in attendance, apart from the instructor and Okafor, and the teacher was demonstrating basic moves—bum isolations and jiggling—without showing the students how to assemble them into a unified whole. "I could hear the beat, but I don't know if she could hear the beat," Okafor says. "Nothing was marrying." She decided that she would take a different approach. Within a few weeks of her first class, her Twerking for Beginners had completely sold out, and the studio added more class sessions to accommodate the increase in demand. Okafor was thrilled. "I was just loving the fact that I could teach people the mechanics of what happens when I dance, and break it down for them and break down the language and the relationship between music and sensuality and show them how to express that physically."

The popularity of the classes and Okafor's growing social media following were exciting for the studio's owners—as was the money her classes were bringing to the studio—but they also wanted to manage the definition of *twerk* in their space and make sure it adhered to what they thought their custom-ers wanted. They asked Okafor if they could rename her class Tribal Twerk, to signal that she was teaching movements that they believed the average white student couldn't execute.

Okafor confronted similar problems at other studios. In an effort to expand her reach, she wrote a studio in Manchester to

see about teaching a workshop. She noticed that they had credited Miley Cyrus as an originator of twerk, an error she found
troubling and was eager to help correct. "I don't enjoy your style
of twerk," the white studio owner said in response. "I find it
basic. When me and my girls twerk, we put our knee pads on
and we throw down."

Okafor posted the studio owner's response on Twitter, and
the tweet went viral, particularly in the United States. "Black
American women were furious," Okafor recalled. "They said:
*This is what's been happening to us for centuries. We are the orig-
inators of something, then it's appropriated by white people, then
it's repackaged for a mainstream consciousness for people to make
profits off of, and we are denigrated in the process.*"

White women's interest in twerk in the 2010s, and in large butts
more generally, is in some ways a curious thing. Although there
have been high-profile examples of white women dabbling in
Black fashion and popular culture before—whether through Bo
Derek's cornrows, Madonna's vogueing, or even the bustle—
white women have often chosen segregation over appropriation, leaving the latter largely to their male counterparts. But in
the 2010s, this began to change, and the center of that change
was an unprecedented and deep engagement with large butts
and twerking.

When I asked Okafor why she thinks so many white women
take her twerk classes, she explained, "It has to do with Western femininity. When white supremacy was evolving, there had
to be something to fight for, and womanhood, femininity, and
white feminine purity became that thing. And so white women
became trapped within that narrative." Okafor further noted
that white men often see it as their duty to protect this mytho-
logical innocent white woman, particularly from the perceived

physical and sexual threat of nonwhite men. "And I think that that is why white women feel called to twerk—because there's still that internal and external battle, to break the chains of white feminine purity.

"We also have to address the intergenerational jealousy from the fact that Black women's bodies were desired by white men during the times of slavery," Okafor continues. She explains that there is a question that must have haunted white women as white men ogled and desired Black women: *"Why are my men desiring this one? If I can emulate her in some way, that desirability [can come back to] me."* This jealousy of Black women's supposed sexual capacity and potency, of course, has a long lineage, back to at least the era of Sarah Baartman, the bustle, and 1814's *The Hottentot Venus; or, The Hatred of Frenchwomen.*

To escape the larger mythology of purity, white women often mimic Black women, buying into stereotypes of hypersexuality. This is the story of many young starlets, including Christina Aguilera, Britney Spears, and, of course, Miley Cyrus. "They have to go through a dirty phase, which is their way of entering a more autonomous aspect of womanhood," Okafor says, but in order to do this, "they emulate an almost bastardized version of Black womanhood. And once they've got their freedom, they throw it away." For Okafor, Blackness was constructed to "accommodate everybody who's been ostracized in whichever way, shape, or form," including white women. "But that isn't fair," she says, "because usually [those people] can leave in a way that Black women cannot."

In 2016, Okafor opened her own studio in London, where she has taught twerk and pole dance classes ever since, offering her students both an academic understanding of the history of dance and biomechanics as well as an intuitive relationship with movement and her lived expertise as a survivor of sexual abuse. For years, Okafor didn't speak about her own history of abuse, but now she sees twerk as a way to override that silence and connect with and take ownership over her body. "I'm reclaiming my body through dance," she says. "I'm able to offer that to people with transparency and vulnerability. There has always been so much violence and trauma around the area of [the hips and bum] when it comes to femmes."

Okafor teaches that twerk doesn't start from the butt, and you don't need a big butt to twerk well. "It starts from your feet and it travels up. That [comes from] the rootedness of West African culture and West African dance. When we look at Senegal, when we look at Nigeria, it's a lot of footwork." When she sees other Europeans twerk—there's a surprisingly large population of Russian and Eastern European twerk teachers online—she thinks they overuse their thoracic vertebrae. "There's a lot of heavy convulsion," she says.

Okafor hopes that students walk away from her classes with an understanding of the ways that different movements have been used in the history of African diasporic dance. "I hope that they get a very thorough understanding of twerk and of its history. I talk to them about where movements originate. How a flick of the foot might have shape-shifted and traveled to New Orleans." She has also built a significant social media presence, as well as a robust career as a writer, podcaster, and actor, hoping that the information and context she provides will spread beyond the community of her studio. "Why not use the space and the communities that I have to educate them so when they go out, the education can pass along?"

Global culture is in many ways driven by borrowing, mixing, and remixing: all music, dance, art, and fashion draws, to some extent, on traditions and experiences beyond the identity and culture of the creator. Without this cultural intermixing, not only would we not have rock 'n' roll, we would not have twerk.

And yet, borrowing can easily become harmful when it occurs unconsciously, without attribution, or without consideration for history. Miley Cyrus is an almost cartoonish example of cultural appropriation: she was frank, and extreme, in her exploitation of twerk to shed her childish image, and she readily cast aside her sexy, faux-big-butted persona when it no longer suited her, instead choosing to reframe the new phase of her career and image around classic rock heroines like Joan Jett and Stevie Nicks. She made huge amounts of money off her performances and apparently never made any public mention of the origins of twerk in Black and queer communities. She also easily sloughed it off post-*Bangerz*.

But the lesson of Cyrus isn't only a lesson about a badly behaved celebrity. It's a lesson about understanding our motives and trying to uncover the desires simmering beneath our initial, conscious reckonings. I didn't spend the 2010s taking twerk classes or snapping belfies for Instagram. But I did enjoy, if that's even the right word, the fruits of changes in beauty standards that evolved over the past thirty years, and how the meaning of and appreciation for big butts had changed in mainstream culture. Men, and women, seemed to see my body differently than they had in the late 1990s. After a meeting at the museum where I worked in the early 2010s, I walked up the stairs a few feet in front of a coworker and he called out: *Look at that butt!* It made me uncomfortable and he shouldn't have said it. But it was also true that a part of me was a little bit thrilled—thrilled that he noticed, thrilled that I was being perceived as sexy. By the time the year of the butt rolled around, three whiskeys in to most of my dates, the person I was with—regardless of gender or race— would usually grab my butt and whisper something about it.

They all seemed to have unleashed the part of themselves that liked big butts, and my body had become more coveted as a result. And I enjoyed it. When I wore tight dresses that showed my butt off, I felt some of its power.

But I also felt its limits. As a teenager, I knew my butt to be only big and gross. All of a sudden, it felt big and sexy. And while this may have constituted an improvement, my butt was still stubbornly *present*. I sometimes wanted to hide it, to make it disappear. I wanted it to mean nothing, to be invisible to the people around me. I wanted to be able to walk up to a podium to give a talk and not think about what people were looking at as I approached the mic. But my body was always there, saying something, meaning something, whether I liked it or not.

What are white women seeking when they dabble in Black culture? The answer may be different for each of us, but for me Kelechi Okafor offers a good place to start: access to sexiness, an opportunity to rebel, a way to push beyond the rigidity of white femininity. But those needs aren't always ones we can articulate easily, or thoroughly, and so we resolve them thoughtlessly.

By turning to Blackness in an attempt to solve these problems of whiteness, white women turn away from the origins of the shame we carry about our bodies, a shame that comes from the construction of whiteness itself, a shame that exists to enforce the idea that some bodies are innocent and others are sexual, that some bodies are better and others worse. In the process, not only do we harm others, but we harm ourselves by never really understanding where our shame comes from.

Conclusion

Last fall, I threw out the only pair of blue jeans I still had left. My thighs had been rubbing together with every step, and the material between my legs had pilled and then frayed, eventually becoming all weft and no warp. Finally, I sat down on a stoop and was greeted by a satisfying and demoralizing tear— the jeans had ripped open entirely along the bottom of my left cheek.

It took many months to muster the courage to shop for a new pair. Since the days of watching my mom try on clothes at Hudson's, I'd been in hundreds of dressing rooms, and almost all seemed to have been designed to foster low-level shame. In some the lighting provided a high-contrast glimpse of the craggy cellulite on my hips; in others, a mirror was strategically angled to make my thighs appear huge. Sometimes, a peppy young salesperson cheered me on from the other side of a thin curtain, convinced I could squeeze myself into a size smaller than the one I'd chosen. I would suck in my stomach and stuff my butt into pants that had no hope of containing it, inexplicably trying to appease a stranger so that she in turn might reassure me that I was good enough.

Finally, after several months of putting off a shopping trip, I dragged myself to lower Manhattan to hunt down the elusive replacement pair. There I ventured into a shop with an all-glass façade, a bright white stoop, and an entire wall of neatly stacked pants in indigo, cornflower, and faded black. I looked up and down, unsure if my size was more akin to a rare, top-shelf bourbon or a cheap wine with a cupcake on the label stashed near the floor. I sifted through one pile and then another, seeing only size 27s and 28s, before finally finding a pair that might fit me at the very bottom of a pile. They were high waisted and acid washed, an updated version of the mom jeans that I swore as a teenager I'd never wear.

I pulled the dressing room curtain shut, studied myself in the large mirror leaning against the wall at an unsympathetic angle, and disrobed. As I fastened the button, I felt the privacy of the moment. It was just me in that room, having an ordinary experience. I was running an errand, checking off a task that had lingered too long on my list.

For a moment, a blaze of hope lifted me, but when I studied myself longer in the mirror, it was clear that the pants were wrong. Even in this age when garment manufacturers promise diversity in size and shape, this store had only one pair of pants in my size, and they bagged weirdly in the legs, felt taut across the butt, and gaped at the waist. They looked big and loose in the mirror, and when I turned around to glance at my butt, I felt a familiar sting of disappointment.

That feeling, I realized, was among those that most interested me when I started writing this book. It is a common, everyday sentiment experienced in a mundane circumstance, one that gnaws away at one's self-image. But it is also so familiar and banal that it's all too easy to ignore.

I was interested in this dressing room angst because it seemed so personal, but I knew it was deeply interconnected with centuries of history, culture, and politics. I had often dismissed anxiety about my body as trivial or shallow. But the politics of race and gender are the politics of bodies, and investigating the thoughts and presumptions we carry about our bodies and the bodies of those around us is crucial and profound. Thoughts like, *My butt is so big!*, *Am I developing a paunch?*, and *Aren't mom jeans supposed to be good for people with my body shape?* bubble up not only from notions of bodies we absorb via Instagram or through ads on billboards or in subways, but from sources deep in our collective past.

After years of researching butts, and coming to a better understanding of the apparently ever-shifting yet somehow always philosophically consistent doctrine of mainstream beauty standards, I know that my feelings about my butt are part of a lineage, informed by Georges Cuvier's autopsy report of Sarah Baartman, Ruth O'Brien's trove of data collected—and discarded—by her measuring squads, Gordon Conway's drawings of freewheeling flappers, and Greg Smithey's VHS tape promising women a way to transcend their fleshy, imperfect forms. These feelings come from the way in which big butts became equated with hypersexuality and Blackness, the way that small butts came to symbolize fashion and freedom, the way strong butts were synonymous with discipline, self-control, and self-respect. And they come from the way that talking about women's butts has, for at least two centuries, been a way to talk about, and around, questions of race, gender, and what bodies mean. It's like getting dressed on a cold winter's day, pulling on two or three pairs of socks, wearing long underwear under sweatpants and ski pants on top of it all. There's a body in there somewhere—a scientific, biological fact—but one that's covered up, made invisible, by the layers heaped upon it. On and in our bodies, we carry histories—those described in this book, and many more besides. Histories of our families, of our lives, and of the world. Our feelings about our bodies are the legacy of people and stories from long ago.

I'd like to say that learning something of these histories freed me from negative feelings about my body, but this sort of knowledge isn't a magic bullet. On the other side of my research, I still feel uncomfortable in the dressing room, still feel like I don't fit when I try on clothes. Ideas and prejudices about bodies imprint early and deeply, and so the first rush of feeling I have when I pull up my jeans still contains a healthy dose of shame, and likely always will. But what this research has offered is a way to understand and contextualize that shame, and it has helped me to question the way I think and the assumptions I make. It has made these large, structural forces seem less vague. It has helped me to articulate, and understand, the way I feel about bodies. And it has given me hope. After the voice in my head whispers, *Your butt is too big*, there is another that asks: *Too big for what? Too big according to whom? Why is big so bad?*

I've often thought about how, despite the fact that this book is very much about butts, it could have been about almost anything. And this gives me hope, too. A close examination of the parts of ourselves that can feel unbearable—whether body parts, emotions, or desires—can be transformative. By growing curious about the sources of shame and by putting that shame in context, we don't excuse ourselves, or even get beyond it. Instead, we turn toward rather than away, a gesture that allows for new possibilities and knowledge.

Understanding the way people of the past shaped the present is also a means of uncovering mechanisms for how we all might shape a future. The fact that human beings from the past created the meanings our different bodies hold shows us that people today can re-create, or discard, those meanings. One of the great gifts of looking closely at the past is that things that once felt inevitable and immutable begin to feel surmountable, changeable, transitory. People create the meanings that are the source of shame, which means that other people—like Rosezella

Canty-Letsome, Deb Burgard, Kelechi Okafor, Vinnie Cuccia, and Alex Bartlett—can change them once more.

Our bodies, by their very nature, resist control, a fact that always has felt paradoxically triumphant when I encounter it. We invent bustles and girdles and exercise videos and cabbage diets and sizing schemes, but our bodies have their own agenda, and so they rarely obey us. Some people want their butt to be big, some people want their butt to be small. But a butt will, for the most part, always remain what it is. As the human mind tries to hammer a body into submission—tries to create meaning, tries to change its shape and appearance, tries to make it something it is not and cannot be—the human body stubbornly refuses to oblige.

It is maybe for this reason that I decided to buy the blue jeans that didn't quite fit. I chose to live with their being just good enough. Sometimes now when I wear them, I feel anxious about the way they look—the tightness in the butt and the looseness in the waist. And sometimes, of course, I feel the familiar pang of annoyance that it's so hard to find a pair of pants that actually fits. But ultimately, I sense a physical reminder of that push and pull between body and mind, between the desire to wrest control and the reality that bodies will always insist on being exactly what they are.

It's been thirty years since I sat on the fleecy toilet cover in my parents' bathroom, watching my mother get dressed, soothed by the warmth and safety I associated with her body and the predictability of her morning ritual, imagining that my body would grow into one like hers. My adult mornings are different from those—I largely work from home and have never been very adept with curlers and lotions and mascara and perfume and all the other high-femme ablutions. But sometimes, when I'm preparing to teach a class or go to a party, I'll lean over the sink with my face close to the mirror to curl my eyelashes, my butt sticking out. I'll dig out a bottle of hairspray and crack the window so it won't stink up the bathroom. And I'll look myself over in the mirror, trying to get a glimpse of my butt. My body does look a bit like my mom's, with its big butt and wide hips. And sometimes, when I'm standing there in my under-wear, before I've pulled on pants or stepped into the world, my butt doesn't feel like a problem or a blessing. It's just a fact.

Acknowledgments

If I've learned anything in my life, it's that creative work happens inside a community of support. I'm so grateful to all the friends, thinkers, artists, and writers who have contributed and been crucial to this project.

The idea for this book started as a little bit of a joke with Damon Locks, whom I'm lucky to call a friend and whose work and life as an artist are a constant inspiration. Damon was one of the many artists I met during my time at the Jane Addams Hull-House Museum in the early 2010s, where some of the most brilliant, warmhearted, hilarious, and creative people I've ever known worked together to make a very special thing. It was from these people—including Isis Ferguson, Lisa Junkin Lopez, Tara Lane, Jen Ash, and the incomparable Lisa Yun Lee—that I absorbed and formed so many of my ideas about politics, history, art, and the possibilities for joy in social movements. This book couldn't exist without them and everything they taught me.

I am extraordinarily grateful to those who believed I was capable of being a writer before I ever could. To Shannon Heffernan, whose friendship, humor, and care has kept me company on both the darkest and most joyful of days. To Lulu Miller, who has shown me how big and beautiful a life could be. To Michelle Boyd, who encouraged me in the moment I needed it most and taught me how to care for myself during times of grief.

Thank you to the teachers I found in Columbia's MFA program, including Leslie Jamison, Hilton Als, Margo Jefferson, Philip Lopate, and Eliza Griswold, whose lessons and support have helped to form me as a writer. To Sam Freedman, who accepted this peculiar-sounding project into his book proposal class and shaped both me and the book over the course of a semester. To the many friends I met during my time at Columbia who became in-the-trenches colleagues, including Noah Shannon, Dan Lefferts, Moeko Fujii, Sasha Bonet, Lisa Factora-Borchers, Harrison Hill, Synne Borgen, Robyn Price, Ari Braverman, Kay Zhang, Maud Doyle, Jonathan Fetter-Vorn, and Jordan Kisner.

Thank you to my agent, Matt McGowen, who had faith in me from the beginning and who always believed that a book about butts could be a serious work of nonfiction. To my editor, Julianna Haubner, whose notes improved the book in innumerable ways, and to all the people at Avid Reader who supported this project behind the scenes.

In the early days of working on the book proposal, I received a grant from the Columbia School of the Arts that allowed me to travel to London and Paris, where I researched the life of Sarah Baartman and the history of the bustle. I'm very grateful for having been able to make that trip and for the reporting opportunities it provided. I'm also indebted to the Metcalf Internship Program at the University of Chicago, which paid for Audrey Fromson, Faryn Thomas, Kitty Luo, Maggie Riviera, Caitlin Lozada, and Bella Costantino to work with me as research assistants. I was thankful every day for the diligence, intelligence, and creativity of these young women who helped to make the book markedly better and the writing process significantly less lonely.

As part of my research, I interviewed many people about their bodies and their butts. I am grateful that these friends, friends of friends, and strangers were willing to be vulnerable and open in talking about their bodies. Those interviews helped me make decisions about what this book would become and helped me to think concretely beyond my own lived experience.

Thank you also to the many scholars who talked to me and whose work I drew upon for this book. A project like this stands on the shoulders of decades of important thinking and research, and I'm grateful to all the people quoted in the body of the text and referenced in the endnotes. Thank you, too, to Joe Tait, archivist at the Cleveland Museum of Natural History, for helping me find materials on Norma and Normman; Sarah Witte, women and gender studies librarian at Columbia University, who helped to track down primary sources; and to the librarians behind Columbia's "Ask a Librarian" feature, who investigated many bizarre inquiries on my behalf.

In the fall of 2019, Matt Kielty picked me up in Phoenix and drove me to Mount Mingus near Prescott where we spent two days together watching a group of humans try to outrun a group of horses. We have been friends and colleagues ever since. I'm very grateful to Matt for his interest in that story and to the geniuses at *Radiolab* for inviting me into their amazing world. Working with the *Radiolab* team has helped me to think in new ways about narrative, character, sound, and nonfiction, and I'm indebted to every one of them for bringing wonder and curiosity to my daily life.

Thank you to the people who read early drafts and sections of this book and offered their brilliant reflections and suggestions: Andrew Semans, Leslie Jamison, Lulu Miller, Robyn Price, Sasha Bonet, Dan Lefferts, Synne Borgen, Emilie Rex, Noah Shannon, Erin Williams, Jonathan Fetter-Vorn, Shannon Heffernan, Lisa Lee, Moeko Fujii, Harrison Hill, Matt Kielty, Becca Bresler, Sasha von Oldershausen, Michelle Boyd, Kathryn Tabb, Marissa Berwald, Julia Hyland Bruno, and Nicole Boettcher. A special thanks to Graham Mason, who came up with the subtitle; to Jane Fletcher, who translated from French to English (and spent a lovely week with me in Paris); to Avery Trufelman, who was regularly willing to talk through questions of fashion; and to Leslie Jamison for the tremendous friendship and constant moral support throughout the process of writing this book.

Thank you to my family, who have always offered love and encouragement: my mom and dad; Mike, Kristi, Ellis, and Ayda; and Ashley Christensen, my first and best friend. And thank you to all my friends from all parts of my life who supported me as I worked on this project. It is because of your emotional, artistic, and intellectual generosity that I'm able to make anything at all. It is a privilege to have such a robust and loving community.

Most of all, thank you to Andrew Semans, who read this book first, last, and most; who has brought me incomparable joy and love; who does not mind that I never remember to put the cap on the olive oil (or anything else). Being able to spend my life with you is the best thing that has ever happened to me.

Notes

INTRODUCTION

4   *As historian Sander Gilman*: "Black Bodies, White Bodies: Toward an Iconography of Female Sexuality in Late Nineteenth-Century Art, Medicine, and Literature," Critical Inquiry 12, no. 1 (1985).

14   *"I personally do not find my butt sexy"*: I conducted interviews with women and non-binary people as background research for this book. These interviews were long and wide-ranging and covered a variety of material about each person's feelings and experiences about their butts and bodies. The quotations here are excerpted from those interviews, which were conducted between 2017 and 2021.

MUSCLE

19   *If you happened to find*: M. D. Rose, "A Hominine Hip Bone, KNM-ER 3228, from East Lake Turkana, Kenya," *American Journal of Physical Anthropology* 63, no. 4 (1984): 371–78.

19   *This creature was closer*: Jonathan B. Losos and Daniel E. Lieberman, "Four Legs Good, Two Legs Fortuitous: Brains, Brawn, and the Evolution of Human Bipedalism," in *In the Light of Evolution: Essays from the Laboratory and Field* (Greenwood Village, CO: Roberts and Company, 2011).

19   *The area he lived in*: Ibid.

19   *The ancestors of* Homo erectus: Rose, "A Hominine Hip Bone."

19   *Several millennia later*: Ibid.

20   *He was there as a member*: Carol Broderick, "Fossil Finders: The Hominid Gang," Leakey Foundation, May 31, 2019, https://leakey foundation.org/fossil-finders-hominid-gang/.

20   *Ngeneo trained his keen eye*: R. E. Leakey, "New Hominid Fossils from the Koobi Fora Formation in Northern Kenya," *Nature* 261, no. 5561 (July 17, 1976): 574–76.

20   *It was Dr. Daniel Lieberman*: I originally reported this section about the biology of human running, the purpose of the butt muscles, and the Man Against Horse Race for WNYC's *Radiolab*. A version of this section can be heard in the show "Man Against Horse," which aired December 27, 2019. For the show, Matt Kielty and I interviewed Daniel Lieberman and Dennis Bramble and attended the race. I've used those interviews and experiences as sources for this section as well. We also interviewed several of the riders and runners, including Nick Coury.

21   *Instead, it was a question*: Daniel E. Lieberman et al., "The Human Gluteus Maximus and Its Role in Running," *Journal of Experimental Biology* 209, no. 11 (April 1, 2006): 2143–55.

21   *Biologists understood human running*: Dennis M. Bramble and Daniel E. Lieberman, "Endurance Running and the Evolution of Homo," *Nature* 432, no. 7015 (November 18, 2004): 345–52.

21   *Because it's impossible*: Ibid.

21   *Usain Bolt*: N. C. Sharp, "Animal Athletes: A Performance Review," *Veterinary Record* 171, no. 4 (2012): 87–94.

21   *an antelope or a horse*: Ibid.

22   *They'd both read*: David R. Carrier et al., "The Energetic Paradox of Human Running and Hominid Evolution" (including comments and reply), *Current Anthropology* 25, no. 4 (1984): 483–95.

22   *Bramble and Lieberman*: Collecting and storing human remains has a long and upsetting history that is deeply tied to the legacies of colonialism and scientific racism, as will be discussed at length in the next chapter. Although the bones that Lieberman and Bramble were looking at were Paleolithic, and in many ways fall into a different category of collecting than the human remains of Sarah Baartman, natural history collections are often housed at Western institutions like Harvard and collected as part of a larger colonial project in, as is the case here, Africa.

22   Homo erectus *was the first:* William J. Cromie, "Running Paced Human Evolution: Anthropologists Conclude Running May Have Helped Build a Bigger Brain," *Harvard Gazette*, November 18, 2004, https://news.harvard.edu/gazette/story/2004/11/running-paced-human-evolution/.

23   *It was also*: Bramble and Lieberman, "Endurance Running and the Evolution of Homo."

23   *He closely examined*: Lieberman et al., "Human Gluteus Maximus."

23   *"If you look at the butt"*: Daniel Lieberman appeared on an episode of *The Colbert Report* that aired on Comedy Central on May 28, 2013.

23   *our gluteus maximus is the biggest muscle*: Andreu Llamas, *Muscles and Bones (Human Body)* (Milwaukee: Gareth Stevens Publications, 1998).

23   *Like the whites of our eyes*: Hiromi Kobayashi and Shiro Kohshima, "Unique Morphology of the Human Eye," *Nature* 387, no. 6635 (June 19, 1997): 767–768, https://doi.org/10.1038/42842.

23   *"Do you feel it"*: Daniel Lieberman on *The Colbert Report*.

24   *the runners would climb 1,700*: Ron Barrett provided me with elevation and course maps, and they are also available on the Man Against Horse website: https://managainsthorse.net/.

25   *never been a human runner*: Information on human endurance and running comes from my interviews with Lieberman and Bramble as well as the following scientific papers: Bramble and Lieberman, "Endurance Running and the Evolution of Homo"; Losos and Lieberman, "Four Legs Good"; Lieberman et al., "Human Gluteus Maximus"; and Dennis Bramble, "How Running Made Us Human: Endurance Running Let Us Evolve to Look the Way We Do," *Nature*, 432. no. 7015, November 18, 2004.

28   *The human butt muscles*: Information in this paragraph and the paragraph above specifically comes from Lieberman et al., "Human Gluteus Maximus."

28   *a breastfeeding mother would have*: Losos and Lieberman, "Four Legs Good," 15.

29   *Dennis Bramble*: This information comes from my interview with Dennis Bramble and his article "How Running Made Us Human."

29   *Another group of scientists*: Information in this section comes from my interviews with Jamie L. Bartlett, as well as Jamie L. Bartlett et al., "Activity and Functions of the Human Gluteal Muscles in Walking, Running, Sprinting, and Climbing," *American Journal of Physical Anthropology* 153, no. 1 (November 12, 2013): 124–31.

29   *One point nine million years ago*: Information in this paragraph comes from Losos and Lieberman, "Four Legs Good."

30   *He feels euphoric*: This information comes from my interview with Daniel E. Lieberman and is also available in Gretchen Reynolds's

article "The Evolution of the Runner's High," *New York Times*, April 25, 2012, https://well.blogs.nytimes.com/2012/04/25/the-evolution -of-the-runners-high/.

30   *the first human in Man Against Horse*: The results for all the Man Against Horse Races are available at https://managainsthorse.net /result.html. The Man Against Horse Race, like all official endurance rides, includes vet checks for the horses where the horses stop, rest, and are checked by veterinarians. These times are subtracted from the horse's final time. Nick Coury was the first human to beat all the horses with the vet check holds subtracted from their times.

FAT

31   *A soft tissue*: This information comes from my interview with Daniel E. Lieberman.

31   *We do know, however*: The information in this paragraph comes from my interview with Duke postdoctoral associate Devjanee Swain-Lenz, as well as Devjanee Swain-Lenz et al., "Comparative Analyses of Chromatin Landscape in White Adipose Tissue Suggest Humans May Have Less Beigeing Potential Than Other Primates," *Genome Biology and Evolution* 11, no. 7 (June 24, 2019): 1997–2008.

32   *According to Morgan Hoke*: Information in this paragraph comes primarily from my interview with assistant professor of anthropology at the University of Pennsylvania Morgan Hoke.

32   *This was necessary:* Losos and Lieberman, "Four Legs Good."

32   *Although all people need fat:* Information in this section comes from my interview with Morgan Hoke.

32   *Studies say the lowest*: George A. Bray and Claude Bouchard, eds., *Handbook of Obesity*, vol. 1, *Epidemiology, Etiology, and Physiopathology* (Boca Raton, FL: CRC Press, 2014).

32   *For men, that number is*: Devi Swain-Lenz also discussed this with me during our interview.

34   *Pregnancy requires*: The information here also comes from my interview with Morgan Hoke.

34   *The most straightforward*: This information comes from my interview with Daniel E. Lieberman.

34   *There is also a body of research*: Information in this paragraph comes from my interview with Morgan Hoke.

FEATHERS

36 *"The sight of a feather in"*: This quotation comes from a letter Charles Darwin wrote to Asa Gray on April 3, 1860. This letter can be found in Charles Darwin, *The Correspondence of Charles Darwin*, eds. Frederick Burkhardt et al. (Cambridge, UK: Cambridge University Press, 1985).

36 *Darwin's theory of natural selection*: Dr. Chris Haufe explained the theories in this paragraph to me in a series of interviews that I conducted in the fall of 2021. However, the theories and questions around natural selection, sexual selection, and ornamentation are spelled out in many of Darwin's works, particularly *The Descent of Man, and Selection in Relation to Sex*. I relied on Richard Prum's *The Evolution of Beauty: How Darwin's Forgotten Theory of Mate Choice Shapes the Animal World—and Us* (New York: Anchor Books, 2017) to understand these theories further, as well as conversations with Prum, Lieberman, and Kathryn Tabb, assistant professor of philosophy at Bard College.

38 *but you'll also find them referenced*: Of course, there are many publications that use evolutionary psychology to explain pop culture phenomena, but here are some examples of evolutionary psychology in *Maxim* and *Cosmopolitan*: Zeynep Yenisey, "New Study Claims to Show Why 'Gentlemen Prefer Blondes,'" *Maxim*, January 7, 2019, https://www.maxim.com/news/men-prefer-blonde-women-study-2019-1/; Zeynep Yenisey, "Why We Love to Hate Villains, According to Science," *Maxim*, December 2, 2015, https://www.maxim.com/entertainment/why-we-love-to-hate-villains-2015-12/; Ali Drucker, "What Do Men and Women Each Regret Most about Sex?," *Maxim*, September 10, 2015, https://www.maxim.com/maxim-man/what-do-men-and-women-each-regret-most-about-sex-study-2015-9/; Meehika Barua, "The Scientific Reason Why Men Ghost You *Exactly* After Three Months," *Cosmopolitan*, May 11, 2021, https://www.cosmopolitan.com/sex-love/a36395867/why-men-ghost-after-three-months/; Zoe Ruderman, "The Move That Makes You Guy-Hot," *Cosmopolitan*, November 29, 2010, https://www.cosmopolitan.com/sex-love/news/a8944/tilted-head-makes-women-attractive-study/. Some of the studies cited by *Maxim*, *Cosmopolitan*, and Reddit include: Jens Kjeldgaard-Christiansen, "Evil Origins: A Darwinian Genealogy of the Popcultural Villain," *Evolutionary*

Behavioral Sciences 10, no. 2 (2016): 109–22; Andrew Galperin et al., "Sexual Regret: Evidence for Evolved Sex Differences," *Archives of Sexual Behavior* 42, no. 7 (November 12, 2012): 1145–61; David C. Matz and Verlin B. Hinsz, "Women's Hair as a Cue to Desired Relationship and Parenting Characteristics," *Journal of Social Psychology* 158, no. 5 (2018): 558–73; Peter Marshall, Amy Bartolacci, and Darren Burke, "Human Face Tilt Is a Dynamic Social Signal That Affects Perceptions of Dimorphism, Attractiveness, and Dominance," *Evolutionary Psychology* 18, no. 1 (January 1, 2020).

38   *long Reddit threads*: Again, there are many examples of evolutionary psychology on Reddit, but one thread where it is easily found is "Evolutionary Psychology / Sociobiology," https://www.reddit.com/r/evopsych/. One study cited in this thread is Rafael Wlodarski and Robin I. Dunbar, "What's in a Kiss? The Effect of Romantic Kissing on Mate Desirability," *Evolutionary Psychology* 12, no. 1 (January 1, 2014).

38   *"High Heels Do Have"*: Thomas Anderson, "High Heels Do Have Power over Men, Study Finds," *Boston Globe*, December 8, 2014, https://www.bostonglobe.com/news/world/2014/12/08/high-heels-have-power-over-men-study-finds/GaOqm3zuAgyrKGcZYZdTSM/story.html?event=event25.

38   *"How Make-up Makes Men"*: University of Stirling, "How Make-up Makes Men Admire but Other Women Jealous," ScienceDaily, www.sciencedaily.com/releases/2016/06/160624155151.htm.

38   *high heels compel a woman*: Farid Pazhoohi et al., "Arching the Back (Lumbar Curvature) as a Female Sexual Proceptivity Signal: An Eye-Tracking Study," *Evolutionary Psychological Science* 4, no. 2 (October 25, 2017): 158–65.

39   *"The Science of Why You're an Ass Man"*: Ali Eaves, "The Science of Why You're an Ass Man," *Men's Health*, September 10, 2014, https://www.menshealth.com/sex-women/a19533624/why-youre-an-ass-man/.

39   *"How the Gluteus Became Maximus"*: Olga Khazan, "How the Gluteus Became Maximus," *Atlantic*, April 2, 2015, https://www.theatlantic.com/health/archive/2015/04/how-the-gluteus-became-maximus/389216/.

39   *"Science Has Finally Figured Out"*: Alanna Núñez, "Science Has Finally Figured Out Why Men Like Big Butts," *Cosmopolitan*, March 6, 2015, https://www.cosmopolitan.com/entertainment/celebs/news/a37405/science-big-butts/.

39 *The experiment was conducted*: David M. G. Lewis et al., "Lumbar Curvature: A Previously Undiscovered Standard of Attractiveness," *Evolution and Human Behavior* 36, no. 5 (September 2015): 345–50.

40 *Paleontologist Stephen Jay Gould described*: Stephen Jay Gould, "The Return of Hopeful Monsters," *Natural History* 86 (June 1, 1977): 22.

40 *evolutionary psychologists often use*: Both Richard Prum and Chris Haufe helped me to understand these critiques of evolutionary psychology, which run very deep among evolutionary biologists.

41 *Another problem with evolutionary psychology*: Amotz Zahavi, "Mate Selection—a Selection for a Handicap," *Journal of Theoretical Biology* 53, no. 1 (1975): pp. 205–214, https://doi.org/10.1016/0022-5193 (75)90111-3.

41 *This may sound counterintuitive*: This information comes from my interview with Chris Haufe.

41 *This mode of thinking*: Stephen J. Gould and Richard C. Lewontin, "The Spandrels of San Marco and the Panglossian Paradigm: A Critique of the Adaptationist Programme," *Proceedings of the Royal Society of London* 205, no. 1161 (September 21, 1979): 581–98.

42 *On a visit to the Peabody Museum*: I visited Dr. Prum at Yale in May 2019 as well as in February 2018 and conducted interviews with him there. The information here also comes from his book *The Evolution of Beauty: How Darwin's Forgotten Theory of Mate Choice Shapes the Animal World—and Us* (New York: Anchor Books, 2017).

43 *But I'm not here to learn about feather pigmentation*: Information in this section comes from my interviews with Dr. Prum and from his book *The Evolution of Beauty*.

45 *In fact, Haufe takes Prum's idea*: This information comes from my interview with Chris Haufe.

LIFE

49 *Life*: The reconstruction of Sarah Baartman's life in this chapter relied heavily on the work of Clifton Crais and Pamela Scully, who wrote the excellent *Sarah Baartman and the Hottentot Venus* (Princeton, NJ: Princeton University Press, 2011), a work widely cited by Baartman scholars. In addition to Crais and Scully, I've also consulted the following texts for general information about Baartman's life and legacy: Anne Fausto-Sterling, "Gender, Race, and Nation: The Comparative Anatomy of 'Hottentot' Women in Europe,

1815–1817," in *Deviant Bodies: Critical Perspectives on Difference in Science and Popular Culture*, eds. Jennifer Terry and Jacqueline Urla (Bloomington: Indiana University Press, 1999), 19–48; Natasha Gordon-Chipembere, *Representation and Black Womanhood: The Legacy of Sarah Baartman* (New York: Palgrave Macmillan, 2016); Janell Hobson, *Venus in the Dark: Blackness and Beauty in Popular Culture* (Oxfordshire: Routledge, 2018); Rachel Holmes, *The Hottentot Venus: The Life and Death of Sarah Baartman* (London: Bloomsbury, 2020); *The Life and Times of Sarah Baartman*, directed by Zola Maseko, Icarus Films, 1998; T. Denean Sharpley-Whiting, *Black Venus: Sexualized Savages, Primal Fears, and Primitive Narratives in French* (Durham, NC: Duke University Press, 1999); and Deborah Willis, ed., *Black Venus 2010: They Called Her "Hottentot"* (Philadelphia: Temple University Press, 2010).

49   *Georges Cuvier was, among other things*: Although most biographies of Cuvier are in French, biographical details of Cuvier are widely available in encyclopedias and scientific histories of the nineteenth century. I relied on scientific encyclopedias from the University of Arizona and the University of California at Berkeley, as well as information in the Crais and Scully biography of Baartman. I also had conversations with philosophers of science Chris Haufe and Kathryn Tabb that helped me understand Cuvier in context.

51   *Her name was Sarah Baartman*: Saartjie is an Afrikaans name and the one that many used for Baartman during her lifetime. She wouldn't come to be called Sarah until she was baptized in Manchester several years after she arrived in England. Although it is nearly impossible to know to what degree any part of her life was choice rather than coercion, it seems in that moment she chose the name Sarah for herself. So it is that name that many scholars choose to call her today. The -tjie suffix is a diminutive with two meanings. It is an endearment used between friends and suggests affection. But it also reduces the size of what it names and suggests enslavement, servitude, subordination. Throughout the history of South Africa, it has been used as a racist form of speech, a way for white people to indicate their authority over Black people. In Baartman's case, there was also likely a mocking in the diminutive: a woman who was known primarily for her full body was being called small every time someone said her name.

52   *The Khoe were*: In some sources, this Indigenous group is called

Khoekhoe, but in conversations with contemporary Khoe people, I was told this is the preferred spelling and the pronunciation is "Quay."

53 *which had become fascinated with butts in general*: This insight comes from Rachel Holmes's biography of Sarah Baartman, *The Hottentot Venus: The Life and Death of Sarah Baartman.*

54 *European Renaissance painting had also commonly represented women's butts*: Sabrina Strings, *Fearing the Black Body: The Racial Origins of Fat Phobia* (New York: New York University Press, 2019).

54 *there were fart clubs*: Edward Ward, *A Compleat and Humorous Account of All the Remarkable Clubs and Societies in the Cities of London and Westminster* (London: 1756), 31–32.

54 *a big-butted woman is merrily taking a bath*: James Gillray, "Sir Richard Worse-than-sly, exposing his wife's bottom;—o fye!," hand-colored etching, March 14, 1782, National Portrait Gallery, London.

55 *Baartman was wearing the same clothes*: Holmes, *Hottentot Venus*, 33.

55 *By the end of the summer*: Crais and Scully, *Sara Baartman and the Hottentot Venus.*

56 *"The Hottentot Venus just arrived from the interior of Africa"*: Holmes, *Hottentot Venus*, 33.

56 *exhibitions featuring albino children and so-called Siamese twins and giants*: For more information on the role of freak shows and human zoos in Europe and the United States, see Bernth Lindfors, *Early African Entertainments Abroad: From the Hottentot Venus to Africa's First Olympians* (Madison: The University of Wisconsin Press, 2014).

56 *She wore no corset or underwear*: Lindfors, *Early African Entertainments Abroad*, 14.

56 *"She is dressed in a color as nearly resembling her skin as possible"*: "The Hottentot Venus," *Times* (London), November 26, 1810, 3.

57 *They very often had her smoke a pipe*: This was both a nod to the long-held stereotype of Khoe women as pipe smokers and a way to further mark Baartman as separate from the women in the crowd. It was rare for English women to smoke pipes at the time, and so this "othered" her in both a gendered and a racial way.

57 *Caesars would lead Baartman around the stage*: "Hottentot Venus," *Times* (London).

58 *"She frequently heaved deep sighs"*: Ibid.

58 *The audience was only too happy to believe Caesars*: Holmes, *Hottentot Venus*, 48.

58 *When abolitionist groups learned of the situation*: Macaulay worked as

an overseer on a sugar plantation in Jamaica before coming to the cause of abolition. In his book on British abolition, *Bury the Chains: Prophets and Rebels in the Fight to Free an Empire's Slaves* (Boston: Mariner Books, 2006), Adam Hoschfield describes him as a priggish and somber evangelical. Along with many others, he actively fought for the abolition of the slave trade, which eventually passed in 1807.

58 *"a foreigner, and a female, too, in worse than Egyptian bondage"*: Holmes, *Hottentot Venus*, 59.

58 *"The Hottentot was produced like a wild beast"*: "The Hottentot Venus," *Times*.

59 *Her defenders—an abolitionist organization called the African Institution*: Holmes, *Hottentot Venus*, 62.

59 *She was shivering onstage*: Harvey Blume, *Africans on Stage: Studies in Ethnological Show Business* (Bloomington: Indiana University Press, 1999).

59 *Until she testified*: The trial transcript is available as an appendix in Martin J. S. Rudwick, *Georges Cuvier, Fossil Bones, and Geological Catastrophes: New Translations and Interpretations of the Primary Texts* (Chicago: University of Chicago Press, 1998).

60 *"whether she preferred either to return to"*: Crais and Scully, *Sara Baartman and the Hottentot Venus*, 100.

60 *"There are persons ready to take her"*: Holmes, *Hottentot Venus*, 62.

60 *"was under no restraint, and she was happy in England"*: "The Hottentot Venus," *Examiner*, December 2, 1810, 768.

61 *"The Venus Hottentot has changed owners"*: Crais and Scully, *Sara Baartman and the Hottentot Venus*, 127.

62 *Cuvier and his colleagues argued*: Holmes, *Hottentot Venus*, 85.

62 *They asked to see Baartman's "organs of generation"*: Sadiah Qureshi, "Displaying Sara Baartman, the 'Hottentot Venus,'" *History of Science* 42 (June 1, 2004): 237–57.

62 *"She kept her apron concealed"*: Rudwick, *Georges Cuvier, Fossil Bones, and Geological Catastrophes*.

63 *"a closer relative of the great apes"*: Crais and Scully, *Sara Baartman and the Hottentot Venus*.

64 *The white, Western understanding of women's butts*: This information comes from my interview with Janell Hobson, professor of women's, gender, and sexuality studies at the University at Albany.

65 *Janell Hobson, professor of women's, gender, and sexuality studies*: Hobson is a Baartman scholar whose book *Venus in the Dark* and papers

"The 'Batty' Politic: Toward an Aesthetic of the Black Female Body," *Hypatia* 18, no. 4 (2003): 87–105, and "Remnants of Venus: Signifying Black Beauty and Sexuality," *WSQ: Women's Studies Quarterly* 46, no. 1-2 (2018): 105–20, were formative to my understanding of Baartman's legacy. I spoke with Hobson twice in the spring of 2021.

65   *"The law basically legitimized rape"*: Many scholars have written on this idea, including Jennifer L. Morgan, "Partus Sequitur Ventrem: Law, Race, and Reproduction in Colonial Slavery," *Small Axe: A Caribbean Journal of Criticism* 22, no. 1 (March 2018): 1–17, and Alys Eve Weinbaum, *Wayward Reproductions: Genealogies of Race and Nation in Transatlantic Modern Thought* (Durham, NC: Duke University Press, 2004).

66   *Her likeness was featured*: Willis, *Black Venus, 2010.*

66   *she was satirized in pantomime*: Untitled article, *Times* (London), January 10, 1811, 2.

66   *As Sander Gilman, a historian*: Sander Gilman's article "Black Bodies, White Bodies: Toward an Iconography of Female Sexuality in Late Nineteenth-Century Art, Medicine, and Literature," *Critical Inquiry* 12, no. 1 (1985), is a foundational piece of scholarship on Baartman and the way that nineteenth-century scientists racialized and sexualized the butt.

66   *"Female sexuality [became] linked to the image of the buttocks"*: Gilman, "Black Bodies, White Bodies," 219.

67   *Baartman wasn't the only large-butted Khoe woman*: Lindfors, *Early African Entertainments Abroad.*

LEGACY

69   *In his 1853 book*: Francis Galton, *Narrative of an Explorer in Tropical South Africa: Being an Account of a Visit to Damaraland in 1851*, 4th ed. (London: Ward, Lock & Co., 1891), 54.

69   *"turning herself about to all points of the compass"*: Ibid.

69   *Although it was primarily the butts of Khoe women*: All the information about eugenics in this chapter comes from the following sources: I interviewed Alexandra Minna Stern, professor of history, American culture, and women's and gender studies, and associate dean for the humanities at the University of Michigan, about the history of eugenics and her book *Eugenic Nation: Faults and Frontiers of Better Breeding in Modern America* (Oakland: University of

California Press, 2016). I also spoke with Kate O'Connor, PhD student in American culture at the University of Michigan, who studies the history and legacy of eugenic sterilization. In addition, I drew from Adam Cohen's book *Imbeciles: The Supreme Court, American Eugenics, and the Sterilization of Carrie Buck* (New York: Penguin Press, 2017), and Lulu Miller's *Why Fish Don't Exist: A Story of Loss, Love, and the Hidden Order of Life* (New York: Simon & Schuster, 2021).

69   *that white people of European descent were the most evolved species*: The information in these pages on classification of whiteness comes from Nell Painter's *The History of White People* (New York: W. W. Norton, 2011), a book that was foundational to my thinking about whiteness and race in this book.

71   *In 1836,* Godey's *hired an editor*: Sabrina Strings, *Fearing the Black Body: The Racial Origins of Fat Phobia* (New York: New York University Press, 2019).

71   *the butt had become a proxy*: Gilman, "Black Bodies, White Bodies," 219.

71   *This association between vulva and butt*: There are ways that the butt and the labia are still linked today. Perhaps the best example is with the peach emoji, which can be a way to represent either the butt or the labia, although it is most commonly associated with the butt.

72   *anthropologist Abele de Blasio advanced this association*: Ibid., 229.

72   *physician and reformer Havelock Ellis*: The information and quotes in these paragraphs come from Havelock Ellis, *Studies in the Psychology of Sex*, vol. 4 (Philadelphia: Butterworth-Heinemann, 1942). Sander Gilman also points to Ellis in his analysis in "Black Bodies, White Bodies."

74   *in the landmark 1927 Supreme Court decision* Buck v. Bell: In 1927, in an eight-to-one decision, the US Supreme Court ordered that Carrie Buck, whom it called feeble-minded, be sterilized under the 1924 Virginia Eugenical Sterilization Act. *Buck v. Bell* set a legal precedent that states could sterilize inmates of public institutions. The court argued that imbecility, epilepsy, and feeble-mindedness are hereditary, and that inmates should be prevented from passing these defects on to their children. Adam Cohen's *Imbeciles* discusses this case further.

75   *As the racial scientists of the nineteenth century*: This section about the repatriation of Sarah Baartman's remains comes from the Crais

and Scully biography as well as Hershini Bhana Young, "Returning to Hankey: Sarah Baartman and Endless Repatriations," in *Illegible Will: Coercive Spectacles of Labor in South Africa and the Diaspora* (Durham, NC: Duke University Press, 2017), 29–72. I also relied on the following contemporaneous accounts: Suzanne Daley, "Exploited in Life and Death, South African to Go Home," *New York Times*, January 30, 2002, https://www.nytimes.com/2002/01/30/world/exploited -in-life-and-death-south-african-to-go-home.html; Obed Zilwa, "S. Africa Buries Remains of 'Sarah,'" AP News, August 9, 2002, https://apnews.com/article/b92223d9da4a13252640e2340899ef1a. In addition, I interviewed Nomusa Makhubu, associate professor of art history and visual culture at the University of Cape Town, about Baartman's legacy in South Africa and South African feminism.

BIGNESS

81   *The effect was that the bustled woman*: Jessica Glasscock, "Nineteenth-Century Silhouette and Support," Metropolitan Museum of Art, October 2004, https://www.metmuseum.org/toah/hd/19sil/hd_19sil .htm.

82   *"The existence of a man-made object"*: Jules David Prown, "Mind in Matter: An Introduction to Material Culture Theory and Method," *Winterthur Portfolio* 17, no. 1 (1982): 1–19.

83   *I expected the archives of the Victoria & Albert*: I visited the Victoria & Albert archive and museum in the summer of 2018. Information about the Victoria &Albert Museum and much of the information about historical fashion comes from their historical archives and collections.

85   *Wearing lots of petticoats*: Kat Eschner, "Although Less Deadly Than Crinolines, Bustles Were Still a Pain in the Behind," *Smithsonian*, April 21, 2017.

85   *Enter the bustle*: Basic information on the bustle can be found in a number of places, including C. Willett and Phillis Cunnington, *The History of Underclothes* (New York: Dover, 2013); Karen Bowman, *Corsets and Codpieces: A History of Outrageous Fashion, from Roman Times to the Modern Era* (New York: Skyhorse Publishing, 2016); and Wendy Tomlinson, "All About the Bustle," Grey Roots Museum & Archives, https://greyroots.com/story/all-about -bustle.

85 *the London* Times *was said to be*: Mary Vivian Hughes, *A London Child of the Seventies* (London: Oxford University Press, 1934), 84.

87 *There are also materialist theories*: The information in this paragraph comes from an interview with Edwina Ehrman, a curator at the Victoria & Albert.

87 *Another theory suggests*: Information in this paragraph comes primarily from an email exchange with fashion historian Heather McNaughton at Truly Victorian.

87 *The bell shape of a crinoline*: Glasscock, "Nineteenth-Century Silhouette and Support."

88 *The day after my trek to the bustle archives*: Information in the rest of this section comes from my interviews with Edwina Ehrman at the Victoria & Albert.

89 *Previously, during the Renaissance*: This theory of Victorian underwear comes from Casey Finch, "'Hooked and Buttoned Together': Victorian Underwear and Representations of the Female Body," *Victorian Studies* 34, no. 3 (1991): 337–63.

89 *"Bustles! What are bustles?"*: "A Short Chapter on Bustles," *Irish Penny Journal* 1, no. 18 (October 31, 1840): 140–41.

89 *In 1814, when Baartman*: The history of Sarah Baartman and the "Hottentot Venus" in this chapter comes primarily from my interviews with Janell Hobson; Holmes, *Hottentot Venus*; and Crais and Scully, *Sara Baartman and the Hottentot Venus*.

89 The Hottentot Venus; or, The Hatred of Frenchwomen: Emmanuel Théaulon de Lambert, Achille d'Artois, and Nicolas Brazier, *The Hottentot Venus; or, The Hatred of Frenchwomen*, November 19, 1814.

91 *"everything but the burden"*: Greg Tate et al., *Everything but the Burden: What White People Are Taking from Black Culture* (New York: Broadway Books, 2003).

91 *In a 1991 interview with critic Lisa Jones*: Lisa Jones, "Venus Envy," *Village Voice* 36, no. 28 (July 9, 1991): 36.

92 *It was mostly men*: Eschner, "Although Less Deadly Than Crinolines."

92 *It was mostly women*: Nancy L. Green, "Women and Immigrants in the Sweatshop: Categories of Labor Segmentation Revisited," *Comparative Studies in Society and History* 38, no. 3 (1996): 414.

92 *Enslaved people in the American South*: Madelyn Shaw, "Slave Cloth and Clothing Slaves: Craftsmanship, Commerce, and Industry," *Journal of Early Southern Decorative Arts*, 42, 2021.

93   *miners in Pennsylvania chiseled*: Arthur Cecil Bining, "The Iron Plan-
      tations of Early Pennsylvania," *Pennsylvania Magazine of History and
      Biography* 57, no. 2 (1933): 117–37.

SMALLNESS

94   *When Gordon Conway*: All information in the following section about
      Gordon Conway and her mother, Tommie Conway, comes from Raye
      Virginia Allen's *Gordon Conway: Fashioning a New Woman* (Austin:
      University of Texas Press, 1997). In addition to offering an excellent
      biography of the Conways, it also provides reproductions of many of
      Gordon Conway's illustrations, which are described throughout this
      section.

94   *As the stiff, cage-like crust of the bustle*: Glasscock, "Nineteenth-
      Century Silhouette and Support."

97   *they were flappers*: Unless otherwise noted, information about flappers
      in this chapter comes from Linda Simon, *Lost Girls: The Invention
      of the Flapper* (London: Reaktion Books, 2017), and Joshua Zeitz,
      *Flapper: A Madcap Story of Sex, Style, Celebrity, and the Women Who
      Made America Modern* (New York: Three Rivers Press, 2006).

98   *took hold with remarkable ferocity*: Anne Hollander, *Seeing Through
      Clothes* (Berkeley: University of California Press, 1993), 155–56.

98   *As one scholar put it*: Kenneth A. Yellis, "Prosperity's Child: Some
      Thoughts on the Flapper," *American Quarterly* 21, no. 1 (1969): 46.

99   *At the end of the nineteenth century*: Bruce McComiskey and Cyn-
      thia Ryan, *City Comp: Identities, Spaces, Practices* (Albany, New York:
      State University of New York Press, 2003).

99   *after decades of anxiety*: Bernarr Macfadden, *The Power and Beauty of
      Superb Womanhood* (New York: The Physical Culture Publications
      Co., 1901).

99   *It began with Paul Poiret*: Information about Poiret and Chanel can
      be found in Linda Simon's *Lost Girls* and Joshua Zeitz's *Flappers* in
      addition to Harold Koda and Andrew Bolton, "Paul Poiret (1879–
      1944)," The Costume Institute, September 2008, https://www.metmu
      seum.org/toah/hd/poir/hd_poir.htm, and Hollander, *Seeing Through
      Clothes*, 156.

100   *"I waged war upon it"*: A well-known quote from Poiret that is quoted
      in Zeitz, *Flapper*, 150.

101   *In the 1925 article "Flapper Jane"*: Bruce Bliven, "Flapper Jane," *The

New Republic, September 9, 1925, https://newrepublic.com/article /113130/bruce-bliven-interviews-flapper.

101 *Others would describe those who*: Emily Spivack, "The History of the Flapper, Part 3: The Rectangular Silhouette," *Smithsonian*, February 19, 2013.

102 *For more than a century*: Hollander, *Seeing Through Clothes*, 155–56.

102 *She is also very much a woman in motion*: This idea also comes from Anne Hollander's *Seeing Through Clothes*.

103 *But even if the typical story of the buttless, fashionable*: Information in this paragraph comes from Valerie Steele's *The Corset: A Cultural History* (New Haven: Yale University Press, 2007), and her other book *Fashion and Eroticism: Ideals of Feminine Beauty from the Victorian Era Through the Jazz Age* (Oxford: Oxford University Press), 1985.

103 *In a study from 1912*: "Dieting, Swaying, Hopping to Make Over the Hip Line," *Washington Post*, December 4, 1910.

104 *Bathroom scales*: Information regarding the study of women's perceptions of their body as well as popular body monitoring and dieting habits comes from Simon, *Lost Girls*, 205–6.

104 *referenced an imagined idea of Japan*: Nancy Hass, "How Japonisme Forever Changed the Course of Western Design," *New York Times*, February 11, 2021, https://www.nytimes.com/2021/02/11/t-magazine /japonisme-paris-western-design.html.

105 *The Japonisme phenomenon ballooned*: Adam Geczy, *Fashion and Orientalism: Dress, Textiles and Culture from the 17th to the 21st Century* (London: Bloomsbury Academic, 2013), 134.

105 *"flat terrain of the cloth"*: Harold Koda and Richard Martin, "Orientalism: Visions of the East in Western Dress," The Costume Institute, October 2004, https://www.metmuseum.org/toah/hd/orie /hd_orie.htm.

105 *In 1912, for example*: This evening coat can be found at https://www .metmuseum.org/art/collection/search/156074.

105 *Page Act of 1875*: The Page Act of 1875, Public Law 43-141, US Statutes at Large 18 (1875): 477–78.

106 *arguably one of the most famous flappers*: Information and analysis of Josephine Baker comes from the following sources: Mae Henderson and Charlene B. Regester, eds., *The Josephine Baker Critical Reader: Selected Writings on the Entertainer and Activist* (Jefferson, NC: McFarland & Company, 2017) (NB: I relied heavily on the

introduction, written by Mae Henderson and Charlene B. Regester, and Michael Borshuk's chapter "An Intelligence of the Body: Disruptive Parody Through Dance in the Early Performances of Josephine Baker"); Marcel Sauvage, *Les memoires de Josephine Baker* (Paris: Editions Correa, 1949); Jean-Claude Baker and Chris Chase, *Josephine: The Hungry Heart* (New York: Cooper Square Press, 2001), 7; Anne Anlin Cheng, *Second Skin: Josephine Baker and the Modern Surface* (Oxford, UK: Oxford University Press, 2013).

106 *"to find freedom"*: Quote comes from *Josephine Baker: The First Black Superstar*, directed by Suzanne Phillips, BBC Four, aired July 9, 2009.

106 *In the midtwenties, Paris was a hub for Black American artists and intellectuals*: Information on Black Paris in the 1920s comes from the following sources: Brent Hayes Edwards, *The Practice of Diaspora: Literature, Translation, and the Rise of Black Internationalism* (Cambridge, MA: Harvard University Press, 2003); Tyler Stovall, *Paris Noir: African Americans in the City of Light* (North Charleston, SC: CreateSpace, 2012); and a talk by Richard Long in April 2014 about the Harlem Renaissance and Paris, which I accessed on YouTube at https://www.youtube.com/watch?v=cGJ9x_PK_pY&t=3307s.

106 *in New York City, flappers like*: Simon, *Lost Girls*.

107 *According to her memoir*: Baker's memoir was dictated to her friend Marcel Sauvage and is in French. I worked with a translator to read the cited section. Sauvage, *Memoires de Josephine Baker*.

107 *"dancing with the hips"*: Sauvage, *Memoires de Josephine Baker*.

107 *In one account of the first performance*: Quotes in this paragraph that describe the reaction to Baker's performance come from Baker and Chase, *Josephine: The Hungry Heart*, 7.

108 *In L'Art Vivant*: Baker and Chase, *Josephine: The Hungry Heart*, 7.

108 *"We've been hiding our butts"*: This famous quote from Baker is often cited in translation from Phyllis Rose and Jazz Cleopatra, *Josephine Baker in Her Time* (New York: Vintage, 1991). I went to the original source, which is the memoir she wrote with Marcel Sauvage, and had a translator look at it again. The difference is slight but meaningful.

108 *"Like Stravinsky's* The Rite of Spring*"*: *Josephine Baker: The First Black Superstar*.

108 *There was even a Josephine Baker doll*: Richard Long, lecture about
     the Harlem Renaissance and Paris.
109 *"All of these moves that in the European"*: *Josephine Baker: The First
     Black Superstar.*

CREATION

115 *Norma's butt*: I first learned about Norma and Normman in a conver-
     sation with Kate O'Connor, a PhD student at the University of Mich-
     igan doing work on the history of eugenics in that state. I've since
     consulted the following sources on the statues: Peter Cryle and Eliz-
     abeth Stephens, *Normality: A Critical Genealogy* (Chicago: University
     of Chicago Press, 2018); Julian B. Carter, *The Heart of Whiteness: Nor-
     mal Sexuality and Race in America, 1880–1940* (Durham, NC: Duke
     University Press, 2007); Dahlia S. Cambers, "The Law of Averages 1:
     Norman and Norma," *Cabinet Magazine* 15 (2004); and Mary Cof-
     fey, "The Law of Averages 2: American Adonis," *Cabinet Magazine*
     15 (2004). Joe Tait, archivist at the Cleveland Museum of Natural
     History, helped me unearth much of the primary source material in
     this chapter. I also spoke with Mary Coffey about her essay "American
     Adonis," published in *Popular Eugenics: National Efficiency and Amer-
     ican Mass Culture in the 1930s* (Athens: Ohio University Press, 2006).
115 *twenty-nine inches across*: Measurements of Normman and Norma,
     1943, Dickinson-Belskie Files, HealthSpace Cleveland Collection,
     Cleveland Museum of Natural History Archives, Cleveland, Ohio.
115 *If* Birthing Series *showed viewers*: Rose Holz, "The 1939 Dickinson-
     Belskie Birth Series Sculptures: The Rise of Modern Visions of
     Pregnancy, the Roots of Modern Pro-Life Imagery, and Dr. Dick-
     inson's Religious Case for Abortion," *Papers in Women's and Gender
     Studies* 9 (2017): 5, https://digitalcommons.unl.edu/cgi/viewcontent
     .cgi?article=1010&context=womenstudiespapers.
116 *a project of American eugenics*: As in chapter 2, all the information re-
     ferring to eugenics in this section comes from the following sources:
     my interview with Alexandra Minna Stern, professor of history,
     American culture, and women's and gender studies, and associate
     dean for the humanities at the University of Michigan, about the his-
     tory of eugenics, and her book *Eugenic Nation: Faults and Frontiers
     of Better Breeding in Modern America* (Oakland: University of Cali-
     fornia Press, 2016). I also spoke with Kate O'Connor, PhD student

in American culture at the University of Michigan, who studies the history and legacy of eugenic sterilization. In addition, I drew from Adam Cohen's book *Imbeciles*, Lulu Miller's *Why Fish Don't Exist*, and Nell Painter's *The History of White People*.

117 *Five years earlier*: Archivist Emily Marsh at the USDA archives wrote an article about O'Brien that is available on the archives' website: Emily Marsh, "Apron Strings and Kitchen Sinks: The USDA Bureau of Home Economics," US Department of Agriculture, https://www .nal.usda.gov/exhibits/ipd/apronsandkitchens/about. I spoke with Marsh, and she pointed me to several primary sources about the study and helped to contextualize it in the broader history of home economics. For more information on the history of home economics, see Cornell University's home economics archive: https://digital.library .cornell.edu/collections/hearth/about.

118 *"There are no standards"*: All the information in the following paragraphs regarding Ruth O'Brien come from her book *Women's Measurements for Garment and Pattern Construction* (Washington, DC: US Department of Agriculture, 1941), 1–73. I primarily used the following chapters: "Foreword," "Measuring Procedures," and "The Schedule."

119 *In his article about Norma and Normman*: Harry L. Shapiro, "A Portrait of the American People," *Natural History* 54 (1945): 248, https:// archive.org/details/naturalhistory54newy/page/248/mode/2up.

121 *interviewed clergy*: Newspaper clipping of Josephine Robertson, "Church Interests Itself in Norma," September 19, 1945, Dickinson-Belskie Files, 1945 Norma Contest scrapbook, HealthSpace Cleveland Collection, Cleveland Museum of Natural History Archives, Cleveland, Ohio.

121 *doctors*: Newspaper clipping of Josephine Robertson, "Norma's Husband Better Be Good," September 15, 1945, Dickinson-Belskie Files, 1945 Norma Contest scrapbook, HealthSpace Cleveland Collection, Cleveland Museum of Natural History Archives, Cleveland, Ohio.

121 *educators*: Newspaper clipping of Josephine Robertson, "Norma's Gym Suit in '90s Covered All," September 12, 1945, Dickinson-Belskie Files, 1945 Norma Contest scrapbook, HealthSpace Cleveland Collection, Cleveland Museum of Natural History Archives, Cleveland, Ohio.

121 *"typical American girl"*: Newspaper clipping of Josephine Robertson, "Our 'Norma' Is Larger Than Her Grandma," 1945, Dickinson-Belskie Files, 1945 Norma Contest scrapbook, HealthSpace

Cleveland Collection, Cleveland Museum of Natural History Archives, Cleveland, Ohio.

121 *talked to artists*: Newspaper clipping of Josephine Robertson, "Norma Is Appealing Model in Opinion of City's Artists," September 15, 1945, Dickinson-Belskie Files, 1945 Norma Contest scrapbook, HealthSpace Cleveland Collection, Cleveland Museum of Natural History Archives, Cleveland, Ohio.

121 *physical fitness instructors*: Newspaper clipping of Robertson, "Norma's Gym Suit in '90s Covered All."

121 *who belonged inside the category of normal*: Although eugenicists were often invested in theories that situated white people as higher than Black and Asian people in a racial hierarchy, their primary racial interest was in policing whiteness itself. As described in the previous chapter, there were myriad ways that scientists classified and ranked people from different parts of the world whom we would call white today. In many of these systems, those considered "less white" were considered more likely to be criminals or feeble-minded, and so the eugenic justification for being suspicious of these groups was part of the larger project of ridding the world of criminality and disability.

122 *The form published by the newspaper*: Newspaper clipping of Robertson, "Norma Is Appealing Model."

122 *Some women measured themselves at home*: Newspaper clippings of tips on how to measure yourself for Norma Contest, September 10, 1945, Dickinson-Belskie Files, 1945 Norma Contest scrapbook, HealthSpace Cleveland Collection, Cleveland Museum of Natural History Archives, Cleveland, Ohio.

122 *On the last day of the contest alone*: Newspaper clipping of Josephine Robertson, "3,700 Send Measurements in Ohio Search for Norma," September 20, 1945, Dickinson-Belskie Files, 1945 Norma Contest scrapbook, HealthSpace Cleveland Collection, Cleveland Museum of Natural History Archives, Cleveland, Ohio.

122 *The following day, the forty entrants*: Newspaper clipping of Josephine Robertson, "Theater Cashier, 23, Wins Title of 'Norma,' Besting 3,863 Entries," September 23, 1945, Dickinson-Belskie Files, 1945 Norma Contest scrapbook, HealthSpace Cleveland Collection, Cleveland Museum of Natural History Archives, Cleveland, Ohio.

122 *The woman who came the closest*: Ibid.

PROLIFERATION

125 *For all its power and staggering profits*: I have previously researched the history of sizes as part of an article I wrote for the *Paris Review* on *Jumpsuit*, an art project created by the Rational Dress Society (Heather Radke, "The Jumpsuit That Will Replace All Clothes Forever," *Paris Review*, March 21, 2018, https://www.theparisreview .org/blog/2018/03/21/the-jumpsuit-that-will-replace-all-clothes-for ever/). One of the co-creators of *Jumpsuit*, Abigail Glaum-Lathbury, also helped me understand the history of size in a series of interviews I conducted specifically for this chapter. Additionally, I looked at Julia Felsenthal, "A Size 2 Is a Size 2 Is a Size 8," *Slate*, January 25, 2012, https://slate.com/culture/2012/01/clothing-sizes-get ting-bigger-why-our-sizing-system-makes-no-sense.html; Laura Stampler, "The Bizarre History of Clothing Sizes," *Time*, October 23, 2014, https://time.com/3532014/women-clothing-sizes-history/; and Gimlet Media, "When Did Pants Become a Thing?," *Every Little Thing* podcast, April 8, 2019, https://gimletmedia.com/shows /every-little-thing/n8hw4d. I also consulted Sarah-Grace Heller, *A Cultural History of Dress and Fashion in the Medieval Age* (London, England: Bloomsbury Academic, 2018).

125 *a truly monumental shift*: Alli Farago, "The Textile Industry During the Industrial Revolution," globalEDGE, October 18, 2017, https:// globaledge.msu.edu/blog/post/54483/the-textile-industry-during -the-industrial-revolution.

125 *Wealthy women hired*: Ava Baron and Susan E. Klepp, "'If I Didn't Have My Sewing Machine . . .': Women and Sewing Machine Technology," in *A Needle, a Bobbin, a Strike: Women Needleworkers in America*, eds. Joan M. Jensen and Sue Davidson (Philadelphia: Temple University Press, 2018), and "History of Sweatshops: 1880–1940," National Museum of American History, August 9, 2021, https://americanhistory.si.edu/sweatshops/history-1880-1940.

126 *did not markedly improve*: Grace Rogers Cooper, *The Sewing Machine: Its Invention and Development* (Washington, DC: Smithsonian Institution Press, 1976), 57–58.

129 *they often call on one in particular*: In addition to Abigail's interviews, I've looked at the following sources to better understand the way contemporary sizing works: Suzanne Kapner, "It's Not You. Clothing Sizes Are Broken," *Wall Street Journal*, December 16, 2019,

https://www.wsj.com/articles/its-not-you-clothing-sizes-are-broken
-11576501384; and Daniel Soyer, "Garment Sweatshops, Then and
Now," *New Labor Forum* 4 (1999): 35–46.

129 *Natasha Wagner, one of the fashion industry's most in-demand denim fit
models*: I interviewed Wagner in September 2020 and all of the biographical information comes from that interview, as does the information about the process that is used for fit models. I have confirmed
these facts with Glaum-Lathbury as well. Natasha Wagner has been
featured in several fashion outlets, including *Vogue* (Olivia Fleming, "Meet the Model Whose Bottom Is Shaping a Nation," *Vogue*,
June 29, 2015, https://www.vogue.com/article/best-jeans-butt-model
-natasha-wagner), Refinery29 (Liza Darwing, "This Denim Model
Literally Has the Best Butt in the Business," Refinery29, June 30, 2015,
https://www.refinery29.com/en-us/2015/06/90010/jeans-model
-natasha-wagner), and WNYC (Jenna Flanagan, "Fashion Fit Models: Rarely Seen but Essential to the Runway," WNYC, February
17, 2011, https://www.wnyc.org/story/115002-behind-stage-fashion
-week-fit-models/). I've drawn on these sources, as well as an interview with Wagner, for this section.

130 *"If you fit with someone who is too curvy"*: Fleming, "Meet the Model."

RESISTANCE

134 *Like almost everything else I encountered*: I attended the Iconic Drag
Competition in the fall of 2019 on the recommendation of Vincent
Cuccia and Alex Bartlett of Planet Pepper.

136 *On a hot July day in 2019*: I interviewed Cuccia and Bartlett in 2019,
and the interviews I used in this section were conducted in their
apartment.

140 *But femininity is not a singular experience*: The analysis of gender and
drag in these paragraphs comes from decades of work done by scholars including Judith Butler, José Esteban Muñoz, and Jack Halberstam. I audited a class with Halberstam in 2019 to help round out my
knowledge on queer performance and have drawn on what I learned
in that class both here and in other sections of the book.

141 *"One is not born, but rather becomes, woman"*: Simone de Beauvoir,
The Second Sex, trans. Constance Borde and Sheila Malovany-
Chevallier (London: Vintage Classics, 2011), 330.

141 *gender as a construction and a performance, rather than as a stable fact*:

Judith Butler, *Gender Trouble: Feminism and the Subversion of Identity* (Oxfordshire: Routledge Classics, 2006).

STEEL

145 *In the first panel of a comic strip from 1994*: Jack Ohman, "Mixed Media," *Denver Post*, May 18, 1984.

145 *It was spoofed on* Saturday Night Live: Brenda Herrman, "'Buns of Steel,'" *Chicago Tribune*, February 23, 1993.

146 *It took me six months to track Greg Smithey down*: The biographical information about Greg Smithey comes primarily from interviews with him I conducted in August 2020. As mentioned, some of the stories and facts about his life weren't possible to verify, but I've done my best to confirm his story when possible.

147 *he claims he trained Sarah Palin*: I couldn't find any evidence on this either way.

147 *According to the website he maintains now*: The website Smithey currently maintains is http://www.originalbunsofsteeldvd.com/. *The Original Buns of Steel* is available for purchase there and also readily available on YouTube.

148 *Throughout the 1960s and '70s*: The information about the history of exercise before 1970 came from my interview with New School professor Natalia Petrzela in June 2020 and Jonathan Black, *Making the American Body: The Remarkable Saga of the Men and Women Whose Feats, Feuds, and Passions Shaped Fitness History* (Lincoln: University of Nebraska Press, 2013), 39.

149 *By the late 1970s*: The idea that the rise of neoliberalism changed the way many Americans thought about their bodies is a fairly common one that comes up in many histories of exercise and came up in my conversation with Dr. Petrzela. It is a complex and difficult thing to define neoliberalism, but I've done my best here with the help of the *Stanford Encyclopedia of Philosophy* and David Harvey's *A Brief History of Neoliberalism* (Oxford: Oxford University Press, 2005).

150 *in 1968, an air force physician*: Kenneth H. Cooper, *Aerobics* (Lanham, Maryland: M. Evans, 1968).

150 *Until that point, most Americans associated*: Information on and analysis of the history of aerobics comes primarily from Cooper's *Aerobics* and also Black, *Making the American Body*; Elizabeth Kagan and Margaret Morse, "The Body Electronic: Aerobic Exercise on Video:

Women's Search for Empowerment and Self-Transformation," *TDR* 32, no. 4 (1988): 164–80; Claire Elaine Rasmussen, "Fit to Be Tied," in *The Autonomous Animal Self-Governance and the Modern Subject* (Minneapolis: University of Minnesota Press, 2011), 137–66; Jenny Ellison, "Not Jane Fonda: Aerobics for Fat Women Only," in *The Fat Studies Reader*, eds. Esther Rothblum and Sondra Solovay (New York: New York University Press, 2009), 312–19; and interviews with Natalia Petrzela.

152 *Jane Fonda, the daughter of screen icon Henry Fonda*: Biographical information about Jane Fonda is readily available in many places, including her own memoir. One of the best sources is the documentary *Jane Fonda in Five Acts*, a 2018 film directed by Susan Lacy and released by HBO. Information on Jane Fonda and her work as an aerobics icon also comes from the sources listed above on the history of aerobics.

153 *as part of a fundraising effort for the Campaign for Economic Democracy*: Robert Lindsey, "Jane Fonda's Exercise Salons Aiding Her Husband's Candidacy," *New York Times*, May 2, 1982, 24.

153 Jane Fonda's Workout Book: Jane Fonda and Steve Schapiro, *Jane Fonda's Workout Book* (London, England: Allen Lane/Penguin Press, 1981).

154 *"a spit and a prayer"*: This quote comes from *Jane Fonda in Five Acts*.

155 *"an Alaska feel"*: Linda Sievers, "Videos to Sweat by Offer Convenient Way to Work," *Anchorage Daily News*, January 15, 1998.

156 *Maier found just that in Tamilee Webb*: The biographical information about Tamilee Webb comes primarily from an interview with her I conducted in June 2020.

160 *It is a fantasy of both hyper-responsibility*: Kagan and Morse, "The Body Electronic," 167, 173–74.

JOY

162 *When I asked Rosezella Canty-Letsome*: The life histories of Rosezella Canty-Letsome and Deb Burgard come from interviews I conducted with them as part of my research in May and March 2020, respectively. Additionally, Jenny Ellison, curator of sport and leisure at the Canadian Museum of History, told me about the fat fitness movement in the Bay Area in an interview with her. I also consulted her scholarship on the subject: "Not Jane Fonda," 312–19, and "Fat

Activism and Physical Activity," in *Routledge Handbook of Critical Obesity Studies*, eds. Michael Gard, Darren Powell, and José Tenorio (London: Routledge, 2021), helped to put that movement in a broader context.

166   *In* Great Shape, *a fitness guide for large women*: Deb Burgard and Pat Lyons, *Great Shape: The First Exercise Guide for Large Women* (New York: Arbor House, 1988).

169   *attracted national media attention*: Marilyn Schwartz, "The 'Plump and Proud' Crowd Is Having Its Day in a Big Way," *Houston Chronicle*, March 27, 1987, and Jane E. Brody, "HEALTH; Personal Health," *New York Times*, September 8, 1988, sec. B, p. 12.

KATE

173   *in 1991, Moss shot*: Calvin Klein, Calvin Klein Jeans advertisement, 1991.

174   *"I didn't want these girls"*: Klein's quotes are from George Wayne, "Calvin Klein," *IRIS Covet Book*, 2017.

175   *In the late nineteenth century, the sickly, tubercular body*: Susan Sontag's "Illness as Metaphor" offers a full accounting of the many ways tuberculosis, and later cancer, became linked to morality and aesthetics. For more information, see Susan Sontag, *Illness as Metaphor* (New York: Farrar, Straus and Giroux, 1978).

175   *"When I was young, I could not have accepted"*: The quote from poet Théophile Gautier and more information on the culture of consumption and sickness in poetry can be found in David M. Moran, "At the Deathbed of Consumptive Art," *Emerging Infectious Diseases* 8, no. 11 (2002): 1353–58, doi:10.3201/eid0811.020549.

175   *and sparked headlines like*: Louise Lague, "How Thin Is Too Thin?," *People*, September 20, 1993, https://people.com/archive/cover-story-how-thin-is-too-thin-vol-40-no-12/; Mark Henderson, "Heroin: A Model Way to Die," *Sunday Star-Times* (New Zealand), June 15, 1997; John Leo, "The Perfect Embodiment of Degraded Pop Culture," *Seattle Times*, June 7, 1994, https://archive.seattletimes.com/archive/?date=19940607&slug=1914393.

175   *in 1997, President Bill Clinton publicly decried*: Christopher S. Wren, "Clinton Calls Fashion Ads' 'Heroin Chic' Deplorable," *New York Times*, May 22, 1997, https://www.nytimes.com/1997/05/22/us/clinton-calls-fashion-ads-heroin-chic-deplorable.html.

176 *When Moss posed with Mark Wahlberg in a Calvin Klein underwear ad*:
     Herb Ritts, *Kate Moss & Mark Wahlberg—Calvin Klein*, photograph,
     1992.

MIX

177 *2. Mix*: I consulted the following sources on the history of hip-hop,
     women and hip-hop, and the butt in hip-hop for this chapter: Jeff
     Chang, *Can't Stop Won't Stop: A History of the Hip-Hop Generation*
     (New York: St. Martin's Press, 2007); Margaret Hunter and Kath-
     leen Soto, "Women of Color in Hip Hop: The Pornographic Gaze,"
     Race, Gender & Class 16, no. 1-2 (2009): 170–91; Joan Morgan, "Fly-
     Girls, Bitches, and Hoes: Notes of a Hip-Hop Feminist," *Social Text*
     45 (1995): 151–57; Evelyn McDonnell, "The Booty Myth," *Medium*,
     November 10, 2014, https://medium.com/cuepoint/the-booty-myth
     -5d524c2ab49d; Janell Hobson, "The 'Batty' Politic: Toward an Aes-
     thetic of the Black Female Body," *Hypatia* 18, no. 4 (2003): 87–105;
     Julia S. Jordan-Zachery, "Inscribing and the Black (Female) Body
     Politic," in *Shadow Bodies* (New Brunswick, NJ: Rutgers Univer-
     sity Press, 2017), 30–51; Bettina L. Love, "Body Image, Relation-
     ships, Desirability, and Ass," *Counterpoints* 399 (2012): 78–87; Tricia
     Rose, "Black Texts/Black Contexts," in *Poetry and Cultural Studies:
     A Reader* (Champaign: University of Illinois Press, 2009, 2009), 194.

177 *"Oh—my—God, Becky, look at her butt"*: Sir Mix-A-Lot, "Baby Got
     Back," 1992, music video, 4:13.

178 *"There was one event that was irritating the shit out of me"*: All quotes
     by Anthony Ray (Sir Mix-A-Lot), Patti Galluzzi, Amy Dorsey-Rivas,
     and Adam Bernstein can be found in a 2013 *Vulture* interview with
     Anthony Ray et al.: Rob Kemp, "'And I Cannot Lie': The Oral His-
     tory of Sir Mix-a-Lot's 'Baby Got Back' Video," *Vulture*, Decem-
     ber 19, 2013, https://www.vulture.com/2013/12/sir-mix-a-lot-baby
     -got-back-video-oral-history.html.

181 *both conservative groups like Tipper Gore's*: Research on the backlash
     to "Baby Got Back" by the PMRC and WAP uses Kory Grow, "PM-
     RC's 'Filthy 15': Where Are They Now?," *Rolling Stone*, Septem-
     ber 17, 2015, https://www.rollingstone.com/music/music-lists/pmrcs
     -filthy-15-where-are-they-now-60601/; Gavin M. Ratcliffe, "Paren-
     tal Advisory, Explicit Content: Music Censorship and the Amer-
     ican Culture Wars," (honors paper, Oberlin College, 2016); and

Christopher Swan, "MTV: Advertisers Carry the Clout. Under Fire for Snarl-and-Seduction Imagery, Producers Leaning Toward Less Threat, but More Flesh," *Christian Science Monitor*, May 8, 1985, https://www.csmonitor.com/1985/0508/lmtv2-f.html.

182 *"That video does not pass the Bechdel Test"*: All quotes from Kyra Gaunt come from my phone interview with Kyra Gaunt (assistant professor of music and theater, University at Albany), August 6, 2020. For my research for this chapter and the next, I also relied on Gaunt's scholarship, particularly Kyra D. Gaunt, "YouTube, Twerking & You: Context Collapse and the Handheld Co-presence of Black Girls and Miley Cyrus," *Journal of Popular Music Studies* 27, no. 3 (2015): 244–73.

183 *Politicians in the 1990s were also busily creating policy*: Stephanie Cornish, "Welfare Reform Garnered for Black Women a Hard Time and a Bad Name," *AFR: The Black Media Authority*, March 18, 2015, https://www.afro.com/welfare-reform-garnered-for-black-women-a-hard-time-and-a-bad-name/. The employment and wage gap statistics were found in Valerie Wilson and William M. Rodgers III, "Black-White Wage Gaps Expand with Rising Wage Inequality," Economic Policy Institute, September 20, 2016, https://www.epi.org/publication/black-white-wage-gaps-expand-with-rising-wage-inequality/, and Callie M. Rennison and Sarah Welchans, "Bureau of Justice Statistics Special Report: Intimate Partner Violence," US Department of Justice, last updated January 31, 2002, https://bjs.ojp.gov/content/pub/pdf/ipv.pdf.

183 *But ethnomusicologist Christopher Smith*: Christopher Smith, *Dancing Revolution: Bodies, Space, and Sound in American Cultural History* (Champaign: University of Illinois Press, 2019), 148.

183 *"a powerfully physical, visible, and independent"*: In his section of *Dancing Revolution* titled "Street Dance and Freedom," Smith elaborates, describing the "Baby Got Back" video as "racially empowering . . . to dance together, to dance a community into existence—if only, as Christopher Small put it, 'for the duration of the performance'—is itself to participate in the invention and reinvention of human liberation."

184 *"Baby Got Back" was number one on the* Billboard *Hot 100*: "The Hot 100," *Billboard*, August 1, 1992, https://www.billboard.com/charts/hot-100/1992-08-01/. The *Billboard* statistics are cited in Stephen J. Horowitz, "Sir Mix-A-Lot on 'Baby Got Back,' the Song of the Summer 25 Years Ago," *Billboard*, May 25, 2017, https://www.billboard

.com/articles/news/magazine-feature/7809400/sir-mix-a-lot-on
-baby-got-back/, and Michael Ellis, "Top 100 Singles Spotlight,"
Billboard, July 11, 1992.

184 *stayed on the charts for seven months*: "Baby Got Back" remained in
the number one spot on the *Billboard* Hot 100 list from the week of
July 4, 1992, to the week of August 1, 1992, before losing its place to
"This Used to Be My Playground" by Madonna.

184 *surpassed only by one of the bestselling songs of all time*: Statistics on
Houston's "I Will Always Love You" can be found at Gary Trust,
"Ask Billboard: Is 'I Will Always Love You' the Most Enduring Hit
of the Rock Era?," *Billboard*, October 4, 2016, https://www.billboard
com/articles/columns/chart-beat/7533218/ask-billboard-is-i-will-always
-love-you-the-most-enduring-hit-of.

184 *the song has earned more than one hundred million dollars*: The one
hundred million dollars figure is from an interview conducted with
Sir Mix-A-Lot, interview by DJ Vlad, VladTV.com, https://www
.vladtv.com/article/261264/sir-mix-a-lot-explains-how-publishing
-beats-out-royalties-flashback.

186 *climbed to number two on the* Billboard *Hot 100*: As per the November 1992 *Billboard* chart, "Rump Shaker" reached the top of
the charts: "Hot Rap Songs," *Billboard*, https://www.billboard.com
/charts/rap-song/1992-11-28.

186 *thwarted by the mighty power of Whitney Houston's*: "Whitney Houston 'I Will Always Love You' #1 in 1992," Whitney Houston.com,
December 9, 2016, https://www.whitneyhouston.com/news/whitney
-houston-i-will-always-love-you-1992/.

186 *Sometimes one of them played a saxophone*: Wreckx-n-Effect Ft. Teddy
Riley, "Rump Shaker," music video, originally published by Future
Entertainment MCA, August 1992, 3:43. Found online at: https://
youtu.be/zdLvauICvPM.

186 *"Rumps ain't dirty"*: Quotes from a 1992 interview with Teddy Riley:
Dennis Hunt, "TEDDY RILEY and WRECKX-N-EFFECT: Shakin'
Their Moneymakers," *Los Angeles Times*, November 29, 1992, https://
www.latimes.com/archives/la-xpm-1992-11-29-ca-2538-story.html.

187 As Nasty as They Wanna Be: 2 Live Crew, *As Nasty as They Wanna
Be*, 1988, Luke/Atlantic Records 91651, 1989, compact disc.

187 *including the 1990 song "Face Down Ass Up"*: 2 Live Crew, "Face Down
Ass Up," track 3 on *Live in Concert*, Effect/Luke Records, 1990, live
album.

188 *"2 Live Crew is engaged in heavy-handed parody"*: Henry L. Gates, "2 Live Crew, Decoded," *New York Times,* June 19, 1990, https://www.nytimes.com/1990/06/19/opinion/2-live-crew-decoded.html.

188 *jumping two Nielsen points in the first week*: McGrath, Tom, *MTV: The Making of a Revolution* (Philadelphia: Running Press, 1996).

189 *"It put us on the same page as rock 'n' roll and music in general"*: Jacob Hoye, David P. Levin, and Stuart Cohn, *MTV Uncensored* (New York: Pocket Books, 2001), 98.

JENNIFER

190 *Jennifer Lopez's butt*: I used the following sources while conducting my research on Jennifer Lopez: Wendy A. Burns-Ardolino, "Jiggle in My Walk," in *The Fat Studies Reader* (New York: New York University Press, 2009), 271–79; Mary Beltrán, "The Hollywood Latina Body as Site of Social Struggle: Media Constructions of Stardom and Jennifer Lopez's 'Cross-over Butt,'" *Quarterly Review of Film and Video* 19, no. 1 (2002): 71–86; Magdalena Barrera, "Hottentot 2000: Jennifer Lopez and Her Butt," *Sexualities in History: A Reader* (New York: Routledge, 2002), 411–17; Priscilla Peña Ovalle, "Jennifer Lopez, Racial Mobility, and the New Urban/Latina Commodity," in *Dance and the Hollywood Latina* (New Brunswick, NJ: Rutgers University Press, 2010), 126–44; Elena Romero, "The Butt Remix: Beauty, Pop Culture, Hip Hop, and the Commodification of the Black Booty," *QED: A Journal in GLBTQ Worldmaking* 4, no. 3 (2017): 190–94.

191 *"If you're raised in this country, since childhood"*: Frances Negrón-Muntaner, "Jennifer's Butt," *Aztlán: A Journal of Chicano Studies* 22, no. 2 (1997): 181–94.

191 *"Jennifer's Butt"*: Ibid.

191 *"Todo eso es tuyo?"*: Mary C. Beltrán, *Latina/o Stars in U.S. Eyes: The Making and Meanings of Film and TV Stardom* (Champaign, Illinois: University of Illinois Press, 2009), 138.

192 Premiere *declared "Jennifer Lopez's ass"*: The interviews with Jennifer Lopez were described in Beltrán, *Latina/o Stars in US Eyes: The Making and Meanings of Film and TV Stardom*, 138–45; Beltrán, "The Hollywood Latina Body"; and Joel Stein, "Interview with Jennifer Lopez," *Time,* October 5, 1998, http://content.time.com/time/subscriber/article/0,33009,989247,00.html.

192 *In 2000, when she wore a revealing green jungle-print dress*: Rachel Tashjian, "How Jennifer Lopez's Versace Dress Created Google Images," *GQ*, September 20, 2019, https://www.gq.com/story/jennifer-lopez-versace-google-images.

193 *In her "Jenny from the Block" video*: Jennifer Lopez, "Jenny from the Block," music video, 2002, 4:04, https://youtu.be/dly6p4Fu5TE.

193 *By the early aughts, they were running articles asking*: The various songs and articles I'm referring to can be found here: Peter Sheridan, "Jennifer Lopez, Bum Selfies and Butt Facials—Are Bottoms the New Boobs?" *Daily Express* (UK), September 23, 2014; Jessica Mehalic, "Bootylicious: Guys Talk Tail," *Cosmopolitan*, (November 2001), 144–47.

194 *an abundant new crop of popular songs*: Sisqó, "Thong Song," 1999, track 8 on *Unleash the Dragon*, Def Soul, February 15, 2000, compact disc; Black Eyed Peas, "My Humps," 2004, track 5 on *Monkey Business*, A&M, September 27, 2005, compact disc.

194 *Department stores even began*: Belinda Luscombe, "When the Fantasy Is a Size 16: Retailers Introduce Voluptuous Mannequins," *Time*, November 8, 2013, https://healthland.time.com/2013/11/08/when-the-fantasy-is-a-size-16-retailers-introduce-voluptuous-mannequins/; Reuters, "Big-Bottomed Mannequins Shake Their Booty," *Today*, November 11, 2004, https://www.today.com/popculture/big-bottomed-mannequins-shake-their-booty-wbna6462911.

194 *the country was in the process of becoming less white*: The census statistics are from the 2000 and 1990 census data (available online from the US Census Bureau). Since the census publishes demographic information in individual reports, multiple reports were used to track the statistics for the growth of individual racial and ethnic groups in the United States between 1990 and 2000.

194 *a trend that would continue through 2010 and is projected to continue*: The data on the projected growth of the Hispanic population was found in Maria T. Mora, "The Increasing Importance of Hispanics to the US Workforce," *Monthly Labor Review*, US Bureau of Labor Statistics, September 2015.

194 *but it did mean that corporate America became increasingly interested*: Robert E. Weems, *The Revolution Will Be Marketed: American Corporations and Black Consumers During the 1960s* (New York: New York University Press, 1998).

195 *In Hollywood, the financial successes of films*: *House Party*, directed by

Reginald Hudlin, was released in 1990 by New Line Cinema; *Boyz n the Hood*, directed by John Singleton, was released in 1991 by Columbia Pictures; *Waiting to Exhale*, directed by Forest Whitaker, was released in 1995 by 20th Century Fox.

195 *"The black population is younger, and is growing faster"*: Karen G. Bates, "They've Gotta Have Us," *New York Times*, July 14, 1991, https://www.nytimes.com/1991/07/14/magazine/theyve-gotta -have-us.html.

195 *Black characters on television also multiplied in the 1990s*: Riva Tukachinsky, Dana Mastro, and Moran Yarchi, "Documenting Portrayals of Race/Ethnicity on Primetime Television over a 20-Year Span and Their Association with National-Level Racial/Ethnic Attitudes," *Journal of Social Issues* 71, no. 1 (March 2015): 12–21.

195 *Hollywood had a more difficult time targeting Latino audiences*: Henry Puente, "US Latino Films (1990–1995): A Three-Tiered Marketplace," *Bilingual Review/La Revista Bilingüe* 31, no. 1 (2012): 51–70.

195 *major corporations increased their efforts to target this demographic group, as well as other ethnic minorities*: Information on the corporate response to the Latino demographics in the 1990s and early 2000s can be found in William M. O'Barr, "Multiculturalism in the Marketplace: Targeting Latinas, African-American Women, and Gay Consumers," *Advertising & Society Review* 7, no. 4 (2006); Eric J. Bailey, *The New Face of America: How the Emerging Multiracial, Multiethnic Majority Is Changing the United States* (Westport, CT: Praeger, 2013); and Silvia Betti, "The Image of Hispanics in Advertising in the United States," *Informes del Observatorio/Observatorio's Reports*, 2015, http://cervantesobservatorio.fas.harvard.edu /sites/default/files/009_reports_hispanic_advertising_0.pdf.

196 *white audiences were ravenously consuming hip-hop music, fashion, and culture*: The 70 percent statistic is from Tricia Rose, *The Hip Hop Wars: What We Talk About When We Talk About Hip Hop—and Why It Matters* (New York: Basic Civitas Books, 2008). However, other sources estimate that the percentage is closer to 60 percent or ranges from 70 to 80 percent. See Christina Montford, "When It Comes to Rap Music, Are White Boys Really Doing All the Buying?," *Atlanta Black Star*, November 6, 2014, https://atlantablackstar.com/2014/11/06/really -listening/, and Ciela Bialik, "Is the Conventional Wisdom Correct in Measuring Hip-Hop Audience?," *Wall Street Journal*, May 5, 2005, https://www.wsj.com/articles/SB111521814339424546.

196 *"When they write the history of popular culture"*: Renée Graham, "Not as Simple as Black and White," *Boston Globe*, April 2, 2002, D9.

196 *"This is the music of a people who have survived"*: "For Centuries, Black Music, Forged in Bondage, Has Been the Sound of Complete Artistic Freedom. No Wonder Everybody Is Always Stealing It," *New York Times*, August 14, 2009, https://www.nytimes.com/interactive /2019/08/14/magazine/music-black-culture-appropriation.html.

197 *Since the Jazz Age, the phenomenon of young white people*: I consulted the following sources when writing about the theory and history of cultural appropriation of Black culture: Toni Morrison, *Playing in the Dark: Whiteness and the Literary Imagination* (New York: Vintage, 2020); Bakari Kitwana, *Why White Kids Love Hip-Hop: Wankstas, Wiggers, Wannabes, and the New Reality of Race in America* (New York: Civitas Books, 2005); Bakari Kitwana (author, journalist, and political analyst) in phone interview with the author, August 7, 2020; Tate, *Everything but the Burden*; Lauren Michele Jackson, *White Negroes: When Cornrows Were in Vogue and Other Thoughts on Cultural Appropriation* (Boston: Beacon Press, 2019). All quotes from Lott's book are found in Eric Lott's *Love & Theft: Blackface Minstrelsy and the American Working Class* (Oxford: Oxford University Press, 2013), 2–103.

198 *whitness as an identity*: Here, I'm, of course, not talking about the kind of white identity espoused by white nationalists and those involved in white pride movements. For those people, there is no shame in whiteness at all. Instead, I'm talking about white people who identify as white and are, in some sense, trying to grapple with the history of that identity.

198 *Minstrel shows have long been seen as one of the primordial moments*: To add another strange twist, minstrel shows weren't primarily representations of Black culture but were white people's parodic renderings of what they saw as the music and dance of Black people. Wesley Morris's essay "For Centuries, Black Music, Forged in Bondage, Has Been the Sound of Complete Artistic Freedom. No Wonder Everybody Is Always Stealing It" gives an excellent accounting of the twists of appropriation that were part of minstrelsy.

199 *"the Afro-Americanization of white youth"*: The phrase specifically comes from Cornel West, *Race Matters* (Boston: Beacon Press, 1993).

199 *As cultural critic Greg Tate put it in his 2003 book*: Tate, *Everything but the Burden*.

200 *Along with this larger adoption of hip-hop culture*: All quotes from Janell Hobson come from my series of phone interviews with Janell Hobson (associate professor of women's, gender, and sexuality studies at the University at Albany), April 8, 2020, and April 13, 2020.

200 *Her ethnic identity was often provided*: Negrón-Muntaner, "Jennifer's Butt," offers a crucial account of how Lopez's butt functioned symbolically, particularly within the Latinx community, just before the release of *Out of Sight*.

200 *But some, like journalist Teresa Wiltz*: Teresa Wiltz, "Butt Seriously, What's Behind Heinie Hysteria?" *South Florida Sun-Sentinel*, October 19, 1998, https://www.sun-sentinel.com/news/fl-xpm-1998-10-19-9810160702-story.html.

KIM

202 *"I wrote that song because I was getting bigger and bigger"*: The original *Newsweek* article quoting Beyoncé is Allison Samuels, "What Beyonce Wants," *Newsweek*, July 28, 2002, https://www.newsweek.com/what-beyonce-wants-147419.

203 *and reached number one on the* Billboard *Hot 100*: "The Hot 100," *Billboard*, August 11, 2001, https://www.billboard.com/artist/destinys-child/chart-history/asi/.

203 *referred to in articles as "G-rated fun"*: "Destiny's Child: Pop Music Pied Pipers," Center for Parent/Youth Understanding, 2001, https://web.archive.org/web/20101116200806/http://www.cpyu.org/Page_p.aspx?id=76738.

203 *"Bootylicious" was a prime example*: All quotes and imagery from "Bootylicious" can be found at Destiny's Child, "Destiny's Child - Bootylicious (Official Music Video) ft. Missy 'Misdemeanor' Elliott," music video, 4:16, October 25, 2009, https://youtu.be/q-qtzhgweLs.

203 *there actually wasn't that much jelly in the video*: "Destiny's Child: Pop Music Pied Pipers."

204 *Several of the costumes referenced the attire of pimps and sex workers*: Aisha Durham, "'Check On It': Beyoncé, Southern Booty, and Black Femininities in Music Video," *Feminist Media Studies* 12, no. 1 (2012): 35–49.

204 *For the past twenty years, scholars and journalists have debated whether or not*: Several of the scholars engaged in this debate include Dayna

Chatman, "Pregnancy, Then It's 'Back to Business': Beyoncé, Black Femininity, and the Politics of a Post-Feminist Gender Regime," *Feminist Media Studies* 15, no. 6 (2015): 926–41, and Ann Power, "In Tune with the New Feminism," *New York Times*, April 29, 2001.

204 *as bell hooks suggested in 2016*: bell hooks, "Beyoncé's Lemonade is Capitalist Money-Making at Its Best," *Guardian*, May 11, 2016, https:// www.theguardian.com/music/2016/may/11/capitalism-of-beyonce -lemonade-album.

205 *The term* bootylicious *first appeared in a song in 1992*: Dr. Dre and Snoop Dog, "Fuck Wit Dre Day (and Everybody's Celebratin')," 1992, track 2 on *The Chronic*, Death Row/Interscope, May 20, 1993, compact disc.

205 *In 2003, when Oprah asked her to define it*: Beyoncé, interview with Oprah, *The Oprah Winfrey Show*, Harpo Studios, 2004.

205 *The following year, it was added to* The Oxford English Dictionary: *The Oxford English Dictionary*, 2nd ed. (Oxford: Oxford University Press, 2004), s.v. *bootylicious*.

206 *Runway models became so consistently, unnervingly thin*: "Danish Fashion Ethical Charter," Danish Ethical Fashion Charter, http:// danishfashionethicalcharter.com/#:~:text=The%20Danish%20 Fashion%20Ethical%20Charter,is%20a%20part%20of%20creating, and Jerome Socolovsky, "Spain Bans Overly Skinny Models from Fashion Shows," NPR, https://www.npr.org/templates/story/story .php?storyId=6103615.

207 *many Armenian Americans do not identify as white today*: Armenians were legally declared white in the 1925 Supreme Court case *US v. Cartozian*, one in a string of cases that was trying to legally determine the whiteness of different Asian ethnic groups because, at the time, only white people could legally immigrate to the United States. The *Cartozian* decision determined Armenians were white based on dubious nineteenth-century racial science, their historical reluctance to "intermingle with the Turks," and their connection to the Caucasian people of Russia. But because race isn't only a legal distinction but also a cultural one, many Armenians still don't consider themselves white, and often experience discrimination and stereotypes specific to being Armenian.

207 *Throughout her career, Kardashian would use her mixed-race identity*: For example, Kardashian referenced her Armenian ancestry in a 2011 episode of *H8R* when confronted about her background and

cultural appropriation. See "Kim Kardashian," *H8R*, CW Network, September 28, 2011, 12:55.

208 *Vivid Entertainment released a homemade, forty-one-minute video*: *Kim Kardashian, Superstar*, video created by Kim Kardashian and Ray J, Vivid Entertainment, March 21, 2007, DVD.

208 *In Kim's first scene of the first episode of* Keeping Up with the Kardashians: "I'm Watching You," *Keeping Up with the Kardashians*, E! Network, October 14, 2007.

209 *a nude photo spread in* Playboy: "Hollywood's Next Sex Star: Kim Kardashian Takes It All Off," *Playboy*, December 2007, https://images-na.ssl-images-amazon.com/images/I/81JxbKAUkkL._AC _SY606_.jpg.

209 *The show was quickly picked up for a second season*: Kimberly Nordyke, " 'Kardashians' Earns Its Keep," *Hollywood Reporter*, November 13, 2007, https://www.hollywoodreporter.com/tv/tv-news/kardashians -earns-keep-154906/.

209 *she was the most googled person in 2008*: "Kim Kardashian Most Goo-gled Celeb of 2008," *Hindustan Times*, January 2, 2009, https://www .hindustantimes.com/entertainment/kim-kardashian-most-googled -celeb-of-2008/story-CYvTJUGdwIv459GktIV9WP.html.

209 OK! *magazine reassured their readers*: "Dancing With the Stars Kim Kardashian: How I Stay Thin . . . But Keep My Sexy Curves," *OK! Magazine*, September 24, 2008, https://okmagazine.com/news/cover -story-kims-fitness-plan/.

209 Cosmopolitan *described her as an entrepreneur*: Shawna Malcolm, "Up in Kim Kardashian's Business," *Cosmopolitan*, November 2009.

209 *she would eventually go so far as to have her butt X-rayed*: "The Former Mrs. Jenner," *Keeping Up with the Kardashians*, E! Network, June 26, 2011.

209 *In general, media stories about Kardashian seemed to suggest*: "Fashion Police," *Us Weekly*, August 11, 2008.

209 *In April 2008, Paris Hilton weighed in*: Paris Hilton, interview by Chet Buchanan, *Chet Buchanan and the Morning Zoo Show*, 98.5 KLUC, April 14, 2008.

210 *In 2009, Kardashian spoke to* News of the World: Polly Graham, "Body & Soul," *News of the World*, October 4, 2009.

210 *"excessive thinness"*: Jessica Bennett, "The Backlash Against Maga-zine Airbrushing," *Newsweek*, May 1, 2008, https://www.newsweek .com/backlash-against-magazine-airbrushing-89805.

210 *In 2006, model and talk show host Tyra Banks*: Shelley Fralic, "A Model of Success Takes on 'Pin-Thin' Culture," *Vancouver Sun*, February 3, 2007.

210 *She appeared on the cover of* People *magazine*: *People* staff, "COVER STORY: Tyra Banks Speaks Out About Her Weight," *People*, January 24, 2007, https://people.com/health/cover-story-tyra-banks-speaks-out-about-her-weight/.

211 *In one 2009* Cosmopolitan *profile of Kim*: Malcolm, "Up in Kim Kardashian's Business."

211 *In the two-minute trailer for her 2009 workout video*: "Kim Kardashian 'Fit in Your Jeans by Friday' 3 DVD Workout Series," posted by Kim Kardashian, Fit in Your Jeans by Friday, YouTube, March 27, 2014 (originally released 2009), 2:55, https://youtu.be/0hP_4RUQNic.

212 *as of 2021, she is the sixth-most-followed person*: "Instagram Accounts with the Most Followers Worldwide as of July 2021," Statista, accessed September 17, 2021, https://www.statista.com/statistics/421169/most-followers-instagram/; "Top Instagram Users: Most Followers," Social Tracker, https://www.socialtracker.io/toplists/top-50-instagram-users-by-followers/.

212 *Instagram's community guidelines banned nudity*: Andrew Griffin, "Instagram Updates Posting Guidelines: Butts Are Out, Breastfeeding Is In," *Independent*, April 17, 2015, https://www.independent.co.uk/life-style/gadgets-and-tech/news/instagram-updates-posting-guidelines-butts-are-out-breastfeeding-is-in-10183882.html.

213 *reaching a new peak in November 2014*: "Break the Internet: Kim Kardashian," *Paper*, Winter 2014.

213 Paper *got what it was asking for*: David Hershkovits, "How Kim Kardashian Broke the Internet with Her Butt," *Guardian*, December 17, 2014, https://www.theguardian.com/lifeandstyle/2014/dec/17/kim-kardashian-butt-break-the-internet-paper-magazine.

214 *It was hardly the only time that Kim made aesthetic choices*: Cady Lang, "Keeping Up with the Kardashians Is Ending, but Their Exploitation of Black Women's Aesthetics Continues," *Time*, June 10, 2021, https://time.com/6072750/kardashians-blackfishing-appropriation/.

214 *provided what critic Allison P. Davis called*: Allison P. Davis, "The End of Kim Kardashian and Kanye West's Wild Ride," *Vulture*, April 26, 2021, https://www.vulture.com/article/kim-kardashian-kanye-west-divorce.html.

TWERK

219 *In* How to Bounce Like the Queen of New Orleans: Big Freedia, *How to Bounce Like the Queen of New Orleans! | Big Freedia's Bounce Etiquette*, video, June 6, 2018, 4:08, https://www.youtube.com/watch?v=wi-eGzxTIjA.

220 *has been twerking and performing*: More on Big Freedia's twerk-shops and TV show (*Big Freedia: Queen of Bounce*) can be found in Christin Marie Taylor, " 'Release Your Wiggle': Big Freedia's Queer Bounce," *Southern Cultures* 24, no. 2 (2018): 60–77. According to Taylor, *Big Freedia: Queen of Bounce* was picked up in 2013 by Fuse TV.

220 *dispensing information about the history of bounce*: One such inter-view occurred with the *Snipe* and can be found in Zoe Christmas, "Interview—Big Freedia," *Snipe*, October 7, 2013, https://www.thesnipenews.com/music/interviews/big-freedia/.

221 *Even before the arrival of Europeans*: Neal Conan, "Joy Harjo's 'Crazy Brave' Path to Finding Her Voice," WBFO, July 9, 2012, https://news.wbfo.org/post/joy-harjos-crazy-brave-path-finding-her-voice.

221 *laws called the Code Noir*: The complete Code Noir is available on-line: "(1724) Louisiana's Code Noir," BlackPast, 2007, https://www.blackpast.org/african-american-history/louisianas-code-noir-1724/.

221 *Wynton Marsalis once declared that*: Nick Douglas, "Black History: Congo Square, New Orleans—The Heart of American Music," *Afropunk*, February 26, 2018, https://afropunk.com/2018/02/black-history-congo-square-new-orleans-heart-american-music/.

221 *The dance was part of a spiritual practice*: In the centuries since the heyday of Congo Square, however, the mapouka and its descen-dants were increasingly interpreted as primarily sexual dances, and their spiritual aspects were overshadowed by angst around exhibi-tions of sexuality. At the end of the twentieth century, the dance was briefly banned in Côte d'Ivoire because it was considered lewd in the devoutly religious country. It is still restricted in Togo, Nigeria, Burkina Faso, and Cameroon.

222 *They also danced the bamboula*: Information on Congo Square dances was found in Makau Kitata, "Sexualising the Performance, Objecti-fying the Performer: The Twerk Dance in Kenya," *Agenda* 34, no. 3 (2020): 11–21; Maureen Monahan, "What Is the Origin of Twerk-ing?," Mental Floss, August 28, 2013, https://www.mentalfloss.com

/article/51365/what-origin-twerking; Gary A. Donaldson, "A Window on Slave Culture: Dances at Congo Square in New Orleans, 1800–1862," *Journal of Negro History* 69, no. 2 (1984): 63–72; and Taylor, " 'Release Your Wiggle.' "

222 *Congo Square represented not only the continuation*: Douglas, "Black History: Congo Square."

222 *happened not only in Congo Square*: Elizabeth Pérez, "The Ontology of Twerk: From 'Sexy' Black Movement Style to Afro-Diasporic Sacred Dance," *African and Black Diaspora: An International Journal* 9, no. 1 (2016): 16–31.

222 *In 1817, the city government of New Orleans*: Donaldson, "A Window on Slave Culture," 63–66.

223 *According to Kim Marie Vaz*: Kim Marie Vaz, *The "Baby Dolls": Breaking the Race and Gender Barriers of the New Orleans Mardi Gras Tradition* (Baton Rouge, LA: LSU Press, 2013).

223 *and was one possible inspiration for Josephine Baker's*: Taylor, "Release Your Wiggle," 65.

223 *Merline Kimble, a granddaughter of a Baby Doll*: The interview with Merline Kimble can be found in "Interview: Merline Kimble of the Gold Digger Baby Dolls," interview with Action Jackson, WWOZ, August 12, 2018, https://www.wwoz.org/blog/418476.

223 *a rebellion against "what was put on women"*: It is this resistance that encouraged Kimble to start her new iteration, and one of the reasons why she encourages children to participate in Baby Doll performances. Although there is an element of sexuality, to interpret the Baby Dolls as only sexy is to misunderstand the role that booty dancing and second lines play in New Orleans culture. The Baby Dolls dress up, dance, and flaunt their butts as a way to celebrate and connect to the women of New Orleans's past.

223 *Another thread in the evolution of twerk comes from Jamaica*: All research on dancehall was found using the following sources: Thomas Vendryes, "Versions, Dubs and Riddims: Dub and the Transient Dynamics of Jamaican Music," *Dancecult: Journal of Electronic Dance Music Culture* 7, no. 2 (2015); Taliesin Gilkes-Bower, "Welcome to Kingston, the World's Dancehall Mecca," Outline, June 28, 2018, https://theoutline.com/post/5125/jamaica-kingston-dancehall-photo-essay?zd=1&zi=jnrp5xln; Sharine Taylor, "The Essential Guide to Dancehall," Red Bull Music Academy, July 10, 2019, https://daily.redbullmusicacademy.com/2019/07/essential-guide-to-dancehall.

224 *where local musicians and dancers, deeply influenced*: Rebecca Trejo, "A Brief History of New Orleans' Bounce Music Style," Culture Trip, July 22, 2021, https://theculturetrip.com/north-america/usa/louisiana/new-orleans/articles/history-of-bounce-music/.

224 *Although undoubtedly used colloquially*: Pérez, "The Ontology of Twerk," 18. The original music video for "Do the Jubilee All" can also be found on YouTube: DJ Jubilee, "Do the Jubilee All," video, 4:21, February 29, 2012, https://www.youtube.com/watch?v=oSCz5RP2gfY.

224 *After "Jubilee," twerk began cropping*: Taylor, "Release Your Wiggle," 66.

225 *Still, it remained mostly a New Orleans phenomenon*: Information on the New Orleans bounce scene was found in Kyra D. Gaunt, "YouTube, Twerking, and You," 256, and Christina Schoux Casey and Maeve Eberhardt, "'She Don't Need No Help': Deconsolidating Gender, Sex and Sexuality in New Orleans Bounce Music," *Gender & Language* 12, no. 3 (2018).

225 *The queer community, in particular*: Gaunt, "YouTube, Twerking, and You," 256; Casey and Eberhardt, "'She Don't Need No Help,'" 318–45; Brett Berk, "New Orleans Sissy Bounce: Rap Goes Drag," *Vanity Fair*, March 11, 2010, https://www.vanityfair.com/culture/2010/03/katey-red-starts-a-band.

225 *"A lot of people think bounce is simply"*: Jason Newman, "Big Freedia Reflects on Miley Cyrus, Coming Out in New Memoir," *Rolling Stone*, July 1, 2015, https://www.rollingstone.com/music/music-news/big-freedia-reflects-on-miley-cyrus-coming-out-in-new-memoir-179654/.

225 *The mass diaspora that resulted*: Gaunt, "YouTube, Twerking, and You," 248.

225 *A group of dancers from Atlanta called Twerk Team*: Information about Twerk Team came from my conversation with Kyra Gaunt.

MILEY

227 Hannah Montana *premiered on the Disney Channel*: *Hannah Montana*, Disney Channel, four seasons, 2006–2011.

229 *In the publicity, music videos, lyrics*: Tracy Clayton, "Miley Cyrus Wants Something That Feels 'Black,'" *The Root*, June 13, 2013, https://www.theroot.com/miley-cyrus-wants-something-that-feels-black-1790884859.

229   *in one of the most controversial live performances of the 2010s*: Even
      months and years later, news sources continued to report on and
      analyze the 2013 VMAs. See Katy Kroll, "Twerk It Out: Miley and
      Robin's VMA Performance, One Year Later," *Rolling Stone*, August
      22, 2014, https://www.rollingstone.com/culture/culture-news/twerk
      -it-out-miley-and-robins-vma-performance-one-year-later-65286/.

229   *It started with a giant space teddy bear*: All descriptions of the 2013
      VMAs come from online recordings of Miley Cyrus's performance,
      e.g., "Miley Cyrus VMA 2013 with Robin Thicke SHOCKED,"
      YouTube video posted by Juan Manuel Cruz, 6:52, August 27, 2013,
      https://youtu.be/LfcvmABhmxs.

230   *Marvin Gaye's "Got to Give It Up"*: Gaye's family won the lawsuit,
      and Thicke and Pharrell had to pay them $5.3 million.

231   *Cyrus would later say*: All quotes and descriptions from Miley Cyrus's
      2013 documentary can be found in *Miley: The Movement*, directed by
      Paul Bozymowski, RadicalMedia, 2013.

231   *the media was ablaze with aghast commentary*: After the VMAs, a host of
      criticism against Cyrus came out, including: Kelly Clarkson (@kelly
      clarkson), "2 words . . . #pitchystrippers," Twitter, August 26, 2014;
      Patrick Kevin Day, "Miley Cyrus's VMA Performance: Media React
      in Shock," *Los Angeles Times*, August 26, 2013, https://www.latimes
      .com/entertainment/tv/showtracker/la-et-st-miley-cyrus-vma-perfor
      mance-media-reacts-in-shock-20130826-story.html; "Sherri Shep-
      herd: Miley Cyrus 'Going to Hell in a Twerking Handbasket'
      (VIDEO)," *Huffington Post*, August 27, 2013, https://www.huff
      post.com/entry/sherri-shepherd-miley-cyrus-going-to-hell-video
      _n_3820742; Jane Timm, "Brzezinski: Miley Cyrus VMA Perfor-
      mance 'Really, Really Disturbing,'" MSNBC, August 26, 2013, https://
      www.msnbc.com/morning-joe/brzezinski-miley-cyrus-vma-perfor
      mance-msna154221; Alexander Abad-Santos, "Creator of the Foam
      Finger Is Deeply Upset with Miley Cyrus," *Atlantic*, August 29,
      2013, https://www.theatlantic.com/culture/archive/2013/08/creator
      -foam-finger-deeply-upset-miley-cyrus/311615/; Jessica Derscho-
      witz, "Miley Cyrus' VMA performance Blasted by Parents Television
      Council," CBS News, August 27, 2013, https://www.cbsnews.com
      /news/miley-cyrus-vma-performance-blasted-by-parents-television
      -council/.

231   *Brooke Shields, who had played Hannah Montana's*: Randee Dawn,
      "Brooke Shields on 'Hannah Montana' Co-star Miley Cyrus: 'It's

a Bit Desperate,'" *Today*, August 26, 2013, https://www.today.com
/popculture/brooke-shields-hannah-montana-co-star-miley-cyrus
-its-bit-8C10995696.

232 *In the documentary, she offers*: Miley: The Movement.

233 *"It's mind-boggling to me that there was even a controversy"*: John
Norris, "Miley Cyrus Breaks Silence on Rootsy New Music, Fiance
Liam Hemsworth & America: 'Unity Is What We Need,'" *Billboard*, May 5, 2017, https://www.billboard.com/articles/news/maga
zine-feature/7783997/miley-cyrus-cover-story-new-music-malibu.

233 *the most mainstream and white of cultural outlets*: Kristin T. Stude-
man, "Starting from the Bottom: Experts Weigh in on the Cultural
Obsession with the Butt," *Vogue*, August 27, 2014, https://www
.vogue.com/article/butts-vma-doctors-weigh-in; Marisa Meltzer, "For
Posterior's Sake," *New York Times*, September 17, 2014, https://
www.nytimes.com/2014/09/18/fashion/more-women-seeking-cur
vaceous-posteriors.html.

233 *As writers like Allison P. Davis pointed out*: Allison P. Davis, "Vogue
Has Just Discovered Big Butts," The Cut, September 10, 2014,
https://www.thecut.com/2014/09/vogue-has-just-discovered-big
-butts.html.

THE YEAR OF THE BUTT

234 *That year 8,654 butt augmentation procedures were performed*: "2013
Cosmetic Plastic Surgery Statistics," American Society of Plastic
Surgeons, 2013, https://www.plasticsurgery.org/documents/News
/Statistics/2013/cosmetic-procedure-trends-2013.pdf. See "Buttock
augmentation with fat grafting" for the 2012 statistics.

234 *The Brazilian butt lift*: A version of the BBL was developed in the
1960s by Ivo Pitanguy, a surgeon who founded the world's first plastic surgery training center in Brazil and is often called the "pioneer"
of the Brazilian Butt Lift. However, this early version of the BBL
was different from what the surgery is today. When he first tried it,
it was more of a butt lift than an augmentation because it removed
excess skin to correct sagging. In the procedure known as a Brazilian
Butt Lift today, a doctor injects fat back into the butt that was taken
from another part of the body.

234 *by 2014 the number reached 11,505*: "2014 Cosmetic Plastic Surgery
Statistics," American Society of Plastic Surgeons, 2014, https://www

.plasticsurgery.org/documents/News/Statistics/2014/plastic-surgery
-statistics-full-report-2014.pdf. For the 2014 statistics, see "Buttock
augmentation with fat grafting," p. 7.

234 *Although a BBL creates a more "natural" look*: "Plastic Surgery Societies Issue Urgent Warning About the Risks Associated with Brazilian Butt Lifts," American Society of Plastic Surgeons, August 6,
2018, https://www.plasticsurgery.org/news/press-releases/plastic-surgery-
societies-issue-urgent-warning-about-the-risks-associated-with
-brazilian-butt-lifts.

235 *but still the number of BBLs performed has continued*: See "Buttock
augmentation with fat grafting" on pages 2 and 7 of the 2019 and
2018 reports, respectively. In 2019, 28,076 buttock augmentations
were reported, compared to 24,099 in 2018. "2019 National Plastic Surgery Statistics," American Society of Plastic Surgeons, 2019,
https://www.plasticsurgery.org/documents/News/Statistics/2019
/plastic-surgery-statistics-report-2019.pdf; "2018 Plastic Surgery Statistics Report," American Society of Plastic Surgeons, 2018, https://
www.plasticsurgery.org/documents/News/Statistics/2018/plastic-
surgery-statistics-full-report-2018.pdf.

235 *In 2013, a Long Islander named Jen Selter*: Ally Jones, "Instagram's
Butt-lebrity: The Bar for Fame Hits Rock Bottom," *Atlantic*, January 3, 2014, https://www.theatlantic.com/culture/archive/2014/01
/instagrams-butt-lebrity-bar-fame-hits-rock-bottom/356677/.

236 *the promotional image from the first season of* KUWTK: *Keeping Up
with the Kardashians*, advertisement, E! Network, 2007.

236 *"Anyone who works hard could be where I am"*: Claire Howorth, "The
Posterior Economics of Motivation Mogul Jen Selter," *Elle*, December 13, 2013, https://www.elle.com/beauty/health-fitness/news
/a14992/jen-selter-interview/. The five-thousand-followers statistic
can also be found in Hilary Sheinbaum, "On Instagram, 'Fitness Inspiration' Is Often an Eyeful," *USA Today*, January 4, 2014, https://
www.usatoday.com/story/news/nation/2014/01/04/fitness-inspiration
-instagram/4295599/.

236 *Jennifer Lopez released the anthem "Booty"*: Jennifer Lopez, Iggy Azalea, "Booty," 2014, track 10 on *A.K.A.*, Nuyorican/Capitol, August
24, 2014.

236 *Beyoncé, the woman who had introduced*: Beyoncé, *Beyoncé*, Park-
wood/Columbia, December 13, 2013.

237 *white singer-songwriter Meghan Trainor offered up*: Meghan Trainor,

"All About That Bass," video, June 11, 2014, 3:10, https://www.you
tube.com/watch?v=7PCkvCPvDXk.

237 *Nicki Minaj released "Anaconda"*: Nicki Minaj, "Anaconda," video,
August 19, 2014, 4:49, https://youtu.be/LDZX4ooRsWs.

237 *Katey Red started recording an album in 1998*: More information on
Katey Red's music career and first-ever music video can be found in
Gaunt, "YouTube, Twerking, and You," 257.

238 *"If a white girl does something that seems to be Black"*: *The Ellen De-
Generes Show*, "Julie Bowen, Nicki Minaj," season 11, episode 15,
directed by Liz Patrick, aired September 27, 2013, on NBC.

RECLAMATION

239 *Kelechi Okafor, one of the most popular twerk instructors*: All quotes
from Kelechi Okafor are from my phone interview with Okafor (actress, director, public speaker, and twerk instructor), November 27,
2020.

Index

About, Nicolas, 76
aerobics, 150–54, 160–61, 165–70
Aerobics (Cooper), 150
Affleck, Ben, 193
Africa and Africans, 12, 51, 52, 54, 61, 65, 71, 106
    Khoe, 51, 52, 56, 57, 67, 68–69, 75, 76, 90, 91, 264–65n
    sexuality of, 54, 58, 61, 65–66, 90
    South Africa, 51, 52, 55, 62, 75–77
African Institution, 59
Alexander, Elizabeth, 75, 91–92
American Museum of Natural History, 115, 117, 119, 120
Anchorage Daily News, 155
androgyny, 173–75
anus, 11, 180
Armenians, 207–8, 290n
L'Art Vivant, 108
Asian women, 105
As Nasty as They Wanna Be, 187
Atlantic, 39, 74

Baartman, Sarah, 10, 51–67, 68, 71, 72, 74–77, 82, 89–93, 109, 123, 182, 200, 213, 243, 249, 264n, 265n
    bustles and, 89–93
    death of, 13, 63, 93
    remains of, 63–64, 75–76, 91, 182, 258n
Baby Dolls, 223, 294n
"Baby Got Back," 177–86, 188, 192, 193, 204, 214, 237
Baker, Jean-Claude, 107–8
Baker, Josephine, 106–10, 223
Banks, Tyra, 210
Barrett, Ron, 24
Barrymore, Drew, 206
Bartlett, Alex, 136–39, 141, 142, 251
Bartlett, Jamie, 29
beauty, 1, 6, 8, 9, 11, 39, 43–44, 176, 200, 245, 249
    in animals, 36, 43–44
    Ellis on, 72–73
    fitness culture and, 160
Beauvoir, Simone de, 141
Bechdel Test, 182
belfies, 235–36
Belskie, Abram, 115, 117, 141
Bernstein, Adam, 180

"better baby" competitions,
        116–17
Beyoncé, 202–6, 212, 236–37
Big Freedia, 219–20, 225, 237–38
"Big Ole Butt," 188
Billboard, 184, 186, 187, 203, 227,
        233, 234
bipedalism, 21, 22, 27
birds, 42–43
    peacocks, 35, 36, 41, 43, 44
Birthing Series, 115, 120
Black Eyed Peas, 194
Black people
    American, in Paris, 106
    appropriation of culture of,
        197–200, 214–15, 233, 238,
        242, 245, 246
    demographic shift and, 194–96
    exoticization of, 106
    lawyers, 163
    television characters, 195
Black women, 12–14, 65, 93,
        182–83, 186, 214
    butts of, 71–73, 91, 108, 177,
        181, 182, 189, 200, 204,
        213–14, 230, 232, 237, 249
    sexuality of, 66, 71, 90, 91, 110,
        183, 204, 232, 243, 249
Bliven, Bruce, 101
"Blurred Lines," 230
Bolt, Usain, 21
bodybuilders, 150
"Bootylicious," 202–5
brain, 22, 28, 32, 43, 73
Bramble, Dennis, 22, 29, 258n
Brazilian butt lift (BBL), 234–35,
        297n
breastfeeding, 33–34
Brinkley, Christie, 156, 174

Brzezinski, Mika, 231
Buck v. Bell, 74, 268n
Buns of Steel, 145, 148, 150,
        155–58, 160, 169, 235
Bureau of Home Economics,
        117–18
Burgard, Deb, 164–70, 251
bustles, 81–93, 94, 98, 100, 102,
        110, 251
Butler, Judith, 141

Caesars, Peter, 52–53, 55, 57, 58,
        59, 60, 62
Campaign for Economic
        Democracy, 153
Campbell, Heyworth, 96
Canty-Letsome, Rosezella,
        162–64, 167–69, 250–51
"Carpool Karaoke," 193
Chanel, Coco, 97, 100–101, 103,
        105, 109, 127, 160
Charnas, Dan, 180
"Cherry Pie," 181, 183
Chicago World's Fair, 117
Chinese women, 105
Christianity, 58, 65, 66, 71, 76, 221
Ciara, 240
cities, 99–101
Clarkson, Kelly, 231
Cleveland Museum of Health,
        120–21
Cleveland *Plain Dealer*, 121, 122
Clinton, Bill, 175
Clooney, George, 191
clothing and fashion, 87–88,
        91–93
    body types and, 114
    bustles, 81–93, 94, 98, 100, 102,
        110, 251

Chanel and, 97, 100–101, 103, 105, 109, 127, 160
Conway and, 94–97, 102, 103, 106, 107, 115, 249
corsets, 81, 86, 89, 94, 100, 103, 160, 202
"Eastern" influences in, 104–5
flappers and, 97–99, 101–7, 110, 116, 175, 249
history and, 88
magazines and, 71, 95–97, 103, 124, 154, 173, 175, 185, 193–94, 205–6, 235
petticoats and crinolines, 84–87
Poiret and, 97, 99–100, 104, 105, 160
ready-to-wear, 101, 118, 123, 125–33
sewing and dressmaking, 87, 92, 125–27, 133
shopping and dressing rooms, 113–14, 124, 247–51
standardized sizes in, 118, 123, 125–33
thinness and, 97–98, 100, 102–4
undergarments, 88, 89, 100, 139–42
Colbert Report, The, 23
colonialism, 65, 67, 93, 258n
Congo Square, 220–22
Connelly, Chris, 196
Conway, Gordon, 94–97, 102, 103, 106, 107, 115, 249
Conway, Tommie, 94, 95
Corden, James, 193
corsets, 81, 86, 89, 94, 100, 103, 160, 202
Cosmopolitan, 39, 193, 209, 211

Coury, Nick, 25–27, 30, 260n
crinolines, 84–87
Crudup, Arthur "Big Boy," 199
Cuccia, Vinnie, 136–39, 141, 142, 251
Cuvier, Georges, 49–51, 62–64, 68, 75, 76, 116, 249
Cyrus, Billy Ray, 227, 228
Cyrus, Miley, 227–33, 234, 237, 238, 242, 243, 245

dancing, 221–24, 244, 293n
Baker and, 107–10
for exercise, 150–51, 153, 166–67
twerking, 219–20, 224–26, 230–33, 237, 239–45
Dancing Revolution (Smith), 183
Dancing with the Stars, 209
Darwin, Charles, 27, 36, 37, 43, 49, 72
Davis, Allison P., 214, 233
de Blasio, Abele, 72
DeGeneres, Ellen, 155
demographics, 194–96, 286n
Destiny's Child, 202–5, 225
Deutsches Hygiene-Museum, 120
Diadem, HMS, 55
Dickinson, Robert Latou, 115, 117, 141
diets, 103–4, 109, 160, 164, 202, 235, 251
Dixon Gottschild, Brenda, 108, 109
DJ Jubilee, 224
Dorsey-Rivas, Amylia, 178, 179
drag queens, 134–39
Dunlop, Alexander, 53–55, 57–60, 62
Durham, Aisha, 204

Ehrman, Edwina, 88
Ellis, Havelock, 72–73
Ellison, Jenny, 168, 169
Emerson, Ralph Waldo, 70
Essence, 154
eugenics, 69, 73–74, 116, 117,
  119–21, 123, 268n, 276n
Everything but the Burden (Tate),
  199–200
evolution, 21–23, 28, 29, 31, 32,
  35, 36, 37, 40, 45, 49
  adaptationism and, 41, 43, 45
  beauty and, 36, 43–44
  natural selection in, 36–37, 43
  sexual attraction and, 38–41,
    44–45
  whiteness and, 69–70
evolutionary psychology, 38–41,
  43, 44, 72
exercise and fitness, 99, 103, 109,
  145–61, 162–70, 235, 236,
  251
  aerobic, 150–54, 160–61,
    165–70
  beauty standards and, 160
  Buns of Steel, 145, 148, 150,
    155–58, 160, 169, 235
  Burgard and, 164–70, 251
  Canty-Letsome and, 162–64,
    167–69, 251
  fat fitness movement, 165–70
  femininity and, 151, 152, 160,
    161
  feminism and, 151–52, 168
  Fonda and, 152–54, 156,
    158–61, 164
  Kardashians and, 211
  Smithey and, 145–48, 154–56,
    249

sports, 151–52
Webb and, 156–58, 161

Farina, Dennis, 200
farting, 54
fashion, *see* clothing and fashion
Fashion Institute of Technology,
  103
fat, 4, 31–35, 148, 205–6, 235
  plastic surgery and, 103, 109,
    206
  use of word, 166
femininity, 2, 11, 13, 14, 34, 73, 93,
  96, 97, 140–42, 190
  drag queens and, 135, 138,
    139
  exercise and, 151, 152, 160, 161
  Norma statue and, 119, 141
  undergarments and, 139–42
  whiteness and, 242–43, 246
feminism, 203–5
  fitness and, 151–52, 168
  MTV and, 180–81, 184
Fisher, Ronald, 43
fitness, *see* exercise and fitness
flappers, 97–99, 101–7, 110, 116,
  175, 249
Fonda, Jane, 152–54, 156, 158–61,
  164
fossils, 20–22, 29–30, 40, 258n
France, 61, 106
  Baker in, 106, 108, 109
  National Museum of Natural
    History in, 49–50, 62–64,
    75, 91
  Universal Exhibitions in, 75,
    91, 104
freak shows, 53, 56
Freedia, 219–20, 225, 237–38

Galluzzi, Patti, 180–81, 183–84

Galton, Francis, 69, 73, 116

Gates, Henry Louis, Jr., 188

Gaunt, Kyra D., 182–83, 185, 186

Gautier, Théophile, 175

Gebhard, Bruno, 120–23

gender, 135, 140, 141

Gender Trouble (Butler), 141

Gibson, Charles, 94–95

Gibson girl, 94–96, 116, 119

Gilman, Sander, 4, 66–67, 71, 75

Glaum-Lathbury, Abigail, 128, 131–33

gluteus maximus, 23, 28, 29, 31

Godey's Lady's Book, 71

Golden Door, 156–57

Google, 192

Gore, Tipper, 181, 187

Gottschild, Brenda Dixon, 108, 109

Goude, Jean-Paul, 213

Gould, Stephen Gay, 40, 41, 43, 45

Gray, Asa, 36

Great Shape (Lyons and Burgard), 166, 168

Greeks, ancient, 54, 89, 90, 119

Griqua people, 75

grunge, 174

Hale, Sarah, 71

Hannah Montana, 227–28, 231, 232

Harlem, 106, 107

Harper's Bazaar, 96

Haufe, Chris, 37, 40, 41, 44–45

Hayden, Tom, 152

Held, John, Jr., 97

heroin chic, 174, 175

Hill, Anita, 183

Hilton, Paris, 206–10

hip-hop, 3, 183, 187–89, 196–97, 199–201, 224, 229, 237

Hispanic and Latinx people, 190–91, 194–96, 200

History of the Anglo-Saxons, The (Turner), 70

Hobson, Janell, 65–66, 68, 200

Hoke, Morgan, 32–34

Hollander, Anne, 102–3

hominids, 19–20, 31, 32

Homo erectus, 19, 22–23, 26–29, 32

Homo sapiens, 31, 50

horses, 28

    Man Against Horse Race, 24–27, 30, 260n

"Hottentots," 51, 54, 69, 72

"Hottentot Venus," 67, 89–91

    The Hottentot Venus; or, The Hatred of Frenchwomen, 89–90, 243

    Sarah Baartman, *see* Baartman, Sarah

Houston, Whitney, 184, 186

Houston Chronicle, 169

Hudson's, 113–14, 247

Hull-House Museum, 10

human remains, displays of, 67, 76, 258n

    of Baartman, 63–64, 75–76, 91, 182

Hurricane Katrina, 225

Icon, 134–36

immigration, 70, 71, 99, 105, 126, 224

Industrial Revolution, 87, 125

In Living Color, 190

Instagram, 124, 135, 211–12, 234, 236

Irish Penny Journal, 89

Irish people, 70, 71, 126

"I Will Always Love You," 184, 186

Jackson, Michael, 188, 207

Jamaica, 223–24

Jane Addams Hull-House Museum, 10

Japan
  aesthetics of, 104–5
  atomic bombing of, 121

Jazzercise, 150–51

Jenner, Caitlyn, 208

Jenner, Kris, 207–9

jokes, 185–86

Jones, Grace, 213

Jones, Lisa, 91

Jones, Lydia, 108

Kardashian, Kim, 207–15, 234–36

Kardashian, Robert, 207, 208

Karl, Stuart, 153–54

Keats, John, 175

Keeping Up with the Kardashians, 208–9, 211, 212, 236

Khoe people, 51, 52, 56, 57, 67, 68–69, 75, 76, 90, 91, 264–65n

Kimble, Merline, 223, 294n

Klein, Calvin, 173–76

Knowles, Beyoncé, 202–6, 212, 236–37

Lake Turkana, 19–20

Latinx and Hispanic people, 190–91, 194–96, 200

Lawless, Lucy, 192

Lawson, Tina, 204

lawyers, 163

Leakey, Richard, 20

Leno, Jay, 192, 231

Levinson, André, 108

Lewontin, Richard, 41, 43, 45

Lieberman, Daniel, 20–29, 40, 49, 258n

Linnaeus, Carl, 52

LL Cool J, 188

London, 53, 54, 56–61, 64

London International Exhibition, 104

London *Times*, 56, 58, 85

Lopez, Jennifer, 190–94, 200–201, 202, 204, 210, 212, 236

Los Angeles Times, 186, 231

Lott, Eric, 198

Love and Theft (Lott), 198

Lover, Ed, 189

Lyons, Pat, 166, 168

Macaulay, Zachary, 58–59, 265–66n

Maier, Howard, 156, 157

Maier Group, 156, 158

mainstream, concept of, 194

Makhubu, Nomusa, 77

Man Against Horse Race, 24–27, 30, 260n

Mandela, Nelson, 75–76

Mardi Gras, 222–23

Marsalis, Wynton, 221

Marx, Gilda, 153

Mbeki, Thabo, 76

Men's Health, 39

"Me So Horny," 187

Middleton, Pippa, 235

military, 117, 126
Minaj, Nicki, 237, 238
minstrel shows, 198
Missett, Judi, 150–53
Mix-A-Lot, Sir, 177–86, 189, 193, 204, 214, 224
Monet, Claude, 104
Morris, Wesley, 196–97, 199
Morrison, Toni, 197, 198
Moss, Kate, 173–76, 206, 207
movies, 102, 190–92, 195
MTV, 180–81, 184, 186, 188–89, 196, 199, 229, 231
muscles, 4, 19, 23, 28, 31, 32
    gluteus maximus, 23, 28, 29, 31
Musée de l'Homme, 75, 76
Musée d'Orsay, 75
Museum at the Fashion Institute of Technology, 103
music, 177–89, 194, 236–37
    "Baby Got Back," 177–86, 188, 192, 193, 204, 214, 237
    Black, 196–97, 199–200
    "Bootylicious," 202–5
    hip-hop, 3, 183, 187–89, 196–97, 199–201, 224, 229, 237
    Jamaican, 223–24
"My Humps," 194

Napoleon, 126
National Museum of Natural History, France, 49–50, 62–64, 75, 91
natural selection, 36–37, 43
Nava, Gregory, 190–91
Nazis, 73, 74
Negrón-Muntaner, Frances, 191
neoliberalism, 149, 152, 279n

New Orleans, La., 219–26, 237, 244, 294n
New Republic, 101
News of the World, 210
Newsweek, 202
New York State Commission for the Blind, 137
New York Times, 74, 169, 188, 195, 233
New York World's Fair, 115
Ngeneo, Bernard, 19–20
normalcy, 117, 121–24, 133, 135, 141, 142
    Norma, 115–17, 119–23, 129, 130, 135, 141
    Normman, 115–17, 119, 120
    perfection and, 119–20, 129

O'Brien, Ruth, 118, 122, 123, 127, 249
OK!, 209
Okafor, Kelechi, 239–44, 246, 251
Out of Sight, 191–92, 200

Paleolithic art, 54
Palin, Sarah, 147
Paper, 213, 234
Parents Music Resource Center, 181, 187
Paris
    Baartman in, 61–62
    Baker in, 106, 108, 109
    Black Americans in, 106
    National Museum of Natural History in, 49–50, 62–64, 75, 91
    slavery in, 61, 106
    Universal Exhibitions in, 75, 91, 104

Parks, Suzan-Lori, 75
Parton, Dolly, 227
Partridge, Kate, 168
Peabody Museum of Natural
History, 42
peach emoji, 268n
peacocks, 35, 36, 41, 43, 44
Pérez, Elizabeth, 222
perfection, 119–20
Petrzela, Natalia, 148–49, 152
petticoats, 84–87
Pharrell, 229, 230
Phil Donahue Show, The, 169
physical fitness, *see* exercise and
fitness
Piccadilly, 53, 56, 57, 59, 66, 74
pigs, 21–22
Plain Dealer, 121, 122
Planet Pepper, 137–39, 141
plastic surgery, 103, 109, 206,
212–13
butt augmentation, 234–35,
297n
Poiret, Paul, 97, 99–100, 104, 105,
160
pregnancy, 33–34, 40
Premiere, 192
Presley, Elvis, 199
Prince, 186
Proust, Marcel, 104
Prown, Jules, 82, 83
Prum, Richard, 42–45, 49
psychology, evolutionary, 38–41,
43, 44, 72

Quintanilla, Selena, 190–91, 200

race and racism, 12, 21, 51, 69–75,
183, 258n

body shape and, 68–69
demographic shift in the U.S.,
194–96, 286n
immigrants and, 70, 71
skull measurements and, 69, 70
thinness and, 71
see also Black people; Black
women; whiteness
Races of Europe (Ripley), 70
Ray J, 208–9
Reaux, S., 61–63
rebellion and countercultures,
173, 175
Red, Katey, 225, 237
Refinery29, 129
Renaissance, 89
Revue Nègre, La, 107–9
Rhodes, Cecil, 77
Richie, Nicole, 207
Riley, Teddy, 186
Rimbaud, Arthur, 175
Ripley, William Z., 70
Robertson, Josephine, 121, 122
Rose, Tricia, 196
Rubens, Peter Paul, 54
"Rump Shaker," 186, 188
Run-DMC, 188
running, 21–23, 26–30
Man Against Horse Race,
24–27, 30, 260n
RuPaul, 137, 141
rural areas, migration from, 99,
101

Saturday Night Live, 192
Second Sex, The (Beauvoir), 141
Selena, 190–91, 200
Selena, 190–91, 194
Selter, Jen, 235–36

Seventeen, 175, 185, 193

sexual attraction and evolution, 38–41, 44–45

sexual characteristics, secondary, 37, 72–73

sexuality, 97, 98

of Africans, 54, 58, 61, 65–66, 90

of Black women, 66, 71–73, 90, 91, 110, 183, 204, 232, 243, 249

butts associated with, 66–67, 71–73, 182, 224

of East Asian women, 105

Ellis's views on, 72–73

sexual reproduction, 33–34, 37, 44, 115

eugenics and, 69, 73–74, 116, 117, 119–21, 123

Shapiro, Harry L., 119, 120, 122

Shepherd, Sherri, 231

Shields, Brooke, 174, 231

Silverstone, Alicia, 206

Simple Life, The, 207

Simpson, O. J., 207

Sir Mix-A-Lot, 177–86, 189, 193, 204, 214, 224

Sisqó, 194

Skidmore, Martha, 122–23

skull measurements, 69, 70

slavery, 52, 55, 58, 61, 65, 92–93, 126, 222, 243

abolitionists and, 58–60, 265–66n

in New Orleans, 221, 222, 226

in Paris, 61, 106

rape and, 65, 66

Smikle, Ken, 195

Smith, Christopher, 183

Smithey, Greg, 145–48, 154–56, 249

Snoop Dogg, 189, 205

social media, 235

Instagram, 124, 135, 211–12, 234, 236

Soderbergh, Steven, 191, 194

Somers, Suzanne, 159

Sorensen, Jacki, 151–53

South Africa, 51, 52, 55, 62, 75–77

Spieker, Lee, 156

sports, 151–52

statuary, 54, 89, 90

Steele, Valerie, 103

stereotypes, 198, 243

jokes and, 185–86

welfare and, 183

sterilization programs, 74, 116, 268n

Stone, Sharon, 192

Strings, Sabrina, 71

Studies in the Psychology of Sex (Ellis), 72–73

Supreme Court, 74, 268n, 290n

Swain-Lenz, Devjanee, 31–32

Target Market News, 195

Tate, Greg, 91, 199–200

Taylor, Henry, 61

television characters, 195

Thicke, Robin, 230

thinness, 54, 71, 97–98, 100, 102–4, 173–76, 206, 210

"Thong Song," 194

Time, 192

Tobias, Phillip, 76

Trainor, Meghan, 237

Turner, Sharon, 70

twerking, 219–20, 224–26, 230–33, 237, 239–45
2 Live Crew, 186–89, 224

underwear, 88, 89, 100
Universal Exhibitions, 75, 91, 104
University of Colorado Boulder, 29
University of Texas, 39–41
Upham, Mansell, 75
urbanization, 99–101
USDA, 117
Us Weekly, 209

Vanity Fair, 96
Vaz, Kim Marie, 223
Venuses, 54, 89, 90, 120
"Venus Hottentot," *see* "Hottentot Venus"
Victoria & Albert Museum, 83–86, 88, 89, 92
Victorian era, 66, 72, 81, 88–89, 95, 99–102
Vietnam War, 152
Vogue, 96, 129, 130, 173, 175, 233
voting rights, 99
Vulture, 178, 179, 181
vulva, 71–72, 268n

Wagner, Natasha, 129–32, 142
Wahlberg, Mark, 176
Warrant, "Cherry Pie," 181, 183
Webb, Tamilee, 156–58, 161

We Dance, 166
weight, 103–4
welfare, 183
West, Cornel, 199
Whistler, James McNeill, 104
whiteness, 246
    Armenians and, 207–8, 290n
    classifications of, 69–70, 276n
    femininity and, 242–43, 246
    as identity, 197–99, 288n
    Kardashians and, 207–8
Wilde, Oscar, 104
Wiltz, Teresa, 200–201
Winfrey, Oprah, 205
Winthrop, John, 163
Wojcicki, Susan, 192
work, 99–101, 121, 148
Works Progress Administration, 118
World's Fairs, 115, 117
World War I, 95, 101, 106, 117
World War II, 73, 74, 117, 223
    atomic bombs in, 121
Wreckx-n-Effect, "Rump Shaker," 186, 188

Yale University, 42
YMCA, 151, 167
Yo! MTV Raps, 188–89
YWCA, 122

Zhu, Huican, 192
Ziglar, Zig, 147

About the Author

Heather Radke is an essayist, journalist, and contributing editor and reporter at *Radiolab*, the Peabody Award–winning program from WNYC. She has written for publications including *The Believer*, *Longreads*, and *The Paris Review*, and she teaches at Columbia University's creative writing MFA program. Before becoming a writer, Heather worked as a curator at the Jane Addams Hull-House Museum in Chicago.

Avid Reader Press, an imprint of Simon & Schuster, is built on the idea that the most rewarding publishing has three common denominators: great books, published with intense focus, in true partnership. Thank you to the Avid Reader Press colleagues who collaborated on *Butts* as well as to the hundreds of professionals in the Simon & Schuster audio, design, ebook, finance, human resources, legal, marketing, operations, production, sales, supply chain, subsidiary rights, and warehouse departments whose invaluable support and expertise benefit every one of our titles.

Editorial
Julianna Haubner, *Editor*

Jacket Design
Alison Forner, *Senior Art Director*
Clay Smith, *Senior Designer*
Sydney Newman, *Art Associate*

Marketing
Meredith Vilarello, *Associate Publisher*
Caroline McGregor, *Marketing Manager*
Katya Buresh, *Marketing and Publishing Assistant*

Production
Allison Green, *Managing Editor*
Sara Kitchen, *Manger, Digital Workflow Specialist*
Alicia Brancato, *Production Manager*
Lewelin Polanco, *Interior Text Designer*
Cait Lamborne, *Ebook Developer*

Publicity
Alexandra Primiani, *Associate Director of Publicity*
Katherine Hernández, *Publicity Assistant*

Publisher
Jofie Ferrari-Adler, *VP and Publisher*

Subsidiary Rights
Paul O'Halloran, *VP and Director of Subsidiary Rights*